# 100 THINGS
# TWINS FANS
# SHOULD KNOW & DO
# BEFORE THEY DIE

Alex Halsted

TRIUMPH
BOOKS

Library of Congress Cataloging-in-Publication Data
100 things Twins fans should know & do before they die / Alex Halsted.
 p. cm.
 ISBN 978-1-60078-554-2
 1. Minnesota Twins (Baseball team)—History—Miscellanea. 2. Minnesota Twins (Baseball team)—Miscellanea. I. Title. II. Title: One hundred things Twins fans should know and do before they die.
 GV875.M55H35 2011
 796.357′6409776579—dc22

                    2010041836

This book is available in quantity at special discounts for your group or organization. For further information, contact:

**Triumph Books**
542 South Dearborn Street, Suite 750
Chicago, Illinois 60605
(312) 939-3330
Fax (312) 663-3557
www.triumphbooks.com

Printed in U.S.A.
ISBN: 978-1-60078-554-2
Design by Patricia Frey
Page production by Prologue Publishing Services, LLC
All photos courtesy of AP Images unless otherwise specified

*For the first two editors who believed in me: Molly Gallatin and John Bonnes. You started all of this.*

*For the people in my hometown of Mason City, Iowa. Twins Territory truly does spread outside of Minnesota, and this is one of many great examples.*

*For Newman Catholic High School: the teachers, faculty, and all of my classmates and friends.*

*For the friends I met at Iowa State University. Without your support and friendship, this would have been much more difficult.*

*Most of all, for my entire family. Especially Mom and Dad and Katelyn and Paige. You're the reason why I am where I am today.*

# Contents

# Introduction

In a sense, baseball, and the fanhood that comes with it, is a journey.

Like life, there are so many different things to see, so many different people to meet, and so many different things to do along the way. As we make stops along the path, we take in incredible moments and put together everlasting memories. Everybody grows up, and as each of us does, it is inevitable that some ways of life and some traditions get left behind. Baseball seems to be one thing that we never let go of, though; it's something that always seems to stick.

For so many different reasons and for so many different people, baseball plays a major role in life. It has the power of connecting people regardless of ethnicity and place of origin, regardless of beliefs, and regardless of what team one might follow. Baseball has the power to connect families and friends and to create bonds. It can act as an aid in time of hurt and suffering, and it can provide some relief when life becomes overbearing. For me, for you, and for so many others, the Minnesota Twins aren't just one of 30 teams in Major League Baseball. The Minnesota Twins are a way of life. No matter how wrong things might go in any given day, baseball is always there in the end, and the game at night can help make things a little better (or sometimes maybe a little worse). Unpredictable it may be, but that's what makes our journey through baseball so great.

From Metropolitan Stadium to the Metrodome, and now from Target Field and maybe even from the couch in front of the television or the chair in front of the computer, we create long-lasting memories and friendships that never seem to fade. As is the case with life's journey, every fan experiences a moment in a different capacity. Each fan has his own set of fond memories and moments, her own set of favorite players, and his own sense of what makes America's pastime so great. But no matter where the fans might come from, and no matter what their paths entail, every journey eventually combines at the same point, and every fan is ultimately connected as a part of Twins fandom.

In a way, this book, *100 Things Twins Fans Should Know & Do Before They Die*, is a guide to that long, eventful, and sometimes crazy journey that we call baseball, and in particular the Minnesota Twins. You could take 100 of the best players in franchise history, you could collect and look back on the 100 best games ever played by the team, and you could find 100 things fans should know about. Or you could combine all three of those things: players, games, moments, and insightful things to know and do, and put them all together in one big collection.

That's what this is, a collection of the 100 things that fans of the Twins should know about; things that will help you look back on the journey and those that will help you create more memories as you move forward. For different people, different sections will bring back different memories. And that's the beauty of it.

This book is a journey that you can control. You can start at the beginning and move through sequentially, or you can hop around to moments that mean the most to you. There are sections on players, ranging from Kirby Puckett to Joe Mauer; famous moments, ranging from the team's arrival in Minnesota to the 1991 World Series to two Game 163s; things to do, ranging from plopping down in the Gold Glove to spending time with family, and so much more. Some things may just be a rehash, but hopefully along the way you'll learn something new and gain a new appreciation for the team you love and the journey they have traveled through their first 50 seasons in the state of Minnesota.

Remember, as is the case with life, every journey is different. The 100 things in this book—the players, moments, things to do, and other facts—might be different than what you would include. But that's what makes this so great. This is really only the beginning of the journey; there is so much more exploring to be done.

Now let's get started, the path ahead is quite long.

# No. 34

As fans, we root for players who do the little things. We root for players who hustle in the field and run out even the easiest ground-outs. We root for the underdogs who overcome difficult odds to succeed. We root for the guys who arrive at the ballpark each day with a smile and greet fans with dignity. We root for the heroes and the players who say things that make us take a step back and reflect. When we wanted to root for all of these things at one time, we rooted for No. 34.

He was so great that his name resonates just by the mention of his number. The great Bob Casey once announced him like so: "And now…the greatest Minnesota Twin ever! Number Thirty-Four…Kirbeeeeee Puckett!" Some called him "Puck," and some left it simply at 34. No matter how anyone referred to him, he was a Twin, and he was the greatest one to ever put on the uniform.

Puckett's underdog story began at a young age. Growing up in the gloomy Robert Taylor Homes on Chicago's South Side, he was one of nine children. And despite tough economics and a dangerous neighborhood filled with narcotics and violence, Puckett eventually prevailed. The city had two baseball teams in the White Sox and Cubs, and naturally Puckett picked up the game. Although there were no area ballfields, Puckett often drew a square on the wall with chalk, playing what he called "strikeout" for hours. He attended Bradley University, where he played one season before dropping out after the death of his father. He would later enroll at Triton Junior College.

It was a summer day in 1981, and with Major League Baseball on strike, Jim Rantz took a trip to Peoria, Illinois, to watch his son

1

play in an Illinois summer college league. What caught Rantz's attention was the short, 5′8″ center fielder. He hit a double, triple, and a home run; he was the first player on and off the field each inning; and he even stayed after the game to greet fans. The kid was Kirby. When the January draft rolled around the following year, in 1982, the Twins listened to the recommendation from Rantz by selecting Puckett with the third overall pick. Little did anybody know, the franchise would soon forever change.

In 1984 Puckett burst onto the scene, becoming just the ninth player in baseball history to collect four hits in his debut. He would play in 128 games that season, and the next he played in all but one. It was in 1986 that he introduced himself to the country, though. That year he collected more than 200 hits for the first of an eventual five times in his career, and he made the All-Star Game.

The following year, in 1987, Puckett led the Twins to their first championship, and in 1989 he added some hardware to his collection as he hit .339 and won the American League batting title.

As the Twins returned to the Metrodome on October 26, 1991, they did so trailing the Atlanta Braves 3–2 in the World Series. The Twins would need to win the next two games to claim their second title. Kirby wasn't worried, though. He told his teammates and his agent Ron Shapiro the same thing.

"I remember in the 1991 World Series when the Twins were down 3–2 in Atlanta," Shapiro said. "Kirby came into a restaurant to meet me and my colleague, Michael Maas. He said, 'Don't worry, I'm going to put the team on my back and carry this team forward,' and darn if he didn't come through. That's what Kirby was all about, carrying a team and doing what it felt like they might not be able to."

His catch against the Plexiglas in left-center that night to rob Ron Gant of extra bases and the Braves of a run in the third inning was the first sign that Puckett was indeed going to carry the team on his back. The next came in the 11th inning, when Puckett became just the ninth player in baseball history to end a World

*Kirby Puckett, the greatest player to ever put on a Twins uniform, made 10 All-Star Game appearances, won six Gold Gloves, and was inducted into the National Baseball Hall of Fame in 2001.*

Series game with a home run, sending the Twins to Game 7 and eventually their second championship.

Years later, as the team wrapped up spring training heading into the 1996 season, Puckett collected two hits in the final tune-up game before the regular season. The next morning he woke up with a dark spot in his right eye, and the diagnosis was glaucoma. He had treatments and surgeries, but by mid-season, as he still sat out, Puckett was told that his career was over at the age of 36, after having spent 12 seasons with the Twins.

While his career was over, Puckett had made his mark; he had become the best player in team history. As he retired, Puckett's name could be found sitting atop the team leader board in hits (2,304), doubles (414), total bases (3,453), at-bats (7,244), and runs (1,071). He made 10 All-Star Game appearances, and his defense in center field won him six Gold Gloves. But Puckett's legacy went much further than his work on the field and in the game of baseball.

"On the field, Kirby was one of the best players in the history of the game and our franchise. He was the heart and soul of two championship teams, and he set a great example on and off the field," said team president Dave St. Peter. "He was always the first guy in the clubhouse and was very accessible to the media. He brought tremendous charisma, and he became synonymous with Twins baseball and was a tremendous ambassador for the game."

There was the trademark catch and home run in the World Series and the many awards throughout his tenure in Minnesota, but some of the greatest memories of Puckett are of his time spent off the diamond.

"There are so many special stories with Kirby, in the times I spent with him, and they all grow out of his joy, his smile, and his making people happy," said Shapiro. "Whether it be surprising a kid with a piece of baseball memorabilia that he knew would make a kid happy, bringing to the city of Minneapolis superstars from all over baseball for his tournament, or just standing up and telling people why it is important to give back."

When Puckett's career suddenly ended, there was sadness and tears. But from Puckett, there was no anger. He ensured everybody that he would be just fine, that he had given everything he had to offer. In 2001 Puckett was elected to the National Baseball Hall of Fame on his first ballot.

The next five and final years of Puckett's life didn't go as well. He and his wife, Tonya, got divorced, and on March 5, 2006, just shy of his 46th birthday, he suffered a massive stroke and passed away. His legacy showed one more time shortly after, when thousands of fans honored him in a Metrodome memorial ceremony despite a blizzard.

Through the years with his catches in center field and heroics on and off the field, Puckett had a lasting effect on many generations. Whether fans remember that October night in 1991 or simply listen to stories about it, when they hear the words "Thirty-Four" or "Kirby Puckett," they think about everything that Minnesota Twins baseball stands for.

"He brought to the game of baseball an infectious joy," Shapiro concluded. "That joy did so much for the game when he played it. Obviously things happened to him off the field when his career abruptly ended, but I don't think those things will define Kirby Puckett."

In a statement following Kirby's death, the late Carl Pohlad summarized things best.

"Kirby's impact on the Twins organization, state of Minnesota, and Upper Midwest is significant and goes well beyond his role in helping the Twins win two World Championships. A tremendous teammate, Kirby will always be remembered for his neverending hustle, infectious personality, trademark smile, and commitment to the community," the statement read.

"There will never be another Puck."

# 2 Welcome to Minnesota!

October 26 is one of the greatest dates in the history of the Minnesota Twins. For many, hearing that date brings back the memories from the night at the Metrodome when Kirby Puckett made his catch and hit a walk-off home run to send the Twins into the final game of the World Series. Had it not been for an October 26 several decades earlier, however, that night in 1991 might have never occurred.

There had been baseball in Minnesota before the Twins, and Metropolitan Stadium had been built before they ever arrived. Baseball in Minnesota, in fact, officially dates back to 1884, when professional baseball in the state first arrived. Up until 1902 the cities of Minneapolis and St. Paul both fielded teams, and for 59 seasons after that year they were rivals.

After the creation of the American Association, the Minneapolis Millers and St. Paul Saints each put teams on the field until 1960. They were the two winningest teams during their tenure in the league, and they played each other in the rivalry a total of 1,303 times, with the Saints taking the series 680–623. Some of the players who took the field for these teams turned out to be great. The Millers saw greats including Ted Williams and Willie Mays come through, and the Saints watched guys like Lefty Gomez and Roy Campanella play. Had it not been for that one afternoon in October 1960, there might have been many more.

The owner of the Washington Senators, Calvin Griffith, was first ready to relocate to Minnesota in 1958, but he eventually changed his mind and kept the team in Washington. One year later, in 1959, it was reported that a move to the Twin Cities was imminent, but that didn't happen either. Finally though, on October 26, 1960, the dream that had taken years of struggles would become a reality.

"The American League by unanimous vote has just decided to expand to 10 teams in 1961," Joe Cronin, president of the American League, announced at a press conference on that afternoon. "The present Washington club will be moved to Minneapolis–St. Paul next year and will play its games in Metropolitan Stadium."

What helped complete Griffith's longtime plan of relocation was that the city of Washington, D.C., would receive an expansion team. Meanwhile, the Twins were headed to Met Stadium for the 1961 season, where plans were already being made to increase seating by nearly one-third before the inaugural season and increase the capacity to around 40,000 by the second year.

It was April 11, 1961, and for the first time in regular season action, players trotted onto the field as representatives of Minnesota. Starter Pedro Ramos of the Twins allowed just three hits

## Player Profile: Camilo Pascual

After playing for the Washington Senators for seven seasons, Camilo Pascual was a member of the original Minnesota Twins team in 1961. At 27 years old, Pascual was just beginning to shine—and in his early years with the team, he was one of the best pitchers in baseball.

In the team's inaugural season in the state of Minnesota, Pascual won 15 games and led the league in shutouts (eight) and strikeouts (221). Over the next three seasons, he continued to excel, twice winning at least 20 games and making a total of three All-Star appearances as a member of the Twins organization.

In 1965, as the Twins won the pennant, Pascual began to deal with arm issues. He would win nine games that year, but his role was relegated to a spot starter. The Twins traded Pascual following the 1966 season, but in his six seasons as a Twin he became one of the team's first bright spots, winning 88 games for the franchise.

*After arriving from Washington, D.C., the Twins still had no logo. To solve the problem temporarily, owner Calvin Griffith drew "TC" on his hat, standing for Twin Cities.* Photo courtesy Minnesota Twins

and no runs over nine innings, and with home runs from Bob Allison and Reno Bertoia, the Twins won their first game 6–0.

As the Twins arrived at Metropolitan Stadium to play their first home game, there was excitement. Not only had fans waited years for that day, but the Twins returned with a 5–1 record, as well. Their opponent carried a familiar name, too; it would be the Washington Senators, a first-year expansion team that had replaced the Twins in the city, arriving in Bloomington, Minnesota.

During that game on April 21, 1961, in front of a then-record crowd of 24,606 fans, the Senators jumped out to a quick 2–0 lead in the first inning. Marty Keough scored the first run on a double-play grounder, and Dale Long hit a home run to push Washington in front. The Twins would score three runs on home runs from Don Mincher and Lenny Green, and the teams entered the ninth inning tied 3–3.

In the top half of the inning, the Senators scored twice to regain the lead at 5–3, but the Twins had one more chance in the ninth inning to win their home opener. With the bases loaded and one out, Hal Naragon popped out to the shortstop, and Pete Whisenant struck out to end the game.

When Minnesota finally got its team prior to that 1961 season, it was getting a franchise about which *San Francisco Chronicle* editor Charley Dryden had once written: "Washington Senators—First in war, first in peace, and last in the American League." But things went differently in Minnesota.

From their inaugural season in 1961 through the 1970 season, the Twins sat near the top of the league in attendance. They made it to the World Series in their fifth season, and they won the American League West in the final two years of that first decade.

What was most important of all, however, was that afternoon announcement in October 1960. Without that, Puckett might have never carried the team on his back some 31 years later, the Twins may have never made the trip to the Metrodome, and the team may have never had a 50-year history.

That day brought baseball to Minnesota and marked the beginning of a long journey.

# 3 Celebrate Good Times

The crowd roared, and the players wept. It was 1987, but it wasn't the World Series, not yet anyway. The Minnesota Twins would eventually win their first championship that year and during that month, but that moment was still days into the future. For now, the fans were celebrating the team's berth in the most coveted series, and the players were taking in every second.

"Returning from Detroit after winning the American League pennant, we had no expectations at all. Word finally leaked to us that there may be as many as 15,000 people in the Dome to welcome us back, which we thought was amazing and very cool," said Roy Smalley, a member of the 1987 club. "We were totally awestruck by the capacity crowd. It was a moment that none of us will ever forget—and rivals the actual winning of the Series in best memories ever."

Just hours earlier the Twins had been celebrating in Detroit after winning the best-of-seven series in just five games. The Twins had scored four runs in the second inning, and they never looked back, winning 9–5. Starting pitcher Bert Blyleven allowed three runs over six innings, and as closer Jeff Reardon tossed the final out to Kent Hrbek at first base, the celebration ensued. The players shouted, jumped with joy, and celebrated with champagne before their departure. While they celebrated, the club's marketing team prepared for a homecoming.

Nothing major, figured Jeff Lowe, the team's postseason coordinator at the time. It was a Monday night, and the event wasn't likely to start until the team arrived around 10:00. In addition to that, there hadn't been much marketing. The announcers mentioned the possibility of a gathering during the broadcast, and a message had scrolled across the bottom of the screen. "If the Twins win," read the crawl that moved across televisions throughout the Upper Midwest, "there will be a welcome-home celebration at the Dome. Gates will open at 7:00."

That was it.

"We thought that it would be 4,000 to 6,000 people," Lowe would later tell the *Minneapolis Star Tribune*. "We were really nervous that we'd get no one, that it might not work. I think there's so much excitement because these people finally have a way to let out their joy after all these years of frustration. You couldn't plan on an event like this. It's awesome."

*After advancing to the World Series by defeating the Detroit Tigers on October 12, 1987, the Twins arrived home to a packed Metrodome. Here, shortstop Roy Smalley points to the crowd.* Photo courtesy Minnesota Twins

After being greeted by a few hundred fans at the airport, the Twins boarded buses and headed for the Metrodome. Suddenly it was clear that this would be no normal welcoming. Horns blared, and fans held signs along the streets as the Twins neared the Dome. Then they arrived, and as players wondered why fans were standing outside, they were told it was because there was no room remaining indoors. *Something crazy must be happening,* was the general thought from the players, and they couldn't have been more right.

What took place under the Teflon roof that night was more than crazy and more than spectacular. Some of the lights were on, and some were off, and where were the aisles? With somewhere around 60,000 fans packed into the Metrodome, the aisles had disappeared, and so too had the ability to hear. Fans cheered and screamed. The Minnesota Twins were headed to the World Series for just the second time in team history.

As the buses pulled into the stadium and the players slowly made their way down the tunnel that led them onto the turf in right field, they were stunned. What they had expected was a small gathering, but what they were looking at was a crowd greater than the possible capacity for a sellout game. Some players cried, while other players simply laughed and smiled. No matter what any of them did, as they wandered around the field, they all took in one of the greatest sights in team history.

There had been many cheers and ovations previously in the season, but nothing like this. Never had there been this kind of crowd or this kind of noise. It was a new experience for everybody. There were some speeches, but mostly there was roaring from the crowd and a sense of jubilation and thankfulness from the players and coaches.

"I speak for all of the guys when I say that I wish we had room on our World Series roster for another person, and I would include all the people here," Twins manager Tom Kelly said to the crowd that night.

In a sense, the fans had become part of the team. The Twins couldn't possibly lose the World Series after the excitement and after the chills that had run through every person in the ballpark that night. They simply couldn't, and they wouldn't. It was quite possibly the greatest celebration ever, and the World Series hadn't even begun.

# 4 1987 World Series

"Championship Drive," read the 1987 Homer Hankies.

That's what it had been for the Minnesota Twins. It wasn't a championship season so much as it was a drive or a run. The Twins hadn't posted a great record, but they had won when it mattered—at the end of the season and in the playoffs—and they found themselves in the World Series for the first time since they had played at Metropolitan Stadium and reached the big stage in 1965. What had happened in the season—their record included—was now irrelevant. This was a drive for a championship, and the Twins were cruising straight ahead.

In the Eastern Division, four teams had won more games than the Twins when the season was all said and done, and the Detroit Tigers, with 98 wins, made the playoffs. But the Twins were in the Western Division, and with just 85 victories, fewer than New York, Milwaukee, and Toronto of the East, they met the Tigers in the first round.

What had guided the Twins to a good portion of their victories was the home-field advantage of the Metrodome. The Twins won more home games that year, 56, than any other team in baseball. And in the first two games of the ALCS, it showed. The Twins won Game 1 and Game 2 at the Dome, dropped a one-run game in Detroit, and then won Game 4 and Game 5, earning a berth in the World Series. The city and the fans went crazy. Around 60,000 fans packed into the Metrodome to greet the team on the Monday night in which they clinched a spot in the World Series, and as players both smiled and cried, there was a feeling that something special was about to happen.

Surely the Twins had gotten lucky. That was the common thought among many who followed baseball. Now up against the St. Louis Cardinals, who were making their third appearance in the World Series in six seasons, their luck was about to run out. Or was it? Sure, the Twins hadn't had the most spectacular season, but they had great pitching with the likes of Frank Viola and Bert Blyleven, and their lineup, which included Kirby Puckett and Kent Hrbek, was no slouch, either.

The Twins fell behind in Game 1 after the Cardinals scored a run in the second inning. But with seven runs in the fourth inning and two more in the fifth, the Twins cruised to a comfortable 10–1 victory to take an early lead in the series. The next night they scored

## The Calls: 1987 World Series

*"Hrbek hits a high drive to deep center...McGee goes back...Grand slam!"*
—Al Michaels calls Kent Hrbek's Game 6 grand slam

*"To Gaetti...for the first time ever, the Minnesota Twins are World Champions!"*
—Al Michaels calling the final out of Game 7

*"Now we know what it feels like!"*
—Al Michaels on the Metrodome, which reached 125 decibels

the first seven runs of Game 2, and as the two teams headed to St. Louis, the Twins had a 2–0 series lead.

But this was where the Twins were supposed to fall apart. All season the Metrodome had been their saving grace, but on the road they went 29–52. The road woes didn't disappear in the World Series, but the Twins weren't blown out by any means. They lost all three games, but two of the losses came by just two runs, and the Twins were still confident as they flew back to Minneapolis.

"Even though we lost three in a row in St. Louis, we weren't really down," said Twins shortstop Greg Gagne after the series. "We still felt we could win at home." That's the way the Twins had reached Game 6 of the World Series, by winning under the Teflon roof. The Cardinals were puzzled; how could the Twins struggle so mightily on the road but be so strong on their home turf?

By the time the 1987 World Series was over, Cardinals manager Whitey Herzog and his team still had no answer. The Twins kept winning, and they continued to prove their critics wrong.

It was October 24, 1987, and in what would prove to be the final day game in World Series history, the Twins took the field on the verge of elimination. They took a 2–1 lead with a pair of runs in the first, but as the game reached the bottom half of the fifth inning, they trailed St. Louis 5–2. At home and with the designated hitter rule in effect, Don Baylor launched a two-run home run to tie the game, and Steve Lombardozzi put them ahead with his two-out RBI single. The next inning Kent Hrbek helped put the game out of reach with a grand slam that pushed the Twins to Game 7.

The last time the Twins had been in Game 7 was in 1965, when they lost the World Series to the Los Angeles Dodgers. Now they were long gone from the Met. This time they had Frank "Sweet Music" Viola on the mound and a 10th player in the stands. During that 1987 World Series, the crowd reached 125 decibels; noise comparable to a jet at takeoff.

The sound at the end of that October night couldn't have been any sweeter.

Viola allowed two runs in the second inning, but the Twins got one back in the bottom half of the inning. They tied the game in the fifth when Puckett doubled home Greg Gagne, and then they took the lead in the next frame when Gagne singled home Tom Brunansky. After tossing eight innings and allowing just two runs, Viola handed the ball to closer Jeff Reardon for the final three outs.

With two outs, Reardon pitched to Willie McGee.

"Gaetti has it," called out Twins broadcaster Herb Carneal, "over to Hrbek, and the Twins are baseball's world champions! The world champion Minnesota Twins!"

For the first time both teams had won every home game in the series. For the first time, a team with so few regular season wins had done it. For the first time ever, the Minnesota Twins were baseball's world champions.

# Tom Kelly

With a record of 59–80 on September 12, 1986, the Minnesota Twins fired manager Ray Miller. Replacing him—with 23 games remaining in the season—was third-base coach Tom Kelly. In the years ahead he would become the man who would change the franchise forever, but initially he was just an interim replacement and a guy hoping for more security at season's end.

"The ball is in the players' court. If they want to see another manager in three weeks, fine," said the 36-year-old Kelly when he took over with three weeks remaining in the 1986 season. "I want to be manager of the Twins next year. If we get a good effort, I have a shot at it. If I don't get a good effort from somebody, maybe they'll sit down a day or two."

The effort that Kelly received in the remaining weeks was good enough. The team finished the season 12–11 under his watch, and at the end of the season he was signed as the permanent manager.

Just months later, on April 7, 1987, Kelly was in the dugout as the manager, and it was the start of a special season. It was just Kelly's first year at the helm, but the Twins finished above .500 with a record of 85–77, won the division, and headed to the playoffs for the first time since 1970. By the end of October, the Twins had won their first championship. As the manager for just 185 regular season games, Kelly had the Twins at the top of baseball.

"Tom Kelly first and foremost was and is still a tremendous organization man; he is focused on being true to this organization," said team president Dave St. Peter. "He got an opportunity from Carl Pohlad and Andy MacPhail in 1986 on an interim basis and was named the manager in 1987. He set the tone to win championships and put the system in place that still exists today."

After the championship in his first full season, the Twins won 91 games in 1988, but they missed the playoffs despite posting a better record. The next illustrious season in Kelly's tenure came in 1991. That year, the Twins went 95–67, and they soared into the World Series, where they met the Atlanta Braves. Trailing 3–2 as the series returned to Minnesota, the Twins won the final two

*Manager Tom Kelly speaks with St. Louis manager Whitey Herzog during batting practice at the Metrodome in Minneapolis before the start of Game 1 of the World Series on October 17, 1987.*

games, and Kelly had helped bring the team its second trophy. That year he was named the Manager of the Year.

In 1992 the Twins won 90 games, but just as it was in 1988, there were no playoffs at the Metrodome. In fact, there would be no more playoffs during Kelly's stay. The Twins finished below .500 for eight consecutive seasons before the rebuilding phase neared an end and the Twins went 85–77 in 2001. At this point in time, Kelly had become the longest-tenured head coach in American professional sports, which included leagues such as the NFL, NBA, and NHL. Surprisingly though, just weeks after the first winning season since 1992, he resigned.

"We were disappointed to see him step down, but we respected the decision and felt he earned the right to go out on his own terms," St. Peter said of the day Kelly called it quits. "Terry Ryan

## All-Time Managers

The Minnesota Twins have existed in the state for 50 seasons, and for half of those years, the man at the helm has been named either Tom Kelly or Ron Gardenhire. But while those two men have led the team much of the way through their first half century, the organization has had 10 other leaders over the years.

1961: Cookie Lavagetto (23–36)
1961–1967: Sam Mele (524–436)
1967–1968: Cal Ermer (145–129)
1969: Billy Martin (97–65)
1970–1972: Bill Rigney (208–184)
1972–1975: Frank Quilici (280–287)
1976–1980: Gene Mauch (378–394)
1980–1981: John Goryl (34–38)
1981–1985: Billy Gardner (268–353)
1985–1986: Ray Miller (109–130)
1986–2001: Tom Kelly (1,140–1,244)
2002–Present: Ron Gardenhire (803–656)

and Bill Smith went with Ron Gardenhire, and he deserved the opportunity. Kelly's impact is significant on the way Gardenhire approaches his role today."

The news came as a shock to the fans and players, too. After nearly a decade full of losing, Kelly had helped reshape the Twins and finally they had nudged their way back into contention during what would prove to be his final year. But at 51 years old, Kelly was done.

"The game is about the players," Kelly said during his good-bye press conference. "It's not about the manager, it's not about the coaches, the trainers, the umpires. I tried to express this to Terry that this wasn't all necessary, but I got overruled."

Like he had done through his entire career, Kelly made sure everybody knew that the players were the story one last time before he left the spotlight, or whatever spotlight there might have been during his 15-plus seasons as the team's leader; Kelly never did make himself the story, even in the biggest moments.

"In 1987, when they won the World Series, he was so focused on the players having that moment," St. Peter recalled. "He stayed behind the scenes and gave the players the credit. That's the type of guy Tom was, he wanted to be behind the scenes and put the light on the players."

Today Kelly remains part of the organization as an advisor. The system he put in place more than two decades ago remains, and as it had always been with Tom Kelly, his work for the team remains out of the spotlight.

# 6 The Homer Hanky

It was the final regular season game in the Metrodome's history, and the entire stadium was white. The Minnesota Twins had just won Game 163, they were headed to the playoffs, and on national television the entire country saw a crowd of more than 54,000 fans bunched together in seemingly one white blob.

The tradition started in 1987 as the Twins reached the World Series that season for the first time since 1965 and for just the second time in team history. Before the team had even reached the World Series that year, more than 200,000 Homer Hankies had been sold, and by the time everything was said and done, more than 2 million had been distributed as people waited in lines for hours just to get their hands on the white cloth that read "Twins 1987 Championship Drive."

The person responsible for the madness was Terrie Robbins, a promotions manager for the *Minneapolis Star Tribune*. To say her idea was a hit would be an understatement. People from around the country tried to get their hands on the hanky, and it showed up on the USS *Arizona* Memorial in Hawaii and on babies in hospital nurseries among other places.

After the world had been introduced to the Twins and the Metrodome crowd waving white hankies during the World Series, more were produced prior to the 1988 season. This time they read, "Just As Great in '88," and they were introduced before the team's home opener one year after they had won their first championship.

By the time the Twins reached their second World Series in 1991, the *Star Tribune* and Minnesota Twins had come to an agreement to produce the hankies together. That year, the third hanky in team history was handed out, and it read, "The Magic Is Back." Indeed it was. As Kirby Puckett put the team on his back, the hankies waved around the Metrodome, and the Twins had their second championship.

For the next 10 years, there would be no playoff Homer Hanky—the Twins fell into a lull, and there was no need for them. Facing the threat of contraction in 2002, the Twins made the playoffs, and the hankies reemerged. That year they read, "Proud and Loud," and there would be a need for many more in the seasons ahead.

The Homer Hanky in 2003 has its own distinction; it is the only hanky to be produced with only the color blue. One year later it was back to red, this time with a large graphic that resembled the layout of the Metrodome.

After taking a year off since the team missed the playoffs, the hanky returned in 2006, paying homage to the team's history with the organization's original logo front and center.

As the national broadcast prepared to turn live to Minneapolis on that October night in 2009, fans waved the final Homer Hanky of the Metrodome's tenure. From the World Series to a one-game playoff some 22 years later, the Homer Hanky became an important part of baseball in Minnesota over the years. When fans waved the white, square cloths, it was with significance.

## Homer Hanky Song

In 1966, one year after the Twins made the World Series for the first time in franchise history, the rock group Tommy James and the Shondells took the song "Hanky Panky" to No. 1 on the charts.

Nobody could have guessed it then, but just more than 20 years later, as the Twins made the World Series and eventually won their first title, that song would make a connection to the team. As fans waved Homer Hankies in the Metrodome that October, a remake of that original song, recorded by the J.D. Steele Singers, hit the air on area radio stations.

The key parts of the jingle were quite catchy:

> I saw her sittin' on the first-base line.
> Yeah, you know she's rootin' for the Twins every time.
> A pretty little girl at the Metrodome.
> Hey, Minny baby, can I take you home?
> In '87, and in '91, yeah, she won!
>
> Yeah, my baby waves the Homer Hanky.
> Yeah, my baby waves the Homer Hanky.
>
> My baby waves the Homer Hanky.
> My baby waves the Homer Hanky.
> My baby waves the Homer Hanky.
> Yeah.
>
> Come on, let's hit it one more time, let's go!
> Yeah, my baby waves the Homer Hanky.
> Yeah, my baby waves the Homer Hanky.
>
> My baby waves the Homer Hanky.
> My baby waves the Homer Hanky.
> My baby waves the Homer Hanky.
> Yeah.

Just like that, the Minnesota Twins had a connection to a famous song from the 1960s, and a song to showcase the hankies that became world famous as the team rose to the top of the league.

*Homer Hankies have been in attendance for the biggest games in team history, including both World Series appearances in 1987 and 1991.* Photo courtesy Minnesota Twins

There would be another Homer Hanky produced after that final Metrodome regular season game. As fans arrived to kick off a new era at Target Field on April 12, 2010, they were handed a commemorative hanky with the team's inaugural season logo.

This had significance, too: the team would continue the long-standing tradition into its new era and trip outdoors. And a hanky with both red and blue made its way outdoors that October for the playoffs. The Homer Hankies signify the best of Twins baseball, they mean the Minnesota Twins are competitive, and as they swirl across the stadium, there is some magic in the air.

# Joe Mauer

He isn't your average Joe.

Born and raised in St. Paul, Minnesota, Joe Mauer became a household name well before he stepped onto the turf at the

Metrodome. At Cretin-Derham Hall, Mauer played baseball, basketball, and football, and he excelled at all three, becoming the first high school athlete to ever be named the *USA Today* High School Player of the Year in two different sports.

With a scholarship offer to play football at Florida State on the table, the Minnesota Twins selected the Minnesota native over college pitcher Mark Prior with the first overall pick in the 2001 baseball amateur draft. Already well known in the Twin Cities, Mauer's name quickly spread. He was rated as the No. 7 prospect by *Baseball America* as soon as 2002, and before he stepped up to the plate to make his major league debut in 2004, he was regarded as baseball's No. 1 prospect.

The accolades for Mauer were well deserved. He had struck out just once in high school, and he moved quickly through the minor league system, never hitting below .300 and skipping Triple A entirely prior to making his debut at the beginning of the 2004 season.

After an injury in his first game, however, he was back in the minor leagues, and a stop at the team's Triple A affiliate was still in store for Mauer during the 2004 season. He went 2-for-3 in his debut with the Twins and collected a hit in his lone at-bat during the second game. While attempting to make a play behind the plate, Mauer collided with the backstop and injured his knee. The injury would require surgery, and while Mauer returned to the lineup for a period of time later that season, his career wouldn't truly get started until the following year.

In 2005, his first full season with the Twins, Mauer appeared in 131 games and hit .294, pretty solid numbers for the then-22-year-old. He was still far from his peak, though, and in 2006 his name became known around the nation. Mauer hit .347 that year, becoming the first catcher in American League history to win the batting title.

*To date, hometown hero Joe Mauer has won three batting titles and was the 2009 American League Most Valuable Player.*

After putting together another good year in 2007 (.293 average) and winning his second batting title during the 2008 season (.328 average), Mauer would miss the first month of the 2009 season with a back injury. He returned to the lineup after missing the month of April, and his first swing went over the left-field wall for a home run. It'd be the first of many home runs over the course of a career year for Mauer. He ended the season hitting .365 with 28 home runs and 96 RBIs.

More than a career year, Mauer's 2009 season was a historic one. His average was the highest by a catcher in baseball history, knocking out Mike Piazza's .362 total from 1997. He became the first player since 1980 and the first catcher ever to lead the league in batting average, slugging percentage, and on-base percentage, and he won his third batting title, matching the total number won by all catchers in baseball history combined. His accomplishments helped him win the 2009 American League Most Valuable Player Award and a hefty new contract.

About to enter a contract year in the team's first season at Target Field, the Twins reached out to Mauer with an offer. After months of rumors and speculation, Mauer became a true hometown hero, agreeing to an eight-year, $184 million deal that would keep him in a Twins' uniform until at least the age of 35.

"Simply put, it means that a hometown superstar valued sticking with his hometown team rather than going to the marketplace for the most money in some other market," said Mauer's agent Ron Shapiro, who was also the agent for Twins great Kirby Puckett. "It reaffirms the special connection between a very special player and his community."

Through the first part of his career, Mauer made appearances on the cover of magazines, including *Sports Illustrated* and *ESPN The Magazine*. He graced the cover of the video game MLB 10: The Show and appeared in commercials for several major companies.

## Mauer's Historic Feat

Kirby Puckett is the only player to ever collect six hits in a game for the Minnesota Twins. Joe Mauer could have become the second. He could have, but he didn't, because after picking up five hits against the Kansas City Royals on July 26, 2010, Mauer was pinch hit for. He might have gotten that sixth hit needed for the rare feat. Nobody will ever know.

What everybody does know, however, is that what Mauer did that night was rare. It was more rare than tossing a no-hitter, and it was more rare than collecting six hits in a ballgame. Along with going 5-for-5, Mauer picked up seven RBIs. He became just the third catcher in baseball history to do such a thing. But his feat is far less common than even that.

In baseball history, there had been 159 no-hitters through that night, and Mauer's feat—collecting five hits and driving in seven runners—had been accomplished only 23 times previously, making it an occurrence that happens on average just once every 5,000 games or so.

"I felt tonight was good," Mauer said after the game that night. "Even the pitches that I was taking, I didn't feel like I was rushed. I felt good even when I didn't swing. Yeah, it was a good night."

Good would be one way to put it.

Selected out of high school as the first overall pick by his hometown team was certainly a lot for Joe Mauer to handle. In the early part of his career he's done more than many could have ever imagined, and he has become not just a Minnesota icon, but also a national one. Still, Mauer has remained the grounded, humble, and quiet player that the team drafted in 2001.

"Joe Mauer is a man of great athletic talent and great human perspective. One of the beauties of Joe is that he doesn't let his accomplishments on the field blur the way he deals with people," Shapiro mentioned. "Becoming a superstar hasn't denied him that special quality of being regular and appreciating the people in his life along the way.

"He is truly a very, very good human being who happens to be a great player."

# 8 1991 World Series

The greatest World Series *ever*.

It was nine days and seven games of pure magnificence. The Twins versus the Braves. Two teams that had finished in last place during the previous season had risen to the top to find themselves representing their leagues in the 1991 World Series. There were the great props; the Twins had the Homer Hankies, and the Braves had their Tomahawk Chop. There was Kent Hrbek's wrestling move, and then there were heroics. First Kirby Puckett put the team on his back and made a magnificent catch and hit a stunning home run to send the Twins into "tomorrow night." Then, finally, it was hometown kid Jack Morris refusing to exit and tossing 10 scoreless innings in what would prove to be one of the best World Series pitching performances ever.

Yeah, I guess you could call it the best ever played.

That 1991 World Series had it all. There was drama, there was tension, there was controversy, there was joy, there was suspense, and it was all topped off with a magical Game 7. It could be said that there really wasn't a loser in the series, but the trophy sitting in Minneapolis would say differently. The series was close, it was back-and-forth, and it certainly was memorable.

"The only thing better," Mark Lemke of the Braves said after their Game 7 loss, "would have been if we stopped after nine innings and cut the trophy in half." That didn't happen, but there had been nothing like this series before. There had never been something so close: four games of the series were decided on the final pitch, five were determined in the final at-bat, five were decided by one lone run, and three games went into extra innings.

"This is storybook," Twins manager Tom Kelly said. "Who's got the script? Who is writing this? Can you imagine this?" Nobody was writing it, but it sure was magical.

The plot had two bottom-dwellers from 1990 sitting atop the league. The series kicked off on October 19, 1991, and the Twins pushed ahead early, getting home runs in the first two games from unsuspected heroes Greg Gagne and Scott Leius, to win the first two games of the series before heading to Atlanta for the next three.

As the Braves and Twins arrived in Atlanta for Game 3, there was trouble for both teams. Native Americans had picketed Atlanta-Fulton County Stadium, protesting Atlanta's use of the nickname "Braves," and their fans' use of the tomahawk chop. Meanwhile, Hrbek and his family, who had been involved in the Game 2 controversy of Ron Gant falling—or according to some being pulled off first base for the final out in the third inning— were receiving threats.

The first two games in Atlanta could have gone either way. Both Game 3 and Game 4 were decided on the final pitch, and unfortunately for the Twins, they were each decided in the home half of the inning, meaning the Braves had evened the series. It was Lemke, who hit .417 in the World Series as the eventual unsung hero, right in the middle of the first two victories for the Braves. First he singled in the winning run in the 12th inning of Game 3. Then, one night later, it was Lemke running home toward Twins catcher Brian Harper and hook sliding around him for the winning run, ensuring the series would return to the Metrodome.

Game 5 was the one game in which the Twins never seemed to have a chance. The Braves went up 5–0 early, and right when the Twins scored three runs in the sixth inning to make it a two-run ballgame, the Braves put nine more runs on the board in the next two innings. The Braves were now within one game of a World Series title as the two teams headed back to Minneapolis for Game 6.

That night, Kirby Puckett met with his agent, Ron Shapiro, and told him not to worry. The next night before Game 6, Puckett told his teammates the same thing. He assured them all that he would carry them on his back, and in a way that seemingly could happen only in a story, he did. Puckett saved a run with his leaping catch in left-center during the third inning, and when he stepped to the plate to lead off the 11th inning, he blasted a pitch into the seats, sending the crowd into an eruption and carrying his team to Game 7.

In some stories, that Game 6 performance by Puckett would conclude the crazy plot that the nation had been watching unfold that week. But as it was said, this was no scripted story, and it was far from normal.

The two teams had arrived on the final night of the 1991 season. The series could go no further, and on that night, there would be just one winner and just one champion. The 36-year-old Jack Morris would face off against the 24-year-old John Smoltz. Morris, the St. Paul native, tossed nine shutout innings, but the

## The Calls: 1991 World Series

*"Puckett swings and hits a blast! Deep left-center! Way back! Way back! It's gone! The Twins go to the seventh game! Touch 'em all, Kirby Puckett! Touch 'em all, Kirby Puckett! And the Twins have won this game 4–3 on a dramatic home run by Kirby Puckett!"* —Twins broadcaster John Gordon in Game 6

*"Into deep left-center, for Mitchell...and we'll see you...tomorrow night!"* —Jack Buck calls Puckett's home run in Game 6

*"The Twins are going to win the World Series! The Twins have won it! It's a base hit, it's a one-nothing, 10-inning victory!"* —Jack Buck calls the final out of Game 7

*"And the pitch to Larkin. Swung on, a high fly ball into left-center, the run will score, the ball will bounce for a single, and the Minnesota Twins are the champions of the world!"* —Vin Scully on the final play of Game 7

Twins hadn't scored, and the game headed to a 10$^{th}$ frame. After some discussion with the coaches, Morris emerged from the dugout for the 10$^{th}$ inning; he had refused to exit the game. After another 1-2-3 inning, Gene Larkin stepped to the plate with the bases loaded in the bottom half of the inning, and his line drive into left field brought the Twins their second championship.

"You get the feeling sometimes that if the Yankees or Red Sox aren't in the World Series, it can't be a classic," David Justice of the Braves said. "But that Series in '91 was a true classic. People talk about it all the time. I mean, come on—four games decided on the final pitch, three go extra innings, five were won in either our last at-bat or theirs, a 1–0 Game 7. I mean, come on, that's amazing."

*More than amazing*, thought commissioner Fay Vincent, "It was probably the greatest World Series ever," he would say after Game 7.

The greatest *ever*. It would be hard to argue.

# 9 "And...We'll See You Tomorrow Night!"

"Guys, I just have one announcement to make," Kirby Puckett told his gathered teammates before Game 6 of the 1991 World Series. "You guys should jump on my back tonight. I'm going to carry us."

And he did.

It was so great that today his home run is deemed one of the greatest in baseball history. It was so great that the performance is regarded as one of the best single-game efforts of all-time. It was so great that Twins radio broadcaster John Gordon shouted not once, but twice, "Touch 'em all, Kirby Puckett!" And it was so great that just the sound of Jack Buck's voice and the playing of his call brings back images and memories of Puckett fist-pumping and screaming his way around the bases.

*Kirby Puckett reacts after hitting a solo home run in the 11<sup>th</sup> inning of Game 6 to win the game and tie the World Series against the Atlanta Braves in Minneapolis on October 26, 1991.*

"And...we'll see you tomorrow night!" shouted Buck as the ball left the bat and headed for the left-field seats. Kirby Puckett had come through on his promise; he had put his teammates on his back and carried them into tomorrow night with his glove and his bat. And when tomorrow night came one day later, the Twins would win their second championship.

"We were in a bad way; we needed someone to step forward in a major way," Gene Larkin would say years later. "He told us to jump on his back. Not many guys can talk the talk and walk the walk, but Kirby always could. After he spoke to us, we just knew that Kirby was going to do something special. We've seen him do that many times. That time it was on the biggest stage."

Puckett had been the hero many times before and had put up big games in the past, too. But never before had he done it in Game 6 of the World Series, and never before had the situation been so dire. The Twins had led the series 2–0 after the first two games at the Metrodome, but as they arrived back in Minneapolis for the game on that October 26 night, they did so on the brink of elimination, trailing the Braves in the series 3–2 and needing two consecutive victories for their second championship.

Four years earlier, in 1987, the Twins were in the same predicament. The St. Louis Cardinals had arrived back in Minneapolis for Game 6, needing just one victory to win the World Series. That year in Game 6, Kent Hrbek had hit a grand slam to help send the Twins to Game 7 and eventually their first championship. Now Puckett was about to swap positions with Hrbek; it was almost like a sequel.

In the first inning Puckett tripled to left, and Chuck Knoblauch, who had reached base ahead of him with a single, scored the first run of the game. The Twins would add another run when Shane Mack singled Puckett home later in the inning, and the Twins had an early 2–0 lead in the must-win game.

The lead was in jeopardy in the third inning, and Puckett's first defining moment ensued. Lonnie Smith stood on first base for the Braves with one out when Ron Gant crushed starter Scott Erickson's fastball toward the seats in left-center field. As it neared the Plexiglas above the outfield wall, Puckett sprinted, caught up with the ball, and leaped. The runner retreated to first as Puckett pulled the ball out of his glove. He had saved a run, and the Braves wouldn't score that inning. It wouldn't be until later that night when everybody would find out how much that catch meant.

Terry Pendleton tied the game at two with a two-run blast in the fifth inning that Puckett had no chance at. In the bottom half of the inning the Twins would reclaim the lead, though. Dan Gladden scored on a sacrifice fly by Puckett, and the Twins were back ahead 3–2. In the seventh inning Gant got some revenge, beating out a double play and allowing teammate Mark Lemke to score the tying run.

Had Puckett not made that leaping catch in the third inning, he wouldn't have been trotting around the bases in the 11th. After the Braves tied the game in the seventh inning, they squandered chances to take the lead. In the final three innings of the game they saw two runners erased on double plays and another gunned down at second base while attempting to steal. And so the bottom half of the 11th inning arrived with the Braves and Twins tied, and the leadoff hitter was one Kirby Puckett.

Lefty Charlie Leibrandt was the pitcher. Puckett was looking for the change-up, and after Leibrandt dropped the first pitch in for a strike, the next two missed the plate. It was the fourth pitch that Puckett swung at, and the fourth pitch that flew into the seats. As the ball left the bat, all 55,155 fans in attendance knew. There would be a tomorrow night.

Kirby Puckett saved a run in the third inning with his glove, and then he sent his team to Game 7 with his blast in extra innings. He had talked the talk before the game, and as he rounded third base, he was now backing it up. The team was now on his back, and they were embracing in celebration as Puckett stomped on home plate for the 4–3, one-run victory.

"This is the game I'll never forget," Puckett said after the game. It's doubtful anybody ever will.

# Seventh Heaven

At last, it was finally "tomorrow night."

Not even 24 hours earlier, Kirby Puckett had taken his team, with his glove and with his bat, and lifted them to this do-or-die situation. There would be one chance and one game on this night of October 27, 1991, to win the second World Series in Minnesota Twins history. Lose, and the season would end with the Twins as nothing more than one of the 25 teams that didn't win the title. Win, and be immortalized forever by fans and in baseball history.

As if the scene hadn't already been set—with two teams that had finished in last place the year before, many close games already in the series, and then Puckett's heroics just one night earlier—the Twins would send St. Paul native Jack Morris to the mound for this winner-take-all Game 7. It would be impossible to match Game 6, figured most. And in the end, most had figured wrong.

Game 4 had seen this very matchup. The young John Smoltz would take on the 36-year-old Morris, who would make his final start for his hometown team in his one lone season in Minneapolis. By the time the night came to an end, Morris had gone out with a bang, providing the Twins with one of the most spectacular pitching performances in not just team history or even World Series history, but in baseball history.

Early on, both Smoltz and Morris were solid. They each tossed 1-2-3 firsts and worked around small threats in the early innings. It was the fifth inning when the Braves put their first big threat together. Mark Lemke led off the inning with a single, and two bunts later—one a sacrifice and the other a single—they had runners on the corners with just one out. But Terry Pendleton popped the ball up in the infield, and Ron Gant was caught looking, causing the crowd to erupt with joy, and sending the game into the next inning with both teams still scoreless.

The eighth inning arrived with zeros all across the line score, but it appeared that it wouldn't be for long. Lonnie Smith reached base with a leadoff single, and Pendleton followed by launching a double into left-center. In hindsight, it appeared that Smith should have scored, but he held at third, and the Braves had two in scoring position with nobody out, and at least one run seemed inevitable.

Gant would tap a ball softly to Kent Hrbek at first for the first out of the inning, but the threat still remained, and the bullpen was warming quickly.

After the first out, and with two runners still on base, manager Tom Kelly stepped from the dugout and headed to the mound. It was decision time. Ultimately, Kelly headed back for the dugout with Morris still standing on the mound. The Twins made the decision to intentionally walk David Justice, and with the bases full, Sid Beam stepped to the plate. He lined the ball sharply to Hrbek at first, who started an inning-ending 3-2-3 double play. The threat had been averted.

Morris was back on the mound for the ninth inning, and after tossing a 1-2-3 inning, Kelly informed him that his night was over. But as the 10th inning rolled around after the Twins failed to end the game in the bottom of the ninth, Morris was headed back to the field. He had refused to exit after his nine scoreless innings, and Kelly told pitching coach Dick Such, "What the heck, it's just a game." When asked later how he could have gotten Morris out of the game, Kelly replied, "Probably a shotgun."

Thankfully for Kelly, he let Morris return to the mound for the 10th frame. The hometown kid worked a quick 1-2-3 inning, and the score remained tied at zero. But the Twins still needed a run, and what would happen if the 11th inning rolled around and Morris wanted to head to the mound yet again?

Dan Gladden pushed such thoughts away with his leadoff double in the bottom half of the inning. Chuck Knoblauch moved him over with a sacrifice bunt, and the Twins had a runner at third base with just one out and Puckett and Hrbek due up. The only move the Braves could make was to intentionally walk both players, and they did. The bases were loaded, and to the plate stepped Gene Larkin.

"And the pitch to Larkin," called out broadcaster Vin Scully. "Swung on, a high fly ball into left-center, the run will score, the ball will bounce for a single, and the Minnesota Twins are the champions of the world!"

There had been pitchers with more strikeouts and bigger numbers, and Morris had gone 10 innings on eight occasions prior to that night. But nobody had ever showed the guts that he did on that fall night. Jack Morris lasted 10 innings, allowed no runs, and his refusal to leave the mound that night led the Twins to their second title.

"I just didn't want to quit, and somehow we figured out a way to win this thing," Morris said after the game.

And because of it, the Twins were in seventh heaven.

 # 11 Home

They say you can always go home, and that's exactly what three players did.

Born and raised in St. Paul, Minnesota, Paul Molitor, Dave Winfield, and Jack Morris were all drafted into other organizations, and they completed most of their careers away from home. But as it goes, they did come home in the end, and all three made some great memories in the hometown uniform.

It was Morris who came home first. He would play for his hometown team at the Metrodome for just one season, but what a memorable season it was. Drafted out of Brigham Young University in 1976 by the Detroit Tigers, Morris would spend the majority of his career, 14 years in fact, playing in Michigan. He joined the Twins on a one-year contract following the 1990 season, and it couldn't have gone much better.

That year, in 1991, Morris won 18 games and posted a 3.43 ERA while tossing nearly 250 innings. He would help lead the

Twins to the World Series that year, and at the age of 36, he was more dominant than ever on the big stage. He made three starts in that World Series, going 2–0 with an incredible 1.17 ERA to lead the team to its second championship in team history.

It was Game 7 that year for which he is best remembered. In a scoreless ballgame through nine innings, Morris refused to end his night. Instead, he headed out for the 10th inning, pitching a scoreless frame. The Twins would score in the bottom half of the inning, winning the World Series and helping Morris take the World Series MVP.

Two years later the second one would come home. This time it was the future Hall of Famer Dave Winfield. Having attended the University of Minnesota, Winfield was selected with the fourth overall pick in 1973 by the San Diego Padres. He spent eight seasons on the West Coast, then nine on the East Coast with the Yankees before moving around for a few seasons and eventually joining the Twins in 1993.

Winfield never put up great numbers in Minnesota. It was near the end of his great career, and at the age of 41, he was on the decline. But there was one memorable moment. The date was September 16, 1993, and after singling in the seventh inning for hit No. 2,999, Winfield singled to left field off pitcher Dennis Eckersley to join a select group of only 27 players to reach the 3,000-hit plateau.

The final homecoming came in 1996 when Paul Molitor signed on to become a Twin. It was supposed to be a fresh start for the Twins after three consecutive losing seasons, but Kirby Puckett would never play again after the final spring training game that year, and the team kept losing.

Molitor would play in Minnesota for three seasons before calling it quits at the conclusion of the 1998 season. He did pretty well, hitting above .300 in two of the years, all while surpassing the age of 40. But the one big moment for Molitor in his time with the team came exactly three years after Winfield collected his big hit. On September 16, 1996, Molitor added his name to the great list. After picking up hit No. 2,999 on a single, Molitor became the only player to collect No. 3,000 on a triple when he went all the way to third base that day in the fifth inning in Kansas City.

Born and raised across the river in St. Paul, Minnesota, Morris, Winfield, and Molitor all eventually found their way back home. Morris may have been the only one to accomplish the childhood dream of winning a championship at home, but all three accomplished great feats in their short time playing in Minneapolis.

# 12 1965: One Game Short

"Last year means nothing now," shortstop Zoilo Versalles told *Sports Illustrated* in early 1966. "In this game, you know, it's easy come, easy go. We got a season to play, and we don't win thinking about last year. We still got to run—that is the name of the game—and we still got to win."

What Versalles was referring to was the best regular season in team history.

It didn't come easy, but by the time the Twins had completed the 1965 season, their fifth season in Minnesota and at Metropolitan Stadium in Bloomington, Minnesota, the team had collected 102 victories and made the postseason for the first time since their name changed from the Washington Senators to the Minnesota Twins in the fall of 1960.

What made the team's accomplishment difficult were injuries, and lots of them. They weren't just nagging injuries, and they weren't to bench players. These were injuries that put players—the team's best—out for weeks and months. Harmon Killebrew, who

*Pitcher Mudcat Grant celebrates as the Twins head to the World Series in 1965. Grant became the first African American pitcher to win 20 games in the American League that season.* Photo courtesy Minnesota Twins

had blasted a league-leading 49 home runs in 1964, missed two months after dislocating his elbow, and starting pitcher Camilo Pascual, who had won 15 games and been one of the team's best pitchers the previous year, went winless for a three-month period as he experienced arm issues. And that wasn't it. Catcher Earl Battey, outfielder Bob Allison, and pitcher Dave Boswell all missed time throughout the season, too.

Luckily for the Twins, others stepped up. Killebrew did play in 113 games and still blasted 25 home runs, but it was certainly a drop from the previous season. So it was Don Mincher who picked up the slack by hitting 22 home runs. Meanwhile, Mudcat Grant became the first black player in American League history to win 20 games, and Jim Kaat picked up another 18 victories.

Just as much as players picked up slack, third-base coach Billy Martin, who had been hired prior to the start of the season, became a key to the team's success. The Twins were still waiting for shortstop Versalles, at 25 years of age entering the 1965 season, to come around. With the help of Martin, who became Versalles' mentor and tutor, the youngster put forth a career year and became one of the biggest keys to their final record. That season Versalles led the league in at-bats, runs, doubles, and triples, and his Gold Glove defense up the middle helped, too.

By the time the season came to an end, the Twins had won 102 games. In no other season in Twins history has a team matched that total, and the record gave the Twins a comfortable seven-game cushion at season's end as they headed to the World Series, where they'd meet the Los Angeles Dodgers in their first trip to the big stage.

## Player Profile: Jim "Mudcat" Grant

There have been three players in baseball history named Jim Grant, but to date there has been just one "Mudcat." That man played four seasons in a Twins uniform over the course of his 14-year career, and during his stay in Minnesota, he became a pioneer for African American players.

After playing seven seasons for the Cleveland Indians to start his career, Mudcat headed to the Twins in a mid-season trade during the 1964 season. The next season he would have a career year.

It was 1965, and the Twins were rolling through the league. That season they won 102 games, and Grant was a big reason why. He went 21–7 with a league-leading six shutouts. Along the way he became the first African American player in American League history to win 20 games, and when he won two World Series games that October, he became the first African American from the American League to win a World Series game.

The Twins hosted the first two games of the World Series, and things went much better than anybody could have anticipated. Up against two Hall of Fame pitchers—two of the best in the league— the Twins won both games. The Twins' best, Grant and Kaat, outdueled Don Drysdale and Sandy Koufax, and the Twins headed to Los Angeles for the next three games with a 2–0 series lead.

But that lead would disappear quickly. Just as the Twins had done, the Dodgers won all of their homes games and moved within one game of a championship as the two teams headed back to the Midwest for Game 6. Grant shined again on the mound. This time he tossed a complete game, a six-hit ballgame, and his three-run home run lifted the Twins to a series tie.

Still at home, and with the series down to a one-game, winner-take-all matchup, things weren't about to get easy for the Twins. While Minnesota sent one of their best to the mound in Kaat, the Dodgers countered with the league's Cy Young Award winner. The Twins' pitchers allowed just two runs, but it wasn't nearly enough. Koufax surrendered three lone hits and struck out 10 batters as the Dodgers took the series and the championship trophy.

When all was said and done, it was still a remarkable season in Minnesota. Not only had the Twins surpassed the 100-win mark, but they also racked up the hardware. Versalles was named the American League MVP, six players had been voted to the All-Star Game that was played at Met Stadium, Tony Oliva won the batting title, and two players (Kaat and Versalles) took home Gold Glove honors.

It won't be remembered for the season of the team's first championship—that honor came 22 years later—but just five seasons into their stay in Minnesota, the Twins were sitting near the top of the league. Versalles may have said that it meant nothing when he looked back on it just months later in 1966, but today no team in the first 50 seasons of Twins baseball has topped that 1965 regular season.

# "Just Don't Take It For Granted"

How could this be happening? Less than 24 hours earlier, Kirby Puckett had gone 2-for-3 and had picked up a hit against Greg Maddux in the final spring training game to up his average for the month of exhibition games to .344. The Twins hadn't made the playoffs since Puckett helped them to a World Series victory in 1991, but with Paul Molitor added to the mix and with Kirby still hitting and making plays in center field, there was excitement in Minneapolis. How quickly that excitement faded.

The Twins were done with spring training, the first regular season game wasn't far away, and they'd soon be leaving their spring home of Fort Myers, Florida, to begin the long 162-game season. There was a problem, though. As Puckett woke up on the morning of March 28, 1996, he couldn't see his wife, Tonya. She wasn't missing, however, she was right there next to him. But all Puckett saw was a black spot in his right eye. Tests would later reveal it to be glaucoma.

"It was an incredible shock to the system [when Puckett's injury surfaced], it was a kick in the teeth," team president Dave St. Peter said when describing the feeling of that moment. "Just based on the fact that he was synonymous with Twins baseball; he was the face of the franchise. It was devastating to Major League Baseball because he was an incredible player and ambassador for the game."

Over the course of the next three months, Puckett underwent many tests and three procedures. By July he still hadn't returned to the field, and he still couldn't see. For one last time, Puckett underwent surgery, and the result would send a sickening feeling across Twins Territory; Puckett's loss of vision couldn't be fixed, his career was over after 12 seasons in a Twins uniform.

On July 13, with gauze over his right eye and glasses over that, Puckett strolled to the microphone wearing his uniform one last time. The team silently made their way to the front rows of the room, where they would watch the greatest Minnesota Twin ever say good-bye.

It was quiet and tense, and as the room looked on and other baseball fans listened intently across the Midwest, Puckett spoke.

"It's the last time you're going to see Kirby Puckett in a Twins uniform," Puckett said calmly. "I want to tell you all that I love you all so much."

Just like that, a great career came to a sudden halt.

"That was a day that was just filled with tremendous sadness for the Twins, the state of Minnesota, and baseball fans across the Midwest," St. Peter said. "Everybody remembers the class and dignity that Kirby had. His words provided a roadmap for how an athlete or individual should handle adversity. I think that day was historic for many reasons, but maybe mostly for the way Kirby handled it."

## Kirby Puckett, Quote Machine

*"Kirby Puckett's going to be all right. Don't worry about me. I'll show up, and I'll have a smile on my face. The only thing I won't have is this uniform on. But you guys can have the memories of what I did when I did have it on."*
—Retirement press conference, 1996

*"I want you to remember the guiding principles of my life: you can be what you want to be if you believe in yourself and you work hard, because anything, and I'm telling you anything, is possible."* —Hall of Fame speech, 2001

*"I was told I would never make it because I'm too short. Well, I'm still too short.... It doesn't matter what your height is, it's what's in your heart."*
—Hall of Fame speech, 2001

*"Just don't take it for granted, because tomorrow is not promised to any of us."*
—Retirement press conference, 1996

As his teammates cried and thousands of fans did the same, Puckett's face remained dry. After stepping to the plate for 7,244 at-bats and collecting 2,304 hits, Puckett's chance at reaching eminent milestones had been halted. But he had no regrets, and he assured everybody that he would be just fine.

"It's time for me to close this chapter of this book in baseball and go on with Part II of my life," Puckett said to his teammates and reporters. "Kirby Puckett's going to be all right. Don't worry about me."

And before he stepped out of the spotlight and into a new phase of his life, Puckett shared some final advice, just as he had done on so many occasions previously.

"Just don't take it for granted, because tomorrow is not promised to any of us."

From a multi-hit game one day to the loss of vision the next and eventually the sudden end to a great career, Puckett found out firsthand how quickly life can change. He never did take it for granted, and his message and spirit that day were certainly enough to remind fans to do the same.

 **Kent Hrbek**

His career was the ideal childhood dream turned into reality.

Growing up in Bloomington, Minnesota, Kent Hrbek lived just two miles from Metropolitan Stadium and could see the lights at night from his yard. He excelled in baseball in high school, scouts noticed, and his hometown team drafted him. And then he played there in his home state for his entire 14-year career, guiding the Twins to several successful seasons and posting numbers to put him with other team greats by the time his career came to an end.

He was the epitome of a hometown hero.

For one man, the guy known by many over the years simply as "Herbie," the common dream was lived; and lived bigger than most could ever imagine. It all began in 1978, when the Twins selected him in the 17th round. Just three years later, at the age of 21, his fantasy became reality.

Sitting in last place in the division, after a strike and during a season that would turn out to be one of the worst in franchise history, Hrbek stepped onto the field in a Twins uniform for the first time on August 24, 1981, at Yankee Stadium. Tied at 2–2 in the top half of the 12th inning, Hrbek led off and blasted his first career home run, an eventual game-winning blast, into the seats. It was all just beginning for Hrbek, and there would be many more blasts in the years ahead.

That 1981 season, in which Hrbek appeared in just 24 games, would be his only chance to play in the ballpark located near his home. But there would be many more seasons—13 of them, in fact—for Hrbek in the state of Minnesota. He became a full-time player during his official rookie season in 1982, and he made his one and only All-Star Game appearance that year, hitting .301 with 23 home runs and 92 RBIs.

Over the next several seasons Hrbek continued to excel. In 1984 he hit 27 home runs and drove in a career-best 107 runners as he finished second in the American League MVP voting. It would be three seasons later that Hrbek would begin capturing the fans' attention as a hometown hero.

For the first time in more than two decades, the Twins were in the World Series in 1987, and Hrbek was still at first base. As the team entered Game 6, they trailed the St. Louis Cardinals in the series 3–2. It was the sixth inning, and with the Twins leading 6–5, Hrbek helped put the game away when he stepped to the plate with the bases loaded. Herbie hit a famous grand slam, and what he did the next morning is just as memorable. With Game 7 and the

*Kent Hrbek hits his sixth-inning grand slam homer in the Metrodome in Minneapolis, October 24, 1987, during Game 6 of the World Series against the St. Louis Cardinals.*

team's chance at a title looming, Hrbek headed out on a duck hunt early on the morning of October 25, 1987. Later that night he and the Twins captured the first championship in team history.

Four years later the Twins were back on the big stage in Game 2 of the 1991 World Series. Leading 2–1 in the third inning, Ron

Gant ripped a two-out single to left field and moved the potential tying run to third base. As he rounded first, the ball was thrown over to Hrbek, who tagged him out as he fell off the base. The Twins would eventually win that game by one run and the World Series by one game. The Braves and their fans felt Hrbek had pulled Gant off the base, and he became so hated in Atlanta that he received death threats when the team traveled there later in the series.

As his career started following a strike in baseball during the 1981 season, it ended prematurely because of a strike in 1994. Hrbek had told reporters that he would call it a career following that season, and when it ended early, he was suddenly done at the age of 34.

"I am tired of hurting all the time," Hrbek said. "This old body is pretty beat up. I don't want to put myself through that again after this year."

For 14 seasons Hrbek lived the childhood dream right where he grew up, and along with his 293 home runs, he also helped lead the team to two championships as he became the hometown hero.

"My career has exceeded my dreams," Hrbek said when he called it a career. "Two world championship parades in my hometown—that's a lot of memories."

Memories that most can only dream about and nobody will ever forget.

# 15 Herb Carneal

"Hi, everybody."

Sitting in the car, strolling down the street, listening to the radio in bed while the team played on the West Coast, or sitting next to the radio on some other occasion, those are the words thousands of

Twins fans heard over the 45 years that Herb Carneal sat in the booth as the radio broadcaster for the Minnesota Twins.

When Terry Cashman wrote the song, "Play-by-Play," he included a part that goes, "I saw it on the radio." That portion refers to Carneal's tremendous ability. He was the Michelangelo of broadcasting, sitting in a group of select broadcasters such as Vin Scully and Ernie Harwell, guys who could paint a picture with words. Fans might not have been able to see Harmon Killebrew hit a home run, Kirby Puckett make a catch, or Justin Morneau scoop the ball at first base, but as Carneal calmly described the scene, it was almost as if a picture were being painted, and the play being visualized impeccably by those listening across the Midwest.

Herb Carneal was the voice of Twins baseball.

"I think Herb's impact has been unmatched," team president Dave St. Peter said. "Multiple generations grew up listening to the voice of Herb Carneal. He was described as the 'Voice of Summer,' and I think that says it best. There was a level of calmness that came along with Herb, he represented everything that is good about Twins baseball: family and the quality of life that we love here in this part of the country."

It was 1954 when Carneal first hit the major leagues. That year, he began calling games in Philadelphia, and he broadcast for the Athletics and Phillies there until his breakthrough opportunity came in 1957. Carneal moved off to Baltimore, where he joined Harwell in the booth calling Orioles games. After spending five seasons on the East Coast, Carneal was offered the position with the Minnesota Twins, and for four and a half decades, he became the voice heard around the Midwest for six months each year.

It was a voice of talent, and Carneal was a man filled with knowledge and passion for both the game of baseball and his job. He rarely missed games until he stopped traveling with the team in 1998 and then restricted his appearances to only home afternoon

*From 1962 until his death in 2007, Herb Carneal was the voice of Twins baseball. He was honored with the Ford C. Frick Award in 1996.* Photo courtesy Minnesota Twins

games in 2003. But even then, his legacy spread across Twins Territory, and that voice was a signature.

There was no signature call or special flair with Carneal, but that's what made him great. His goal was to paint a picture of the game's every moment; allowing those words, and not some particular

## Carneal's Calls

*"Here's the set, the two-strike pitch...swing on a little pop-up back into shallow left field. Washington the shortstop under it, and the game is over. Roy Smalley has made the final out here at Metropolitan Stadium with a pop-up to the shortstop U.L. Washington in shallow left field."*
—Metropolitan Stadium, September 30, 1981

*"Gaetti has it...over to Hrbek, and the Twins are baseball's world champions! The world champion Minnesota Twins!"* —1987 World Series

*"His first pitch to Larkin...swung on, there it is, a long fly ball into left-center field, and it is going to be a hit for Gene Larkin. Gladden scores, and once again the Minnesota Twins are baseball's world champions. For the second time in five years, it's the world champion Minnesota Twins...and the crowd loves it!"*
—1991 World Series

*"Erickson taking the sign from Walbeck...from the set, he delivers. A swing and a high fly ball to left field, Cole is coming in...has it, and it's a no-hit, no-run game for Scott Erickson."* —Scott Erickson no-hitter, April 26, 1991

*"Eric Milton into the windup...and the pitch. Swing and a miss, he struck him out! A no-hit, no-run game for Eric Milton; being mobbed by the Twins coming out of the third-base dugout."* —Eric Milton no-hitter, September 11, 1999

style, to be the show. He once said that the keys to broadcasting were to describe the play, let the audience hear the crowd, and then explain what happened. That's exactly what he did, and even without an exclusive mark, he became regarded as one of the best.

In 1996 Carneal was honored with the Ford C. Frick Award, the highest honor a baseball broadcaster can receive, and an honor that effectively placed him in the broadcaster's wing of the National Baseball Hall of Fame in Cooperstown, New York. Five years later, the Twins added him to their Hall of Fame, and he still resides as the only broadcaster in that prominent group.

On April 1, 2007, one day before the team's first regular season game, Carneal passed away at the age of 83. He had spent more than a half-century as a broadcaster, and most of those years as the voice of Twins baseball. His incredible talent and voice were gone, but his legacy and the memories for several generations of Twins fans have carried on well into the future. When fans heard the words, "Hi, everybody," they knew they had tuned in to the right station, and that Herb Carneal was about to tell them a story in a way only he could.

He was the Voice of Summer, and nothing will ever change that.

## Mentoring in Minnesota

The players who have patrolled center field in Minneapolis over the course of the past two decades have a lot in common. Kirby Puckett, Torii Hunter, and Denard Span all rose through the Twins' farm system, they were all highly regarded, and each became a mainstay in the team's lineup. The three all share something much greater than their talents though; all three are connected in a chain of mentoring.

It was 1994 in Fort Myers, Florida, and standing there in front of Torii Hunter was the legend himself, the World Series hero, Kirby Puckett. When he helped guide the Twins to a World Series victory in 1987, Puckett was just a 27-year-old kid. Now, with a young center field prospect in spring training, he had become a 34-year-old veteran leader.

The previous year, in the summer of 1993, Hunter had been drafted with the team's first-round pick, the 20th overall selection in the draft. He quickly became the guy many thought would one day replace the greatest Minnesota Twin ever. Puckett helped Hunter, he took him out for dinner that spring, he helped him on the field, and he provided him with advice. Never did Puckett look

51

for anything in return, he only asked Hunter to some day in the future pay the favor forward.

Soon after Puckett was forced to retire with glaucoma prior to the 1996 season, Hunter took over center field at the Metrodome, playing his first full season with the Twins in 1999. Hunter quickly established himself as one of the game's best center fielders, making the All-Star Game in 2002. That same summer, the Twins selected center fielder Denard Span with the 20th pick in the amateur draft.

The similarities from the beginning were astounding. Each player had been selected with the 20th pick in the first round, about one decade apart, they were both quickly regarded as highly touted prospects, and in the years following their selection by the Twins, they'd each carry on the mentoring tradition in Minnesota.

In almost the same scenario, Hunter had gone from the 18-year-old youngster in 1994 to the 26-year-old leader when Span arrived at the Metrodome to visit for the first time in 2002.

"Torii began mentoring me the day I first met him at the Metrodome in 2002," recalled Span. "It was a surreal feeling to have an All-Star actually keep in touch with me."

Following the team's comeback season in 2006, Hunter had just one year remaining on his contract. That off-season he met with Span, brought him to his home, and provided him with advice just as Puckett had previously done.

After the 2007 season Hunter left for Anaheim, California, and in stepped Span. He wouldn't make the team out of spring training, but by the end of the 2008 season, he was leading off in Game 163 for the Twins as they attempted to make the playoffs.

In the years since the team selected Span, they have drafted two more outfield prospects, including Ben Revere in 2007 and Aaron Hicks in 2008. As has been the case over the past two decades of Twins baseball, the players are similar. Both Revere and Hicks were first-round selections and both quickly became highly regarded across baseball.

At the age of 26, entering the team's first season at Target Field, Span had already taken up the role of mentoring. He took Revere and others out for dinner, and in the shadow of both Puckett and Hunter, he's providing advice.

"I keep in touch with Ben throughout the season and also a little during the off-season," said Span. "Last spring training was the first time that I was able to take him and some others out to eat and mentor them like Torii did with others and me when I was younger."

It's a tradition that has spanned nearly two decades in team history, and with more young prospects on the way, there's no reason to believe that the trend will soon come to an end.

"I believe it must continue," Span concluded. "Torii always told me that when I got older and took his job, to pass the torch to the next guy."

# The Comeback

Who would have thought?

The Twins lost to the Seattle Mariners on June 7, 2006, pushing their deficit in the American League Central to 11½ games behind the first-place Detroit Tigers. That one-run loss, in which the Twins allowed an 11th-inning run, would become a tremendous spark.

Over the course of the remaining games in June, the Twins would go 18–2. They went 18–8 in July, and then slowed down in August, going 16–12 before picking it back up and going 18–9 in September, heading into the final series of the season.

After going a combined 70–31 from a day after their extra-inning loss in early June, the Twins entered the final weekend of the season tied atop the American League Central. Each game would be critical. The Twins would host an eventual 90-win Chicago White Sox team at the Metrodome while the Tigers would host a last-place Kansas City Royals team in their home ballpark.

The first two days in Minneapolis were filled with frustration. In the first game of their three-game series with the White Sox, the Twins rallied for two runs in the bottom half of the ninth inning, but came up short and lost a one-run ballgame. In Game 2 the Twins rallied for three ninth-inning runs, but yet again came up short, this time by three runs.

The Twins had lost the first two games of their final series of the season, but the Tigers lost, as well, and the two teams headed to October and the final regular season game of the 2006 season with a division title on the line.

One goal was on the mind of the Twins as they entered Game 162: win. If the Twins could come away with a victory, they'd force at the very least a tie for the division. Starting pitcher Carlos Silva allowed a first-inning run, but Torii Hunter's home run in the fourth inning gave the Twins a lead that they would never surrender.

The Twins had won their 96th game of the season, but the Tigers played on about 700 miles east in Detroit, Michigan. Fans remained seated at the Metrodome, with all eyes locked on the video boards around the stadium.

After nine innings in Detroit the score was tied, and the Tigers and Royals headed to extra innings. Two runs in the top half of the 12th inning would push Kansas City to a series sweep and set in motion an eruption from the remaining fans at the Dome.

Joe Mauer won his first American League batting title that day, ending the season with a .347 batting average. The comeback, combined with strong season performances, would also soon net starting pitcher Johan Santana and first baseman Justin Morneau their own hardware. Santana took home his second

Cy Young Award and Morneau the American League Most Valuable Player Award that off-season.

In the end, the Twins would be swept out of the playoffs, and the Tigers eventually would be headed to the World Series as the American League wild-card. But the Minnesota Twins had pulled off one of the greatest comebacks of all-time, winning 71 of their final 104 games, creating memories that fans will forever remember, and a season that will forever be etched into the best of Twins history.

 **Bob Casey**

His voice was heard through generations of Twins baseball. Every fan has one memory or another about him. He mispronounced names, he was seldom serious, he had his signature phrases, and players and fans from around baseball looked up to him. His name was Bob Casey, and after spending 44 seasons as the public address announcer of the Minnesota Twins, it's a name that won't soon be forgotten.

Casey began his announcing career in 1947, when the Minneapolis Lakers hired him, and he started doing Minneapolis Millers games in 1951. When the Washington Senators moved to Minnesota in 1961, Casey had a new job. It would be his last. That year, on April 21, he was the announcer for the first regular season game at the Twins' home of Metropolitan Stadium. Over the course of four decades and more than 3,300 Twins games, he became a signature voice at the ballpark and a memorable one for all fans and players of several generations.

"His voice certainly was synonymous with Twins baseball," team president Dave St. Peter said of Casey. "From Harmon

Killebrew and Tony Oliva to Rod Carew and Roy Smalley to Kent Hrbek and Kirby Puckett to Joe Mauer and Justin Morneau, Bob Casey announced them all in one generation or another."

When you spend as much time as a public figure as Casey did, there are bound to be many memories. But the recollections that arise from his legacy don't stem from a long tenure with the team, but rather from a special talent that Casey and few others have ever possessed.

From his yell of, "There is n-o-o-o-o-o-o smoking in the Metrodome!" before every game, to his sometimes-intentional, sometimes-accidental mispronunciations of a player's name, to his humorous and witty side, to the way he bellowed, "Kir-beeeee Puckett!" every time No. 34 stepped to the plate, Casey was always an essential and illustrious part of baseball in Minnesota.

There were many friendships over the years. Casey became especially close with Kent Hrbek and Kirby Puckett, as well as a guy who never played in Minnesota, Alex Rodriguez. While he'd announce every other player from the opposing team casually, Casey always put more emphasis into Rodriguez's name. And when others stepped to the plate, sometimes he just said it all wrong. Who else announced Omar Vizquel as Ozzie Virgil, Nomar Garciaparra as Garcia Parra, or Carlos Baerga as Carlos Viagra? The answer is nobody, but the examples are the reason Casey was beloved and one-of-a-kind.

"He's one of the great announcers of all-time," said Rodriguez in 2005. "He and I grew very fond of each other, became very close, and I have a lot of respect for this man."

When remembering Casey, there are always two stories that tend to arise. One comes from a moment on August 25, 1970, when a bomb threat surfaced at Metropolitan Stadium. Casey's job was to evacuate the ballpark and keep fans calm. So he said over the speakers, "Ladies and gentleman, please do not panic…there will be an *explosion* in 15 minutes!" And then there is the memorable

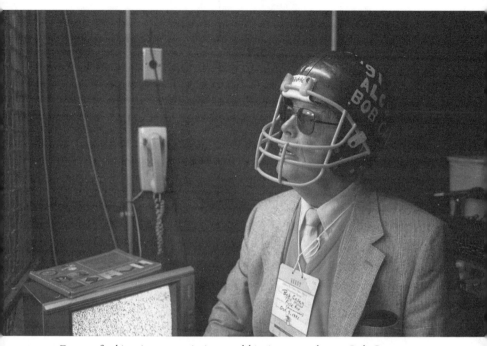

*Famous for his mispronounciations and his signature phrases, Bob Casey spent 44 years as the Twins' public address announcer. Here, Casey shows off his humorous side by wearing a football helmet.* Photo courtesy Minnesota Twins

moment during Game 7 of the 1987 World Series when the players locked Casey in the dugout bathroom during a TV break. When he got out, Casey rushed back to his booth to answer a ringing phone. As he put it up to his ear, he found that it contained shaving cream.

For almost the entire first half-century of Twins baseball, when you thought of the team, you thought of Bob Casey, too. He was an indispensable part of the game. Fans waited to hear his pregame introductions and announcements, and with each at-bat there was a chance something entertaining might occur. That was Casey, and that was the experience in Minnesota until he suddenly passed away on March 27, 2005, just shy of his 80th birthday and what was to be his final season in his hut behind home plate at the Metrodome where he made his magic.

"Bob Casey was a dear friend and mentor to me," said the team's public address announcer, Adam Abrams, when he took over for Casey in 2006. "He will forever be remembered as one of the great voices in professional sports. I have tremendous respect for his legacy and what he meant to the Twins organization and fans. I'm humbled to be given this opportunity but can never replace Bob."

There is nobody who could ever fill the shoes that Bob Casey left open when he passed away, but with all the memories he created over the years, they certainly won't ever disappear.

 # Game 163: Take I

If it wasn't apparent previously, the Minnesota Twins found out how big of an impact one game can really make on a season. On that day, September 30, 2008, the Twins were getting ready to play in an extra regular season game, Game 163, to decide a winner of the American League Central after tying with the Chicago White Sox at the conclusion of their initial schedule.

It didn't have to be that way, though: the Twins could have avoided that eventual dreaded trip to Chicago.

The downfall began in the final weeks of August that season. With the Republican National Convention in town, the Twins were forced to the road for two weeks of nonstop action with 14 consecutive games. The first part of the road trip would put the Twins on the West Coast for 11 straight games against the Los Angeles Angels, Oakland Athletics, and Seattle Mariners. It would conclude with a three-game series in Toronto, where the Twins would face the Blue Jays before at last returning to the comfortable confines of the Metrodome in Minneapolis.

After all was said and done, things hadn't gone anywhere near the way the Twins would have liked. They went just 5–9 on that trip, with eight of the losses coming by two or fewer runs. Joe Nathan, at that point arguably the best closer in the game since having joined the organization in 2004, went just 2-for-5 in save opportunities, blowing an uncharacteristic three saves in a short span.

That run of poor play would be what many would look back on as the reason this Game 163 was happening. So often, the saying goes, "It's just one game, there's always tomorrow." Most of the time that turns out to be true—one game doesn't always make the difference. But in this year it did. Had the Twins won just one of those games—just one at any other point that year—they would have avoided that night. Then again, the White Sox could have said the same thing.

On the mound for the Twins was Nick Blackburn; the youngster who had gone 11–10 to that point in his rookie season. It turned out that Blackburn couldn't have been much better. Through the first six innings, he held the White Sox scoreless and scattered two harmless singles and three walks.

Unfortunately for Minnesota, Blackburn's opposition, John Danks, was even better. He allowed just one hit through the first two-thirds of the game and scattered three walks to keep the Twins out of the run column.

In the top half of the seventh inning, slugger Jim Thome stepped to the plate. Before he joined the Twins for their inaugural season at Target Field in 2010, Thome had blasted 57 career home runs against them, and one of them came as the leadoff batter in this inning. It was the one bad pitch by Blackburn that night.

The White Sox would never score again, but neither did the Twins. Danks kept dealing, allowing just a single in his final two innings of work, ending his night with eight scoreless, two-hit innings. The ball would be handed to Bobby Jenks for the ninth, and one game defined the team's entire season as the Chicago closer shut the door, making the White Sox the 2008 American League Central division champions.

One pitch defined the season. The fly ball off Thome's bat that flew an estimated 461 feet into the hedges at U.S. Cellular Field ended the Twins' run at the playoffs, leaving them one game short of the divisional crown.

But it didn't have to be like that.

Had the Twins found a way to pull out one other game along the way, they'd have been celebrating well before that day, and they would have avoided that painful trip back to Minneapolis. In the end, the loss on that September night would come as practice. The Twins now knew how much of a difference one game could make, and they'd soon have a chance to prove it.

 Game 163: Take II

"This game is going to live forever," manager Ron Gardenhire would say after the game. "People are going to talk about this forever."

It was a game so great that today it needs no title other than "163." It was so good that it has been called the greatest regular season game in Minnesota Twins history. That extra regular season game on October 6, 2009, the final regular season game in the Metrodome's history, was the embodiment of baseball at its best.

Nobody could have scripted it any better. Shouldn't the eventual American League Most Valuable Player get the walk-off hit? Shouldn't arguably the best closer in baseball get the final out? "No," said the baseball gods, "they shouldn't."

Just one year and about one week earlier, the Twins had flown to Chicago to play in this very game—a one-game playoff to determine the winner of the American League Central. That day the

Twins would lose 1–0, and they found out how much one game really meant, how one lone win or loss could define an entire season's work.

As was the case during the 2008 season, the reason for this one-game playoff couldn't be traced back to a bad two-week stretch. The Twins had been up and down for much of the season, but with no Justin Morneau, they rallied in the final three weeks, winning 16 of their final 20 scheduled games to catch the Detroit Tigers.

In the team's final seven games, they'd play the Tigers four times. They needed at the very least a split to stay in contention, and after losing two of the first three games in Michigan, they won the series finale and remained two games back with three still left to play. Catching the Tigers was still improbable. The Twins would need to somehow gain two games in a three-game span. They'd do it, though. While they swept the Kansas City Royals at the Metrodome, the White Sox provided some help, taking the first two games from the Tigers before falling in the finale.

For the second straight season, one game would decide the division.

The game would have been played a day earlier, but the Minnesota Vikings were hosting the Green Bay Packers on that Monday night, and since this wasn't an actual playoff game, football took precedence over baseball, giving both teams a day off to prepare for battle.

Things didn't start the way the Twins would have hoped. The Tigers put a three-spot up in the third inning, and while the Twins would get one run back in the bottom half of the inning on a Rick Porcello error, the crowd was rather silent.

For the next two innings, nothing happened. The Twins remained down 3–1 heading into the sixth inning. After Orlando Cabrera and Joe Mauer were retired, Jason Kubel hit a two-out home run, bringing the Twins within a run and bringing the crowd back to life.

The next inning Nick Punto led off with a single to left field. After Denard Span struck out, the Twins' mid-season acquisition, Cabrera, stepped to the plate and launched a deep fly ball into left field. The ball cleared the wall by mere inches.

Twins 4, Tigers 3.

For the remainder of the game, fans would be on their feet. With two more innings and a strong bullpen, it was going to be tough for Detroit to come back now, right? Not so much. As the first batter of the eighth inning, Magglio Ordonez homered off reliever Matt Guerrier.

Twins 4, Tigers 4.

After the home run that inning, Guerrier would get just one out and walk two hitters. The Twins were forced to summon closer Joe Nathan from the bullpen, and he'd end the inning, getting third baseman Brandon Inge to pop to second and then striking out catcher Gerald Laird to end the threat.

Nathan remained on for the ninth inning, allowing a perfectly placed leadoff bunt single. Curtis Granderson singled next, and the Tigers had runners on the corners with nobody out. The crowd sighed; there was no way the Twins wouldn't allow a run. Except they didn't. Nathan struck out Placido Polanco, and Ordonez lined to Cabrera at shortstop, who then caught Granderson off first base for the final out.

The Twins did nothing in the ninth, and the game headed to extras. After Aubrey Huff was hit by a pitch with one out, Inge doubled to left, scoring a run. The Metrodome magic seemed to be nearing an end. After 28 seasons, the team's tenure could soon be over.

Tigers 5, Twins 4.

There was more magic, though. In fact, the Metrodome seemed to have a message for the baseball world. Michael Cuddyer hit a sinking line drive to left field to lead off the bottom half of the 10th, and the ball skipped under the glove of left fielder Ryan Raburn, rolling all the way to the wall and sending Cuddyer all the way to third base. Brendan Harris would walk, and Alexi Casilla came on to run. With runners on the corners, Matt Tolbert singled; the Twins were back in it.

Twins 5, Tigers 5.

There was still just one out in the inning, and the Twins had runners on the corners. When Punto lifted a fly ball into left field, it seemed that the Twins might end the game. Raburn was seeking some revenge, though, and after getting a late jump, Casilla was thrown out at the plate. The Twins wouldn't take the lead that inning.

Nothing happened through 11 innings, so the game headed to the 12th. With basically nobody left to pitch, Bobby Keppel

*Carlos Gomez (22) scores the game-winning run as his teammates follow during the 12th inning of a game against the Detroit Tigers on October 6, 2009, in Minneapolis. The Twins won 6–5 to take the AL Central title.*

remained on the hill and worked into a bases-loaded jam. With one out and the bases packed, Keppel got a groundball from Inge, and Punto played it perfectly, firing to home plate for the second out. The next batter, Laird, struck out swinging. Inning over.

Carlos Gomez, who had come on as a defensive replacement in the eighth, singled to lead off the bottom half of the inning. After Michael Cuddyer grounded out, Delmon Young was walked intentionally to set up the double play. There would be no need for it, though, as Casilla stepped in, having had only two at-bats in nearly a span of one month. With Detroit closer Fernando Rodney still on the mound for his fourth inning of work, Casilla hit a grounder that slipped into right field, sending Gomez home for the winning run and sending the crowd of 54,088 fans into an eruption.

Twins 6, Tigers 5.

One season after missing the playoffs by one game, the Twins had come out on the other end, making an improbable comeback and winning the American League Central. Not only was it the best regular season game in team history, it was baseball at its best. Bobby Keppel collected the win, and two players who had started on the bench, Casilla and Gomez, combined for the winning run.

Ron Gardenhire was right: the number 163 won't soon be forgotten.

# 21 Carl Pohlad

A famous writer once wrote, "The way you get meaning into your life is to devote yourself to loving others, devote yourself to your community around you, and devote yourself to creating something that gives you purpose and meaning." Carl Pohlad did all of those things and more.

Born in 1915, Carl learned about hard work from a young age. During the tough times of the Great Depression, Carl worked in the cornfields, where he first became a businessman. He'd gather up local boys to pick weeds, collecting five cents' commission of each boy's wages.

While it was often nonstop work for the boy, Carl took great pride in his sports, including football. Pohlad played two seasons at Gonzaga University before returning to Iowa after his senior season.

Upon his return to the Midwest, Carl continued to work until he was drafted into the Army in 1942. While he was in Europe, however, Carl's businessman-like ways continued as he used a tent to continue his small-loans occupation.

Pohlad was injured in the war, returned to Iowa where he received a Purple Heart, and in 1947 he married his wife, Eloise.

After years of being an entrepreneur in several industries, including the Pepsi-Cola bottling company and many banks, Carl Pohlad for the first time became a widely known figure when he purchased the Minnesota Twins from Calvin Griffith in 1984 for $34 million, effectively keeping the Twins as Minnesota's team. At the time of the purchase, there were rumblings of the team possibly being moved to Florida. Pohlad helped dash those thoughts, and better things for the baseball franchise located in Minneapolis were in store.

"I believe Carl did save baseball in Minnesota," said Minnesota Twins assistant general manager Rob Antony. "Calvin Griffith was poised to sell the team, and we would have been moved to Florida. Mr. Pohlad stepped in and purchased the club and looked at it as entertainment value, not only for his family, but also for the people of Minnesota and the Upper Midwest."

That's how Carl was; while he was a businessman at heart, Pohlad cared deeply about the community, and when he purchased the Twins, his intent was to keep the team a local product.

"No one can know for sure what would have happened had Mr. Pohlad not purchased the team, but the fact remains that he did keep the Twins in Minnesota," said Twins president and good friend Dave St. Peter. "Mr. Pohlad knew that the Twins were a community asset. By buying and owning the team, he enabled this community asset to remain here [in Minnesota] for the long term."

Within the first few seasons under Pohlad's wing, the Twins won World Series titles in 1987 and 1991. Carl loved to win and was even more keen on building a solid foundation for the organization.

"His biggest contribution to the Twins, in my estimation, was his ability to foster continuity, and he created a solid base for the organization," said Antony. "He didn't panic when things weren't going well, and he hired good people and let them do their jobs."

Letting his people do the work was another thing that Pohlad strongly believed in. While some baseball owners take pride in running the show and being in the spotlight, Pohlad didn't care for the attention.

Aside from being a great businessman who was careful with his money, Pohlad was strong on respect and showed that in the way he treated his staff.

"Mr. Pohlad was a very thoughtful man and respected his employees," St. Peter said. "He was a big fan but never interjected too much in the operation of the franchise. He was very supportive of his employees and trusted them to do their jobs well. When he was at games, he always had a smile and a handshake for everyone. He often enjoyed stepping into the manager's office for a kind conversation and a vote of confidence."

And it wasn't only the staff that Pohlad cared for, he loved his players, and it was always important to him that his organization was a model for other teams.

"He and his wife, Eloise, genuinely cared about the players and wanted to win," Antony said, "but they were most proud of having

*Carl Pohlad, shown here with an early model of a newly proposed ballpark in 1997, kept baseball in Minnesota when he bought the team in 1984. Pohlad passed away just one year before his team began playing in Target Field.*

an organization they could be proud of and one that was respected in the game."

Pohlad was never criticized for being unkind or trying to steal the spotlight. The biggest mark against Carl in his years as the team's owner was for being cheap.

## A Story About Carl Pohlad

Team president Dave St. Peter remembered one of his fondest memories of longtime owner Carl Pohlad: "When the team clinched the division title in 2006, Mr. Pohlad was wearing his lucky red socks to the game. He went into the clubhouse where the players were celebrating and joined in that celebration. But what he also did was what was most impressive. In an adjacent dining room, front-office employees assembled for their own celebration. Mr. Pohlad—always thinking about the employees—wheeled into the dining room and thanked all the front-office employees for their hard work, dedication, and sacrifice and reminded everyone that this celebration wouldn't be happening if it were not for all the hard work they put in, too. He then made a toast. Unfortunately, we didn't have any champagne glasses in that dining room...so we poured some in a paper Pepsi cup, and he hoisted that in the air!"

Many blamed Pohlad for not spending money and for simply putting a team on the field to be semi-competitive rather than a team promised to win it all. Carl was, after all, one of the richest owners in the game; *Forbes Magazine* estimated Pohlad's fortune at $3.8 billion shortly before his death, making him one of the richest men in America. Yet what many fans never understood was that Carl was a businessman at heart and had many other investments in addition to the Twins.

"Mr. Pohlad was not a cheap owner," Antony said. "Mr. Pohlad was willing to pay what he needed, setting benchmarks when we signed Kirby Puckett for $3 million a year and again when he got $6 million per year. Many fans and media look at his overall net worth and think he should spend whatever it takes to have a championship team. The Pohlads have always been very competitive and want to win, but they also believe in running the organization as a business in that it should be self-sustaining."

Carl Pohlad passed away prior to the 2009 season, leaving the team in the family and leaving fans with two championships and a new ballpark to create many new memories.

# Brad Radke

Brad Radke wasn't a big-name pitcher. He didn't possess a high-velocity fastball that blew hitters away, and he made just one All-Star appearance during his 12 seasons at the major league level. But Radke was the epitome of Minnesota Twins baseball. He was quiet, he was loyal through and through, and the righty from Eau Claire, Wisconsin, had heart.

In 1995 Radke made his debut with the Twins, winning 11 games as a member of the team's starting rotation for the entirety of his rookie season. It would be the start of a long and very consistent career for Radke.

Over the course of the next 12 seasons, Radke would put a double-digit number up in the win column 10 times, and he topped the 200-inning mark nine times. The consistency for Radke helped put him at the top of the organization's leader board when he called it quits following the 2006 season. After putting on a Twins uniform for just over a decade, Radke finished his career sitting at third in franchise history with 377 games started, fourth with 148 victories, and fifth with a total of 2,451 innings pitched and 1,467 strikeouts.

Those are the numbers on Brad Radke, but numbers don't tell his whole story. More than a consistent pitcher who ended his career with numbers that put him in a group of elite players from Twins history, Radke was tough.

During the 2006 season, the one that would prove to be Radke's last, toughness showed the most. After getting off to a slow start to the tune of an 8.89 ERA, Radke improved as the days

*In the course of his 12-year career with the Twins, Brad Radke pitched more than 200 innings nine times. Known for his consistency and his toughness, Radke ended his career with 377 games started and 148 wins. He was inducted into the Twins Hall of Fame in 2009.*

moved to summer. In the end, he'd complete his final season with a 12–9 record and a 4.32 ERA.

In his mid-thirties, those numbers were respectable. More respectable was the fact that Radke did most of his pitching that season with a torn labrum, staying on schedule with cortisone shots between starts. This didn't surprise many people, though. It was the same Radke who stayed a Twin when he could have bolted for a larger market and more money during free agency, and the same Radke who played with a total of 197 different Twins in his career, including two Hall of Famers.

For many players, numbers define a career. How many wins or strikeouts are racked up over the course of a career oftentimes characterize how successful a player was. Radke could have won more games on better teams, but he was fine with less fame, and he was committed to and was an essential part of turning the Twins back into a contender during the 2000s.

When Brad Radke was inducted into the Twins Hall of Fame during the 2009 season, he apologized to fans for not bringing Minnesota a championship. He may not have won a title and he isn't headed for baseball's Hall of Fame, but his career will be remembered for more than numbers and accomplishments— Radke had the heart and toughness of a champion.

# "We're Gonna Win, Twins!"

When you've gone to a baseball game in Minnesota, or in any other location for that matter, there has long been the expectation to hear "Take Me Out to the Ball Game" during the seventh-inning stretch. At a Twins game exclusively, though, there is yet another expectation. Since the team first moved to the state in 1961, the song "We're Gonna Win, Twins" has guided players onto the field for each home game.

The song was originally a collaboration between a man named Ray Charles (not *that* Ray Charles) and Dick Wilson, two local jingle writers who worked for the ad agency Campbell Mithun. It first debuted in a commercial as the jingle for a local company, Hamm's Beer:

*Sing out for Hamm's beer,*
*Sing out the name,*
*Sing out for Hamm's beer,*
*Of sky-blue waters fame.*

After the Twins made the move from Washington to Minnesota in the fall of 1960 to play their first season in the state the following year, owner Calvin Griffith purchased the rights to the tune for just $1, and the words were changed to fit the Twins:

*We're gonna win, Twins*
*We're gonna score*
*We're gonna win, Twins*
*Watch that baseball soar.*
*Crack out a home run*
*Shout a hip-hooray*
*Cheer for the Minnesota Twins today!*
*We're gonna win, Twins, give it our all!*
*We've got the guys who'll knock the cover off the ball!*
*Let's hear it now for the team that came to play!*
*Cheer for the Minnesota Twins today!*

Since its inception during the team's inaugural season in Minnesota, the song has undergone one small transformation. In 1990 it was made more modern with some additional length, supplementary background, and overall minor touches. Nevertheless, it still remains as the introduction for the team for each home date every season.

From Harmon Killebrew to Rod Carew to Kent Hrbek to Kirby Puckett to Torii Hunter to Joe Mauer, and from Metropolitan Stadium to the Metrodome and now to Target Field, "We're Gonna Win, Twins" has been the team's identity for each of the franchise's first 50 seasons in Minnesota. From Opening Day to the regular season games that follow, and even in the much-anticipated playoff games, fans have stood and clapped as the song plays above and as the players scamper from the dugout to their positions at the start of each game.

The jingle is short and to the point, but when it plays over the speakers each game, and as fans rise to their feet to greet the players, there is no better place to be. The song is enough to get a fan pumped up and ready for America's pastime, and when the Twins fulfill the lyrics sung in the tune by providing fans in attendance with a victory, it only gets better.

# 24 Harmon Killebrew

They called him "Killer."

Half of the time the title fit just fine, the other half, not so much. On the field, Harmon Killebrew became one of the most feared hitters of his generation. He hit monstrous home runs and annihilated opposing pitchers by day and night. Off the field, he couldn't have been more different. It isn't to say he was a bad guy on the field, but his nickname stems from what he did with his bat and not his actions or personality. Killebrew was bashful and quiet in reality, much different than many would expect based on the way he blasted the ball from home plate throughout his illustrious 22-year career.

"Harmon Killebrew was one of the classiest people I've ever met in my life," former Twin Rich Reese once said. "He treated people with respect, even with the stature he had."

That stature would in time become legendary.

Born in Payette, Idaho, in 1936, Killebrew was signed as a bonus baby in 1954 by the Washington Senators. Through the first five seasons, he sat on the bench, but in 1959, at the age of 23, he played a full season and burst into the league as an everyday player in a big way. He led the league that year with 42 home runs, and it would be just the beginning of an eventual Hall of Fame career.

After one more season in Washington, in which Killebrew continued to provide a power threat with 31 more home runs, the team was moved to the Midwest, becoming the Minnesota Twins. It would be there, in Bloomington, Minnesota, and at Metropolitan Stadium, where Killebrew would spend 14 of his final 15 major league seasons and become an iconic figure in both team and baseball history.

"The important thing for me is to drive in runs and score them," Killebrew told *Sports Illustrated* in 1970. "I think I should take the hardest swings I can every time I'm at the plate."

With the physique of the mythical Paul Bunyan, Killebrew fit perfectly in Minnesota, and he certainly swung hard. He swung so hard, in fact, that he hit the farthest home runs in two different ballparks by the time his career came to an end. It was May 24, 1964, in Baltimore when Killebrew hit the first. On that day Killer hit a shot to straightaway center field that measured 471 feet; it turned into the longest home run in the history of Baltimore Memorial Stadium. Three years later, on June 3, 1967, the Twins were back at home in Metropolitan Stadium. That day Killebrew launched the longest home run in both the ballpark's history and the team's. The blast went 520 feet.

Through his career with the Twins, Killebrew belted 475 home runs. He had hit 84 when the team was in Washington and 14 in his final season with the Kansas City Royals. In all, Killebrew hit

*Harmon Killebrew's 520-foot home run on June 3, 1967, was the longest home run in both the team's and Metropolitan Stadium's history. Over his 22-year career, he hit a total of 573 home runs. In 1969 he won the American League MVP Award.*

573 home runs during his career. When he retired, Killebrew was the all-time leader in home runs by a right-handed batter, although that record has since been broken.

Killebrew led the league in home runs six times during his career, and he belted at least 40 home runs eight times, including 49 home runs in two different seasons. One of those seasons was in 1969, when Killebrew put forth his best season. That year he hit .276, and along with the 49 home runs, he racked up 140 RBIs and also led the league with 145 walks as he played in each of the team's 162 games on the way to his one and only American League MVP Award.

It was Killebrew who became the team's first true power hitter, and franchise player, too. Today he holds team records for games played (1,939), home runs (475), RBIs (1,325), walks (1,321), and, as a guy who so often went for all or nothing in the batter's box, strikeouts (1,314).

The name Killer fit perfectly for Killebrew at the plate. On so many occasions he killed the ball and with that the opposition's hopes. But while many players looked for fame, Harmon Killebrew fit perfectly in Minnesota: he didn't smoke, he didn't drink, and he was not once ejected from a game in 22 seasons. There is no doubt he was a Killer, he was just a type nobody had ever seen.

 ## Bringing Home the Hardware

Baseball is the true epitome of a team sport. A team can score 10 runs, but if the pitching staff allows more, the team still loses. Or a pitcher can put forth a quality outing, but if the offense can't score, the end result is again a loss. It takes an entire team effort at the plate, in the field, and on the mound to win a game and in the end make a run at the one big goal for each of baseball's 30 teams— winning a championship.

Whether a team wins it all or misses the playoffs entirely, the top performers are rewarded for their efforts each season with baseball's two most prestigious individual awards, the Most Valuable Player and the Cy Young Award.

Through the first 50 years of baseball in Minnesota, five players from the Minnesota Twins have won the American League Most Valuable Player Award. The MVP has been given out since 1922, but since 1931 the Baseball Writer's Association of America has awarded it, with the writers picking a winner annually.

Before the Twins made the move from Washington in 1961, two players from the Senators won the award a total of three times. Walter Johnson took the honor twice, while Roger Peckinpaugh took it home once.

The first Twins player to win the award was Zoilo Versalles in 1965. Looking to break through, the team needed big things from Versalles, and he delivered, hitting .273 with 19 home runs and 77 RBIs while playing an integral part as the Twins reached their first World Series.

Harmon Killebrew and Rod Carew would win the next two in team history. Killebrew's came in 1969 as he blasted 49 home runs and drove in 140 runners. Carew collected the award in his masterful 1977 season when he hit .388 and kept fans wondering if a .400 batting average would ever again be reached.

For almost three decades, no Twins player would be tabbed as the best from the American League. But after helping the team to one of the best comebacks of all time in 2006, Justin Morneau became the fourth player in team history to win the award. Joe Mauer would win the fifth MVP award in Twins history during the Metrodome's final season as he put forth some of the best numbers by a catcher in baseball history.

Through the first 50 seasons of Twins baseball, five players were selected as the best from the American League as they put up astonishing numbers and helped the team make a run at the postseason. The Cy Young Award, named after the righty who collected 511 career victories, has been received four times in team history by three different players.

## Player Profile: Jim Perry

Jim Perry spent 17 seasons as a major league pitcher, but none were greater than the 10 that he spent as a member of the Minnesota Twins pitching staff, and especially two seasons in the later part of his career.

In 1969 Perry was one of the best pitchers in the American League. That season he went 20–6 with a 2.82 ERA, leading the Twins to an American League West title along the way. The next season, at 34 years old, he did better. Perry went 24–12 with a 3.04 ERA that season and became the first Twin in team history to win the Cy Young Award.

Through his decade-long tenure with the Twins, Perry won a total of 128 games and made two All-Star appearances. His brother, Gaylord Perry, was a Hall of Famer, and the brothers combined for 529 victories throughout their careers.

The year 1970 would mark the first Cy Young Award for a pitcher from the Minnesota franchise. Jim Perry, a guy who pitched in 10 seasons for the Twins, won 24 games that year after having won 20 the previous season. In 1988, a year after the Twins won their first World Series, Frank Viola won 24 games, too, and received the second Cy Young Award in team history.

The next two and final Cy Young Awards collected by a player from the Twins in the team's first five decades of existence in Minnesota would be won by Johan Santana. After beginning to establish himself in the two previous seasons, Santana won 20 games in 2004 and won his first honor. The second would come along with Morneau's MVP in 2006 as Santana won the pitcher's triple crown, leading the American League in wins, ERA, and strikeouts.

Baseball may be the pinnacle of a team sport, but the nine major awards won by Twins through the team's first 50 seasons have rewarded some of the top individual performances in team history, and the team has done well in those season, as well, making the playoffs in six of the eight seasons in which a player has received the top honor.

## 26 Metropolitan Stadium

Oh, the colors.

Lined across Metropolitan Stadium were colorful panels: shades of blue, red, and yellow. They were distinctive and memorable. Those panels, and specifically those colors, are what many remember when they think back to the team's first home. Known by most simply as "The Met," it was somewhat like the team's birthplace; it was their first home, the place where the Washington Senators became the Minnesota Twins, and the place where baseball in Minnesota got its start.

As the saying goes in the film *Field of Dreams*, "If you build it, *he* will come." It turned out that *he* was Calvin Griffith, and what he would bring with him was a baseball team that would settle in Bloomington, Minnesota. Metropolitan Stadium was built for $8.5 million on a cornfield in 1956 as the home for the American Association's Minneapolis Millers. But the ultimate goal, and the ultimate vision, was having a team from Major League Baseball some day grace the field.

When it opened, Met Stadium had a capacity of 18,200. By the time the Twins left after the 1981 season, the ballpark could hold more than 45,000 fans. It had been patched together over the years to take the park from a minor league facility to a major league one, but it was the home of the Twins, nevertheless. Over the years permanent bleachers were added along the left-field line, and the first and second decks were extended down the right-field line. Finally in 1965 the expansion was complete when a large double-deck grandstand was installed in left field.

Patched together or not, Met Stadium became home for the Twins. It was a place for baseball outdoors in the greatest outdoor state. It was the place to watch some of baseball's greats, such as Harmon Killebrew, Rod Carew, Tony Oliva, and Bert Blyleven, all while catching some sun. The smell of concession food filled the air, and some will say that the smell resembled that of a carnival. There was entertainment and a baseball team, and over the team's 21-year stay, there were memories that will forever remain in the minds of those who saw the games, and in team history for those who didn't.

The year 1965 was a big one for the Twins, and it was the best year for The Met. As the Twins rolled through the division on their way to 102 regular season victories, the team hosted the All-Star Game at the season's midway point, seeing stars such as Hank Aaron, Willie Mays, Pete Rose, and Willie Stargell arrive in the Midwest for the event. Then the Twins played the Los Angeles Dodgers there in four World Series games that October. And mixed in along the way that year was that night on August 21 when The Beatles played in front of 25,000 fans.

The 1965 season may have been host to some of the biggest events during the team's tenure and some of the biggest moments, but there were 20 other seasons and many other memories to be had.

Harmon Killebrew played most of his career at The Met, and he accomplished two of his greatest feats there. First there was the longest home run in both the ballpark's history and the team's. On that day, June 3, 1967, Killebrew blasted a ball 520 feet into the stands. Then four years later, on August 10, 1971, he hit career home run No. 500. The Twins were never no-hit, but two of their pitchers threw no-hitters at the home ballpark. In 1962 it was Jack Kralick, and then, in 1967 it was Dean Chance (in a rain-shortened five-inning game). And in addition to those moments, there were great seasons, both by the team and players. Rod Carew and Tony Oliva combined for 10 batting titles, Zoilo Versalles, Killebrew, and

Carew won the MVP, Cesar Tovar played all nine positions, and in addition to that World Series season in 1965, the Twins won the division in both 1969 and 1970 and competed in "the Great Race" in 1967.

Only 15,900 fans showed up for the final game at Met Stadium on September 30, 1981. There was no great sendoff, and no big crowd to say good-bye. By that time, the stadium was falling apart; the railings in the upper deck in left field were a safety hazard, and fans could no longer sit there. Finally on that Wednesday afternoon radio broadcaster Herb Carneal made one last call from that booth.

"Here's the set, the two-strike pitch…swing and a little pop-up back into shallow left field. Washington the shortstop under it, and the game is over. Roy Smalley has made the final out here at Metropolitan Stadium with a pop-up to the shortstop U.L. Washington in shallow left field."

Just like that, the team's tenure at Metropolitan Stadium came to an end. The ballpark would eventually become a shopping mall. The stadium never lasted long enough to become a Fenway Park, Dodger Stadium, or Wrigley Field, nor did the Twins win a title there. But a large portion of team history stems from the era of The Met, and the plaque of home plate that lies on the floor of that mall

## Metropolitan Stadium Facts

Cost to build: $8.5 million
Years of operation: 1956–1981
Capacity: Original (1956): 18,200; 1st Season (1961): 30,637; Final Season (1981): 45,919
Dimensions (Final): LF: 343 ft.; CF: 402 ft.; RF: 330 ft.
All-time record: Wins: 910
Losses: 759
Winning %: .545
Firsts: Game: April 21, 1961 (Senators 5, Twins 3); HR: Dale Long; Grand Slam: Mickey Mantle
Lasts: Game: September 30, 1981 (Royals 5, Twins 2); HR: Clint Hurdle

is the root of many of those memories. It continues to keep The Met alive and those moments from being forgotten.

Then again, who could ever forget those colors?

 ## Sit in the Glove

The glove that sits on the plaza just outside of Gate 34 at the Twins' new home of Target Field signifies multiple key parts of the team's history, and after just one year of existence, it's one of the most popular pregame destinations for fans of all ages.

Sitting 520 feet from home plate, the glove is placed at the exact distance of the longest home run in both Minnesota Twins history and Hall of Fame slugger Harmon Killebrew's career. The date was June 3, 1967, and with two outs and two runners on, Killebrew would hit a three-run home run off pitcher Lew Burdette of the California Angels to give the Twins a lead they'd never surrender. More than a game-changing home run, Killebrew's blast was a historic one, not because it marked any particular milestone in his illustrious career, but because of its massive distance.

In addition to marking the great blast by "the Killer," the glove represents the organization's longstanding commitment to both hustle and defense. In front of the gigantic seven-foot-wide, 10-foot-tall gold glove—the team says it would hold 630 baseballs—is a plaque honoring every Rawlings Gold Glove winner in team history.

The Gold Glove was first given out in 1957, and since then it has been given to a player at each position, as voted by both managers and coaches, who shows superior individual fielding performance.

Since its inception, a total of 12 different players in Twins history have taken home the award a grand total of 41 times through 50 seasons of baseball in the state.

*The glove outside Target Field is exactly 520 feet from home plate, marking the distance of the longest home run in Twins history.* Photo courtesy Alex Halsted

It should come as no surprise that the center-field position is right at the top with the most awards in team history, having had Torii Hunter (7) and Kirby Puckett (6) take home the honor a total of 13 times. With Jim Kaat's 12 and Johan Santana's one Gold Glove award, the pitchers sit even with the two Twins players known quite possibly best for their game-changing catches.

At catcher, Joe Mauer won his third honor during the 2010 season, and Earl Battey won it twice with the Twins, although Battey also won the award in 1960 before the Twins moved to Minnesota. First baseman Vic Power, the first Puerto Rican to play in the American League, won two with the Twins, while Doug Mientkiewicz took home the honor one lone time in 2001. Rounding out the team's impressive list of Gold Glove winners is second baseman Chuck Knoblauch, shortstop Zoilo Versalles, right fielder Tony Oliva, and the guy nicknamed "G-Man," Gary Gaetti, who took home four in his time spent in Minnesota.

## Player Profile: Earl Battey

He was the Gold Standard in the early 1960s.

After playing five seasons for the Chicago White Sox to begin his career, Earl Battey was traded to the Washington Senators prior to the 1960 season, and when they moved to Minnesota for the following 1961 season, he became a Twin and an essential part of their success.

At catcher, Battey was one of the best in team history. He won his first Gold Glove during his lone season in Washington, and then he won two more in his first two seasons in Minnesota. No catcher in team history would match Battey until Joe Mauer won his first Gold Glove in 2008.

Throughout his seven seasons as a Twin, Battey caught a total of 142 runners attempting to steal on him, and he made four All-Star Games. Best known for his defense, Battey wasn't a slouch at the plate. He averaged nearly 11 home runs per season as a Twin and hit .278 during his tenure with the team.

Battey was the first catcher in team history and one of the best to date.

The most players the team had win the award in a single season was in 1962, the Twins' second season in Minnesota. That year, Battey and Kaat became the first of an eventual five pitcher-catcher combos in baseball history to win the award, and Power joined them.

Thousands of Twins fans have waited in long lines stretching to the entrance of the plaza and then stepped up the curb just to plop down inside the enormous glove. Taking a picture inside the glove, by yourself or with a group, is a commemorative part of the ballpark experience, and more than a popular destination, the glove marks two of the many distinguished aspects of Twins history.

 **Bert Blyleven**

His career is well remembered for his pranks and joking personality, but above all else, it is remembered for his actions on the mound. What Bert "Be Home By Eleven" Blyleven did on the rubber through the entirety of his 22-year career is more than most pitchers in the history of baseball have ever accomplished. And for half of those seasons, he did it on the mound in Minnesota.

Born in Zeist, Netherlands, Blyleven moved to Garden Grove, California, where he grew up listening to Vin Scully and watching Sandy Koufax and his curveball with the Los Angeles Dodgers. Because of this, it's no wonder that Blyleven became enamored with the game of baseball or that he taught himself how to throw his own hook, one that would in time become the best of his generation and one of the best in baseball history.

It was 1969 when the Twins drafted Blyleven out of high school, and after only 18 minor league starts (21 appearances overall), the Twins brought him to Minnesota with starters Luis Tiant and Dave Boswell injured. During his rookie season in 1970, at the age of just 19, Blyleven made 25 starts on the hill and went 10–9 along the way to being named the American League Rookie Pitcher of the Year by the *Sporting News*.

Over the course of the next five-plus seasons, Blyleven continued to succeed. He won no fewer than 15 games in any of the next five full seasons with the Twins, and in 1973 he put forth one of the best seasons of his career, winning 20 games, including nine shutouts, on the way to his first All-Star Game appearance. But Blyleven and owner Calvin Griffith began to disagree soon after the implementation of free agency in 1976.

"I was going to become a free agent at the end of the year, and Twins owner Calvin Griffith didn't have any interest in negotiating a new contract with me," Blyleven wrote in 2010. "In fact, at the start of the year, he sent me a contract for the exact same amount I had made the previous year. I rejected it, hoping to get a raise, but his next offer was for 20 percent less, which was allowed as I was under team control. Obviously, that was a sign that the Twins weren't going to keep me around."

*The Twins drafted Bert Blyleven out of high school in 1969, and though the team traded him in 1976, he returned to Minnesota nine years later. Over his 22-year career, he had 287 career wins and 60 shutouts.*

And soon after, the Twins traded him.

It wasn't a pretty exit from the team for Blyleven. Making what he already knew was his final start with the team, Blyleven made an obscene gesture as he left the mound for the final time.

The fallout made the team's move on August 1, 1985, somewhat of a surprise for fans. With a new owner in Carl Pohlad, the Twins reacquired Blyleven, and his second stint with the organization would go much smoother.

After finishing the remainder of the 1985 season by going 8–5, Blyleven won 17 games in 1986. Then in 1987 Blyleven went 15–12 as the Twins made the playoffs. It was on the big stage that Blyleven shined the brightest during his career, especially in 1987. Overall, he went 3–1 that year in the ALCS and World Series combined, and helped lead the team to its first championship in franchise history.

When his career came to an end after the 1992 season, in which he played for the California Angels, Blyleven retired with 287 career victories, 4,970 innings pitched, 3,701 strikeouts, 242 complete games, and 60 shutouts.

His overall numbers place him with the best pitchers in baseball history, many of whom are in the Hall of Fame. But for his first 13 years of eligibility, Blyleven couldn't get through the door. Many voters pointed to his long career as the reason for his vast numbers or the fact that he never finished higher than third in voting for the Cy Young Award and won 20 games in just one season.

On 178 occasions during Blyleven's career, he lost or received a no-decision, despite putting forth a quality start. Had just 13 of those games gone in his favor, Blyleven would have been a lock for the Hall of Fame long ago.

In his 13th year on the ballot, in 2010, Blyleven received 74.2 percent of the vote, leaving him less than one percentage point short of the 75 percent required for admittance into the most coveted place in baseball history. With two years remaining to finally join his legendary counterparts, Blyleven was voted in on his 14th ballot on January 5, 2011.

And finally, after many years of waiting, Bert Blyleven will be home by '11.

## Get Circled By Bert!

Sometimes things happen by accident, and the next second they take off beyond expectations. That's how it happened for Bert Blyleven and the "Circle Me, Bert" phenomenon that follows him and the team's broadcasts through every stop and every city each season.

It was a slow game in Kansas City during the 2002 season, and being the same guy fans came to know and love during his playing career, Bert used the newly purchased telestrator, which had been bought to help the broadcasters describe plays, to circle a Twins fan in the upper deck. As he did it, he called out, "You are hereby circled."

During the next stop on the road trip with the team playing in Detroit, a fan brought a sign to the ballpark asking Bert to circle them, too. He did, and by the time the Twins returned to the Metrodome, there were bunches of signs in attendance looking for Bert to put the telestrator to use.

"I run into a lot of people [who] introduce me, 'Hey, it's Circle Me, Bert.' The heck with my baseball career, I'm the guy who circles people," Blyleven once told WCCO of Minneapolis.

The trend continues today as fans arrive at the ballpark for each game with unique signs. The more unique the plea for being circled, the better chance fans have to get their face with Bert's trademark blue circle around it broadcasted all across Twins Territory.

# The Gold Seat

It's just a seat, right? Not exactly.

The seat that once graced the outfield at the Metrodome in section 101, row five during baseball games might have been just one of more than 50,000 blue chairs at the ballpark when it was built, but in reality this was a special seat, an iconic one. Now the question probably arises: how can a piece of blue plastic, one that has thousands of duplicates everywhere you look, be so special?

The answer is quite simple: when the Twins left the Metrodome following the 2009 season after 28 seasons under the roof, that seat was no longer blue. That's why it's distinctive, that's why fans flocked to see it, and that's why it's a piece of history fans should know about.

This chair that originally had the No. 27 placed on it marked the location of one of the greatest home runs in both team and baseball history. This chair inspired the memorable call, "And...we'll see you tomorrow night." And when tomorrow night came one day later, another fan sat in this chair and watched the Twins win the World Series for the second time.

Sitting in the general admission area, it was this chair that fans rushed to each regular season game, and sometimes pushed and shoved to get. They wanted to be the one to sit down where history had been made years earlier. So often when you saw a fan take a picture with something at the Metrodome, you saw them placed in the outfield, in that section, row, and seat. It was the one seat that deserved special recognition on September 7, 1996, when Kirby Puckett said good-bye to fans and announcer Bob Casey called out over the speakers, "And now...from the exact seat in which his game-winning home run landed...the greatest Minnesota Twin ever...No. 34, Kirbeeeeeeee Puckett!"

That seat was Golden.

Not just figuratively. Sure the seat was golden in the sense that it brought the Twins their second championship trophy, and sure it marked the location of one of the greatest home runs ever. But this seat was actually golden. In color. The seat was changed by the team after the 1991 World Series when in Game 6, Puckett put the team on his back just as he had said days earlier, and carried it to the final game with an 11th-inning blast to left-center, to seat 27 in section 101 and row five.

You can retire the numbers of your greatest players, and the Twins did. They have six players who were so good their numbers will never be worn again. But how do you retire a chair? You can't, really, and so the next best thing is to memorialize it, to make it special. So the Twins did. They changed the color, and then the number was changed to 34. The seat that was once so normal and ordinary became anything but. It was almost a tourist attraction within a stadium that had played host to so many other special moments, and one that already had enough extraordinary features and quirks.

Today left-center in Minneapolis is filled with bleacher seats, and the Twins no longer play at the Metrodome where that game-winning home run once landed. But fans won't soon forget the chair that started off just like the others when the ballpark was opened in 1982, and nine years later, when magic filled the air on October 26, 1991, became iconic. The original blue seat with the No. 27 sits in the Puckett atrium at Target Field, and the "replacement" gold chair with the No. 34 remains in the Metrodome to this day (although team curator Clyde Doepner hopes to one day add it to the team archive). It was the lone seat that deserved to be "retired." And in a sense, it was. That seat is the only golden chair in team history.

 # Baseball and Healing

In the end, it was just a typical ballgame. With the Minnesota Twins and Kansas City Royals tied at three runs apiece after nine innings on August 1, 2007, they headed to extra innings. Eventually Alex Gordon would launch a two-run home run off of reliever Juan Rincon with two outs in the 11th inning, and the Twins would lose the division battle 5–3. But there was no care for the final score that night; something much greater had taken precedence.

As pregame festivities began, about one hour before the first pitch, Minneapolis was scurrying. At 6:05 PM, the I-35W bridge had collapsed, leaving hundreds in the waters below and sending panic and anxiety throughout the Upper Midwest. Some on the bridge had been heading home from work; others were on their way to the Metrodome for that night's game.

Across the city, and for that matter across the nation, eyes were glued to televisions as live video footage showed the catastrophe, and news networks replayed the frightening videos of the bridge falling. The Twins, meanwhile, were preparing for a game, even though it was one they would have liked to postpone.

"That was a horrific night for all Minnesotans. We were getting ready to play a game, and our thought was that we shouldn't play that night," said team president Dave St. Peter. "Ultimately, the Twins made the decision to play based on the fact that we had 25,000 fans there, and having fans leave would have created traffic issues. We didn't want to play, but we felt it was the best thing to do."

In the end, 13 people lost their lives on that horrific day, and in the first 40 hours after the collapse, nearly 100 more were sent to the hospital. The day was unfathomable and sickening, and baseball plays a very little part in it. But no matter how minimal it may have been, baseball did play a role.

While the Twins postponed the next day's game, they took the field at the Metrodome on August 3 against the Cleveland Indians. For those who watched on television or sat in the blue seats that night, the final score likely had little importance. That night was about healing and about a community coming together for the first time just days after that very dark evening.

"As we played games later that week, we hoped we could help provide support and healing after what happened," St. Peter said of playing for the first time after that night.

Baseball is America's pastime. It's a way for friends and families to connect, and a great way to spend a summer afternoon or evening. There are so many great things about baseball, but one of the greatest might be the way it allows a community, and sometimes a nation, to join together in times of difficulty.

Six years earlier, on September 11, 2001, a group of terrorists attempted to tear the country apart. We remember where we were when that first plane struck the World Trade Center, and where we were when another struck the other. We remember where we were when one hit Washington, D.C., and where we were when a group of heroes took one down in Pennsylvania.

What we also remember about that time of difficulty is baseball.

After a layoff in professional baseball, the players took the field a short time later, and the citizens packed the parks from sea to sea. The games were not meaningful because of what was on the scoreboard, but because they showed strength, and for three hours, allowed a nation to join together and remember.

Nobody will ever forget where they were when they saw the bridge collapse that night, and the final scores of the games the Twins played during that time period likely will never hold any significance. But what also won't be forgotten is the way the community joined together at the Metrodome days later, and for a short period of time returned to normalcy with America's pastime acting as a shield from reality and helping friends, family, and a society heal.

# 31 Visit Spring Training

The feeling isn't quite the same as a ballgame from April through October, but there is something about spring training that makes it great. For just more than one month, players head south to the Minnesota Twins' spring home of Fort Myers, Florida. Some are stars or proven players simply tuning up for the upcoming season, some are newly acquired players looking for a fresh start, and the rest are minor leaguers looking to prove their worth to the organization.

## Hammond Stadium
Cost to build: $14 million
Years of operation: 1991–present
Home of: Minnesota Twins (Spring Training), Fort Myers Miracle (Class A),
 GCL Twins (Rookie League)
Capacity: 7,500
Dimensions (Final): LF: 330 ft.; CF: 405 ft.; RF: 330 ft.

**Spring Training Pregame Schedule**
*1:05 PM Start*
Twins hit: 10:15–11:15
Visitors hit: 11:15–12:15
Twins infield: 12:15–12:30
Visitors infield: 12:30–12:45
Field preparation: 12:45–1:05
*7:05 PM Start*
Twins hit: 4:15–5:15
Visitors hit: 5:15–6:15
Twins infield: 6:15–6:30
Visitors infield: 6:30–6:45
Field preparation: 6:45–7:05

As you pull into the parking lot at Hammond Stadium, the first thing you'll see is rows of parking with each aisle named after former players such as Harmon Killebrew, Bert Blyleven, Kirby Puckett, and Tony Oliva. Walking up the sidewalk lined with palm trees toward the entrance, the stadium resembles Churchill Downs, the venue most known for hosting the Kentucky Derby. Farther into the complex, though, is where fans can see baseball at its best.

Spring training is the place where you'll see the true side of baseball. Players taking groundball after groundball, pitchers fielding practice, coaches joking with players as they hit grounders, and countless other drills. Some of it still happens during the season, but fans never see it. Spring training is different, though; it's a chance for fans to get up close, an opportunity to see a side of baseball that often goes unnoticed.

There is more than the major league aspect at spring training. In fact, at the Lee County Sports Complex, where Hammond Stadium lies, there are several fields for minor league sessions. This is where you can learn more than the casual fan cares to know. Some of these players may someday surface as a well-known prospect or make the trip north, and you'll have seen them, maybe even talked to them, before they become the next big star.

And the stars are another reason why a trip to spring training is so essential. The Twins have a unique bond with their former players, and each year in Fort Myers you can traditionally find the likes of Paul Molitor, Harmon Killebrew, Rod Carew, Tony Oliva, and a host of other Twins greats signing autographs and chatting before games and between practice sessions.

The snowstorms and bitter cold should be reason enough for a Twins fan to escape the Midwest, but if you're from another part of Twins Territory or you just need one more reason to visit, it shouldn't be too hard to find. There is no place better than spring training. It's the place where you'll get that first whiff of freshly cut grass and the first sight of America's pastime. Whether you spend one day or one week watching baseball in February and March at Hammond Stadium, you'll leave with a new appreciation for the "little things" in baseball, and, who knows, maybe that guy you'd never heard of from the eighth inning will be the next big thing.

# The 1990s: The Downfall

The Twins had won the World Series the year before, and their second title in a four-year span had fans excited as Minnesota brought back a large group from the championship team for the 1992 season.

After a slow start in the season's first month, the Twins surged, and as the team neared the end of July, they were 60–38 and in first place in the American League West. Into town during the final week of July came the Oakland A's, at the time the second-place team in the division. They'd sweep that three-game series at the Metrodome, and then they'd do it again when the Twins visited the West Coast later that season in September. In the end, those six games would be the difference. The Twins were 90–72 that season, but they finished in second place by six games, missed the playoffs one year after winning it all, and the years ahead were about to get worse.

Sure, the Twins hadn't made the playoffs in 1992, but they were just five games worse than they were when they won the title in 1991, and their popularity was still soaring as they drew nearly 2.5 million fans to the Metrodome that year. In that off-season, however, things took a turn for the worse. The team did retain its star, Kirby Puckett, but lost Greg Gagne, a member of both World Series teams, as well as Chili Davis and John Smiley, the pitcher the Twins had acquired just prior to the season.

The next season the result of many core players moving on showed in the standings. Instead of battling for first place with the A's, the Twins were battling with them to stay out of last place. Despite the struggles, there was one highlight that year. Dave Winfield, the hometown boy from St. Paul, had been signed before the season, and that year he collected hit No. 3,000 at the Metrodome. In the end, though, that would be the lone bright spot, and while the Twins did avoid last place, they went 71–91 in the first of what would prove to be eight consecutive losing seasons in Minnesota.

When the players went on strike on August 12, 1994, there had been some highlights to the team's season. Starter Scott Erickson had tossed a no-hitter, and Puckett was hitting .317 with 20 home runs and 112 RBIs. Despite a few positives, the pitching staff had a league-worst 5.68 ERA, and when the season ended prematurely, the Twins were just 53–60, good for fourth place in the newly formed American League Central.

To make matters worse, following that shortened season Kent Hrbek, the Minneapolis native who had played his entire 14-year career with the hometown team, hung up the jersey for the final time at only 34 years old. Andy MacPhail, the man who built the team's two championship teams soon left, too, heading for the Chicago Cubs and leaving Terry Ryan with a team in need of a remodel.

With the 1995 season, things would only get worse. Sure, Marty Cordova became the fifth Twin to win the Rookie of the Year Award, but the Twins finished in last place in the division, 44 games behind the first-place Cleveland Indians. At the trade deadline, the Twins began the rebuilding process, trading three pieces from the 1991 World Series team: Kevin Tapani, Scott Erickson, and Rick Aguilera. Later that year, on September 28, Puckett was hit in the face by a pitch, and little did anybody know at that moment, it would be the last time he'd ever step to the plate in a regular season game.

Looking to put an improved product on the field after three straight losing seasons, the Twins brought back Aguilera on a three-year contract that off-season and then signed Minnesota native Paul Molitor. There were still question marks, of course, but there was finally some excitement surrounding the team.

Much of that changed, however, when on March 28, 1996, shortly before Opening Day, Kirby Puckett awoke with no vision in his right eye. For just over three months, the organization and fans held out hope that Puckett would play again, but on July 12 that year he announced to the world that at the age of 36, his career was over.

Molitor had one of the best seasons of his career that year. He hit .341 and led the league with 225 hits. But with no Puckett roaming center field, the team kept losing, going 78–84 on its way to a fourth consecutive losing season.

Following the 1996 season, the Twins began pushing harder for a new stadium. After a committee killed the hopes by voting against a referendum for a new ballpark, commissioner Bud Selig opened the gate for the team to search for alternatives—even if that meant moving the team to a new city.

During the 1997 off-season, the Twins yet again brought in a Minnesota native. This time they signed catcher Terry Steinbach. Now in his third season with the Twins, 24-year-old pitcher Brad Radke won 20 games, but it wasn't enough to help the team improve, and it finished below .500 for yet another season.

By the end of the off-season that year, the Twins had moved Chuck Knoblauch, the second baseman from the 1991 championship team, for what turned out to be two future All-Stars in Eric Milton and Cristian Guzman, as well as two other players.

The next year in 1998 the Twins suffered another losing season, and in 1999 they fell to last place in the American League Central. The team still couldn't get legislation passed for a new ballpark, and it had just finished their seventh consecutive season with a losing record. In 2000 players such as Torii Hunter, Jacque Jones, and Matt Lawton began to form a formidable outfield, but the Twins finished in last place, nonetheless.

The decade that had started so well with a championship in 1991 had ended with seven straight losing seasons, and the new decade didn't get off to a great start, either, as that streak was extended to eight with the team's dismal performance in 2000.

But out of nowhere, the Twins played well in 2001. They didn't make the playoffs, but they ended their streak of losing seasons when they finished 85–77, just six games back of Cleveland and good for second place in the division. After the season, the team endured another loss when manager Tom Kelly, who had led the organization to two titles in his 16-year tenure, resigned.

Ron Gardenhire would take over, and he had what would prove to be a good nucleus. Despite the team's promising 2001 season, though, the Twins were in danger of being contracted.

Just 10 years earlier, the Twins were baseball's best, but in a downfall that included the end of a career for the greatest Minnesota Twin ever, the loss of several other stars, and eight straight losing seasons, the team was at an all-time low.

And worst of all, the Minnesota Twins were in danger of extinction.

 **Escaping Contraction**

After posting a losing record in eight consecutive seasons before they finally cleared .500 in 2001, the Minnesota Twins were on the verge of extinction. At the conclusion of the World Series that year, the players received a letter from ownership in November 2001, telling them that the Twins were one of two teams, along with the Montreal Expos, up for contraction; that the final game of Twins baseball may have already come and gone.

"It was a very difficult time for the organization. The franchise was in a much different place, and there was a strong feeling of hopelessness," said team president Dave St. Peter of the feeling at the time. "I think, as an organization, we certainly had a high level of concern but remained hopeful that a solution would emerge."

Months of rumors and updates would follow the initial shock. On November 16, 2001, Hennepin County District Judge Harry Crump ruled that the Twins had to honor their Metrodome lease;

thus forcing the team to play the 2002 season in Minnesota. After appeals by the league, on February 5, 2002, commissioner Bud Selig announced that there would be no contraction for the upcoming 2002 season, but the possibility would again arise for the following season in 2003.

With the guarantee of playing, for one more season at least, the Twins pressed on. They got off to a quick start in 2002, and by the midway point, they sat atop the American League Central. On August 30 of that year, with the Twins still leading the division, baseball avoided a strike by agreeing to a deal with the players' union in the final hours. One big thing emerged from the agreement: baseball assured the union that there would be no contraction until after the 2006 season at the earliest. The Twins were safe.

"It would have been devastating [had the Twins been contracted]; there are so many people in the Upper Midwest who follow the Twins on a daily basis," St. Peter said of the possibility of Twins baseball disappearing. "We mean so much to the quality of life in the Midwest, and it would have been very hard to imagine life without the Twins."

Just two weeks after learning that they were safe, the Twins took the field at the Metrodome on September 15 with a chance to claim the division. After beating the Cleveland Indians 5–0, the team waited for the Chicago White Sox to fall in New York before erupting in celebration.

In less than one year, the Twins had gone from being on the brink of disappearance; they had turned the C-word into a good thing, it was no longer *contraction* for them, but *champions*. The Twins had returned to the top. As they celebrated on that September day, some players held back tears, while others, such as outfielder Jacque Jones, let it all out.

"Bud Selig couldn't get rid of us," Jones told the media after the game. "The White Sox couldn't get rid of us. The Cleveland Indians couldn't get rid of us. Here we are, and we're staying."

## Contraction Timeline

November 6, 2001—At a meeting in Chicago, Illinois, the owners vote 28–2 in favor of contracting two of the league's 30 teams sometime before the 2002 season. The Minnesota Twins seem to be an early leader for contraction.

November 7, 2001—The players' union files a grievance claiming the vote to eliminate two teams violates the collective bargaining agreement.

November 16, 2001—Ten days after the vote, Minnesota judge Harry Crump orders the Minnesota Twins organization to honor the final year of their lease to play in the H.H.H. Metrodome. Major League Baseball appeals.

December 4, 2001—An arbitrator hears arguments from the league and union about the grievance filed by the players' association.

December 6, 2001—Commissioner Bug Selig tells Congress that baseball is in financial difficulty and the best way to solve the problem is to eliminate two teams from the league.

February 4, 2002—After a quiet month in January, the Minnesota Supreme Court upholds the ruling that obligates the Minnesota Twins to play out their lease at the Metrodome and play there for the 2002 season.

February 5, 2002—With the Twins needing to play the 2002 season by court ruling, commissioner Bug Selig announces that there will be no contraction prior to the 2002 season but says the league will try again following the season, aiming for eliminating two teams prior to the 2003 season.

The Twins weren't just staying; they were about to prove how big of a mistake eliminating them would have been to begin with. Over the course of the remainder of the decade, the Twins won four more division titles and moved to a new ballpark that would further ensure their existence for many decades into the future.

So many memories had been made previously, and many more have been made since that ominous November day in 2001. And to think: had a judge not ordered the team to stay in the Metrodome that winter, and had the Twins not surged to the top the next spring, so many memories would never have happened; there would be no need for a book like this.

# 34 The 2000s: Rising to Contention

After the threat of contraction had subsided, for the 2002 season at least, the Twins attempted to move forward. The gloomy possibility still loomed heading into spring training, though; it seemed that baseball would again look into contraction for the 2003 season. The Twins marched on, regardless. The previous year they might not have made the playoffs, but their eight-season losing streak was over, and new manager Ron Gardenhire had a young group to proceed with.

By the time the Twins reached the midway point in the 2002 season, they were already sitting comfortably in first place in the American League Central. But the lead in the division was almost good for nothing. Baseball neared a strike on August 30 of that year, and the Twins' success was nearly for naught. At the last minute, though, the season was saved, and it turned out baseball in Minnesota was, too. The deal that the players and owners agreed to would put contraction talks to rest for five seasons, keeping the Twins alive well into the future.

After the threat of a mid-season strike went by the wayside, the Twins continued to move through the remainder of the season as the leader in the division, and by the time it was over, they had made the playoffs for the first time in 10 seasons with a record of 94–67. After winning the final game of the first round of the playoffs against the Oakland A's to advance to the second round, the Twins lost to the eventual World Series–champion Los Angeles Angels in the ALCS. But just one season after sitting at the bottom of baseball, the Twins were back near the top, and it was just the start of a new trend in Minneapolis.

Finally back in the playoffs, the Twins were looking to begin a new streak of competitive baseball in Minnesota. It wouldn't be easy during the 2003 season, though. After the Twins elected not to offer slugger David Ortiz arbitration, they got off to a slow start. Heading into the All-Star break, they lost eight consecutive games and found themselves 7½ games back in the division. At the trade deadline, general manager Terry Ryan traded for outfielder Shannon Stewart, and things quickly turned. Stewart hit .322 during the remainder of the season and provided a spark at the top of the lineup. In the end, the Twins turned their mid-season deficit into a second-consecutive divisional title.

It would be a first-round exit for the Twins this time, but they finally had baseball's attention, and their success was beginning to be mimicked by other struggling teams around the league. As the Twins continued to lose in 1999, they did make one strong move when they acquired pitcher Johan Santana during the Rule 5 Draft. After being inserted into the rotation in the second half of the 2003 season, Santana pitched his first full season in 2004, and the result was both a Cy Young Award for him, and back-to-back-to-back division titles for the team.

Almost unimaginable, the Twins, in a matter of just a few years, had risen from the cellar to win three straight American League Central titles. With the core of the pitching staff back for the 2005 season, expectations remained high. Santana put forth strong numbers again and led the league in strikeouts. But the offense was last in the league in runs scored, and Santana won just 16 games because of it and failed to win a second Cy Young Award. The Twins still finished above .500, but they moved down to third place in the division, and for the first time in three years, there were no playoffs to be played at the Metrodome.

For nearly half of the following 2006 season, it seemed as if the Twins would miss the playoffs again. At one point in June they were sitting 12 games back in the division. After a one-run loss to the

Seattle Mariners on June 7, though, the Twins surged. They won 71 of their final 104 games and made the playoffs on the final day of the season. The run was fueled by Joe Mauer, who would win his first batting title; Justin Morneau, who took home the American League MVP; and Johan Santana, who won his second Cy Young Award.

The strong second-half run didn't carry the Twins far in the playoffs. It was another first-round exit for the team. During the 2007 season, the Twins finished below .500 for the first time in six seasons. That was far from the big story, though. After the season, longtime center fielder Torii Hunter headed to the Los Angeles Angels via free agency, and in fear that they might not retain him the next off-season, the Twins shipped Santana to the New York Mets. After the Twins had finished 17 games back in the division that previous season, it now looked like they were headed into rebuilding mode.

There would be no playoffs in 2008, but the story of that season isn't so simple. While the Twins had lost Hunter and

## Glenn Williams: 13 Games, 13 Hits

On June 7, 2005, with the Twins in Arizona to play the Diamondbacks, third baseman Glenn Williams stepped to the plate as a pinch-hitter for pitcher Brad Radke. He singled that night in his first major league at-bat, and that was just the start of what would be an incredible month-long career with the Twins.

Twelve more times during that month of June Williams played in a game for the Twins, and he continued to hit. He had hit in 12 consecutive games as the Twins took on the Kansas City Royals on June 28 in Minnesota. Williams collected a hit that night, but in the fourth inning, he dislocated his shoulder while sliding into third base.

Williams wouldn't play the rest of that season, and he wouldn't play in the majors again. The Twins invited him to camp the next year, but he never made it back to the Show. But in those 13 games that Williams did appear in, he went 17-for-43 to give him a .425 career batting average. Now retired, the Australian native is still in the midst of a 13-game hitting streak.

Santana, two of their key players, along with Matt Garza and Carlos Silva from the rotation, they still enjoyed success on the field. Through the summer, the Twins battled with the Chicago White Sox, and in the end, 162 games weren't enough. The two teams met in Chicago for a one-game playoff, and the Twins fell 1–0, missing the playoffs for the second straight season.

That Game 163 would prove as practice in a sense, though, as the Twins headed to their final season under the Teflon roof of the Metrodome. The Twins went 16–4 in the final weeks to close out the season and put themselves in a second-consecutive one-game playoff with a chance to return to the playoffs after a two-year hiatus. This time the game was at the Metrodome, and in the final regular season game indoors, the Metrodome provided some final magic. The Twins won in 12 innings and made the playoffs for the fifth time in the final eight years of the decade.

There would be just one more playoff game indoors, with the Twins falling in the first round to the New York Yankees. But as the first decade of the 2000s came to a close, the franchise had taken a tremendous leap forward. From eight straight losing seasons to five division titles, the Twins were ready to head outdoors as one of the league's better teams. After the threat of extinction at the start of the decade, the Twins ushered in a new era safe in Minnesota as they packed and moved across town to Target Field.

# 35 The Great Race

All or nothing, win or go home. That was the scenario back in 1967, when only two divisions existed in baseball and the winner of each headed directly to the World Series. There were no individual divisions or wild-card, and no early rounds in the playoffs. The regular season standings put two teams in the championship series, and the remaining teams headed home for the winter.

And so the final week of that 1967 season was more intense than any other before.

As that week began, four teams in the American League had a chance to win the pennant, and three of them—Detroit, Boston, and Minnesota—were still in the hunt on the final day of the season. It had taken a strong run, but there the Twins were at Fenway Park on September 30, 1967, ready to begin a two-game series against the Red Sox and holding a one-game lead in the division.

Two seasons removed from their World Series appearance in 1965 against the Los Angeles Dodgers, the Twins had acquired pitcher Dean Chance prior to the season, and they received strong performances from sluggers Harmon Killebrew, who hit 44 home runs and drove in 113 runners, and Bob Allison, who added another 24 home runs. Rookie second baseman Rod Carew stepped up and hit .292, and three pitchers, Chance, Jim Kaat, and Dave Boswell, all struck out more than 200 hitters to become the first three pitchers to accomplish the feat while playing for the same team. But the road to that final weekend, where the Twins found themselves still in contention, wasn't quite that simple.

The Twins started the season 5–10 through the first three weeks, and on June 8, they blew a lead in the ninth inning and fell to 25–25. The next day, owner Calvin Griffith fired manager Sam Mele after just over six seasons as the club's leader. Mele was replaced at the helm with Cal Ermer, the manager at Triple A Denver.

"Sam had been around a while, we'd had some success, and it seemed like he changed some the last couple of years," pitcher Jim Kaat told the *Minneapolis Star Tribune* years later. "There was a feeling in the clubhouse that he was taking too much credit for the good and none of the blame for the bad. There was a little discord starting to form. Cal Ermer was a great guy. I don't know if he ever had control over big-league players, but he was a different presence than Sam, and it worked for the rest of that season."

The move did work, but not necessarily immediately.

Through the remainder of June, following the arrival of Ermer, the Twins went 11–9. Then along with the month of July came a spark. The Twins were on an eight-game winning streak by July 5, and at the end of the month, they took three out of five games against the Red Sox. From there, the Twins won 17 of 23 games.

The Great Race was officially on.

By the beginning of September, the race had become almost unimaginable. It was September 6, and four teams sat tied atop the division. Both the Red Sox and Tigers held records of 79–62, while both the White Sox and Twins had played two fewer games, but were even in games back with records of 78–61 with just under one month remaining in the race to the finish.

At last, the final week arrived. The White Sox fell out of the race first, and as the Twins entered their final series of the season, a two-game matchup with the Red Sox, they held a one-game lead over both Boston and Detroit. Needing just one win, and with Kaat and Chance headed to the hill, the team's chances of reaching its second World Series looked good.

It was September 30, 1967, a Saturday ballgame, and to the mound trotted Kaat. He had gone 7–0 through the month of September, and he would later call it the best month of his career. The Twins scored first and led 1–0 in the third inning with one out, and then came the noise. It had nothing to do with the bat connecting with the ball, but rather from a pop in Kaat's left elbow. He had torn his tendon.

Kaat would leave the game, and the Red Sox would score six runs in the middle innings off the Twins' relievers, including a three-run home run off the bat of eventual American League MVP Carl Yastrzemski to cap things off.

The Twins had effectively lost Kaat, the game, and their lead in the league. Along with the Red Sox, they were now tied atop the AL, with the Tigers a half-game back as the month shifted to October and the final regular season game of the 1967 season.

It was Sunday now, and a do-or-die situation for all three teams remaining in the race. The possibility of a tie still loomed, but it would have to be between the Tigers and only the Twins *or* Red Sox. The Twins would send Chance to the mound, a 20-game winner, for that final game.

Leading 2–0 heading to the bottom half of sixth inning, only 12 outs stood in the way of a potential trip to the World Series for the Twins. Things were about to get complicated, however. The Red Sox picked up four consecutive singles to lead off the inning, and by the time the side was retired, they had forced Chance off the mound and taken a 5–2 lead.

The Twins would get one back with three straight singles of their own off the bats of Killebrew, Tony Oliva, and Allison in the eighth inning. But the threat was ended when Yastrzemski threw Allison out as he attempted to stretch his base hit into a double. The threat had been stopped, and so had the Twins. The season was effectively over.

The Tigers would win one of their two games that day, but the one loss that came with it meant that Boston was headed to the World Series, while both Minnesota and Detroit finished tied for second place. It had been a back-and-forth race, and for Boston fans it became known as "the Impossible Dream," as they won the pennant for the first time in 21 seasons.

Through the long and strenuous season, the division lead shifted hands many times. Chicago spent 91 days in first; Detroit spent 41 days at the top; the Twins were the leaders for 39 days; and Boston held the lead for the shortest time with just 24 days at the helm. But they were sitting in first when it counted; they had won the Great Race, with the Twins right behind.

# The Metrodome

For 28 seasons, the Minnesota Twins called the Metrodome home. With seats angled for a football game and no natural elements, it may not have been the best place to watch a baseball game, but it sure did give the team a home-field advantage and played host to many memorable moments.

Built for $68 million and named after former vice president Hubert H. Humphrey for his dedication to the state of Minnesota, the H.H.H. Metrodome roof was inflated on October 2, 1981, and the Minnesota Twins stepped foot on the SuperTurf for the first regular season game on April 6, 1982, losing to the Seattle Mariners. It would be just the first of more than 2,000 games played at the Metrodome.

With a white roof and a cement-like surface, the Metrodome played host to a lot of quirky moments. There were many balls lost in the roof and many balls that hit seams in the turf or simply bounced so hard at home plate that the infielder could make no play. Many opposing teams and managers hated the Dome, and there were thoughts by some, such as managers Alan Trammell and Bobby Valentine, that the Twins would use the air-conditioning system to alter the flight of the ball, turning it on when the team was at the plate, and turning it off when they were in the field.

No matter what anybody might have thought about it, the Metrodome certainly was loud. Containing the screams of up to about 56,000 fans, with no escape, the Metrodome is one of the loudest sports venues in the world. During the 1987 World Series, the Dome reached its loudest decibel level ever for a baseball game, measuring at 125 dB, comparable to standing next to a jet at

## H.H.H. Metrodome Facts

Cost to build: $68 million

Years of operation: 1981–2009 (final Twins game)

Capacity: 55,883

Dimensions (Final): LF: 343 ft.; CF: 408 ft.; RF: 327 ft.

Field Surfaces: SuperTurf (1982–1986); AstroTurf (1987–2003); FieldTurf (2004–2009)

All-Time Record: 1,214–1,028

Winning %: .541

Firsts: Game: April 6, 1982 (Mariners 11, Twins 7); HR: Dave Engle; Cycle: Kirby Puckett (1986)

Lasts: Game: October 6, 2009 (Twins 6, Tigers 5); HR: Magglio Ordonez; Win: Bobby Keppel

takeoff and putting it right at the Threshold of Pain—it's no wonder why so many ears were throbbing for days after Game 7.

The 1987 World Series was a big reason for fans to get loud inside the Metrodome, but the venue played host to many other big events, too. The Twins hosted the All-Star Game in 1985; there was the team's second World Series in 1991; there were playoffs for the Twins on five different occasions during the first decade of the 2000s; there was a sad good-bye to Puck, the greatest Twin ever; and the last ever regular season game at the Dome was an extra one to decide who'd represent the American League Central in the 2009 playoffs.

With its odd features and with the help of thousands of screaming fans, the Metrodome became a lot like a 10th player over the team's near–three decade stay. In 2,242 games at the Metrodome, the Twins posted a winning percentage above .540, winning 1,214 games and losing 1,028 games on the turf. And maybe most importantly, the team was 8–0 in two World Series at the Metrodome, winning both of their championships in front of the home crowd.

The Metrodome was also consistent. No matter how hot, cold, dry, or wet the weather was in downtown Minneapolis, baseball went on at a comfortable 68 degrees indoors. There were only two delayed games during the team's tenure at the Dome. On one occasion, a snowstorm kept the then California Angels from arriving, and the one other game was delayed after the devastating collapse of the I-35W bridge.

While some people loved the Metrodome for its oddness, others loved to hate it. All feelings aside, there is no doubting that the Dome allowed fans to share in some of the most unique and most memorable moments in not just baseball history, but in sports history.

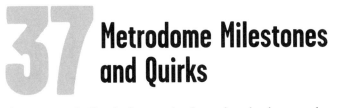

# Metrodome Milestones and Quirks

Playing in a ballpark for nearly three decades leaves a lot of room for the occurrence of milestones, and in 28 seasons at the Metrodome, there were several. With a white Teflon roof and a hard turf, there was also a good chance some odd things would occur, and fans saw plenty of quirky moments during the team's tenure at the Dome.

Only 27 players in baseball history have ever collected 3,000 or more hits in a career, and three of those players reached the big milestone under the roof in Minneapolis. On September 16, 1993, it was St. Paul native Dave Winfield who accomplished the feat. Two years later, on June 30, 1995, Eddie Murray, the slugger for the Cleveland Indians, reached the milestone, and then, on April 15, 2000, Cal Ripken Jr. singled to become the third and final player in the ballpark's history to reach No. 3,000.

Fans witnessed two no-hitters at the Metrodome, and thankfully both were thrown by their own. Scott Erickson tossed the first no-no in the stadium's history on April 27, 1994, as the Twins beat their border rival, the Milwaukee Brewers, 6–0. Five years later, on September 11, 1999, the Twins beat the Anaheim Angels 7–0 behind Eric Milton's no-hitter, the fourth in team history.

Bert Blyleven played for the Twins on two different occasions during his career, and a total of 11 separate seasons. One of the biggest moments in his storied career came on August 1, 1986, when he struck out Mike Davis to record strikeout No. 3,000. Blyleven would record 701 more strikeouts through the remainder of his career, but it was in front of the Metrodome crowd that he joined a select group of only 16 players to accomplish the feat.

One final Metrodome milestone came on June 28, 2007, when Frank Thomas stepped to the plate against Twins starter Carlos Silva. Thomas, known in baseball as the "Big Hurt," had hurt the Twins on several occasions through his career, having blasted more home runs against Minnesota when all was said and done (52) than any other team. On this day, Thomas joined the 500–home run club when he blasted a home run into the stands in left field.

The milestones were aplenty over nearly three decades of baseball at the Metrodome, and there were a few odd plays that stuck out from the team's tenure when it had played its final game indoors in October 2009.

It was May 4, 1984, when Dave Kingman hit a monstrous pop-up. Had the game been played at any other ballpark, it likely would have been a casual out. At the Metrodome, that wasn't the case. The ball went up, and as fans and players stared into the air, they saw nothing. The ball didn't come down, it instead went into a drainage hole in the roof, where it stayed. After some discussion by the umpires, Kingman was awarded a double.

While Kingman received a double, former Twin David Ortiz wouldn't be so lucky when he hit a blast during the 2006 season. After hitting a ball headed for Kirby Puckett on the upper deck sheet, Ortiz momentarily admired the blast. The only problem was,

## Met Flagpole

Metropolitan Stadium may be long gone with a shopping mall in its place, but 50 years after the Twins played on those grounds in Bloomington, Minnesota, a piece of that era and that ballpark remains with the team. Now at Target Field, standing tall in right field, is the original flagpole that once graced the grounds at Met Stadium.

For nearly 30 years after the Twins bolted for the Metrodome beginning in 1981, the flagpole displayed the Stars and Stripes at Richfield's American Legion. They paid just $150 for the 100-foot steel pole, and it stood untouched for nearly three decades before the Twins moved back outdoors for the 2010 season.

As is the case all around Target Field, the Twins have made the connection to their past by bringing the flagpole back into their possession. They paid the legion $10,000 for the pole, and to meet their needs, cut it to 45 feet.

Before each home game, a member of the armed services raises the American flag, reminding fans of both Metropolitan Stadium and the reason they can sit in the stands and watch America's pastime.

the ball never reached its destination. Instead, a Metrodome speaker stopped the path of the hit, sending the ball to the feet of Torii Hunter in center field. A disappointed Ortiz would gain just a single on what could have been one of the longest home runs in the ballpark's history—if only the speaker didn't get in its way.

Nobody can say the Metrodome was the greatest place to watch a baseball game, but it sure did host some of baseball's great milestones, and without it we wouldn't have some of the most awkward plays in team history.

 Rod Carew

It was a president, Theodore Roosevelt, in fact, who once said, "Speak softly and carry a big stick; you will go far." His implication with this saying had nothing to do with baseball, but by the time

Rod Carew finished his 19-year major league career, it might as well have been he who professed it. He was everything that the quote stood for.

His stick was a 32-ounce, about 34-inch bat. He spoke softly, too. And when his career came to an end after the 1985 season, he had accomplished more in the game of baseball than many would ever dream about. Carew was the personification of that quote.

"He still looks lackadaisical. It's his style. He's so smooth, he seems to be doing it without trying," the great Ted Williams wrote in *Sports Illustrated* during Carew's marvelous 1977 season. "Some guys—Pete Rose is one, and I put myself in this category—have to snort and fume to get everything going. Carew doesn't."

Carew was loose as the plate, always calm. He was so calm and nonchalant, in fact, that his batting stance at times made it appear as if he were sleeping. He was graceful and masterful and about every other perfect adjective you can think of. By the time he was inducted into the Hall of Fame in 1991 on his first ballot, the results proved it.

In 1978, his final season with the Twins, he won his seventh and final batting title. The season prior, in 1977, Carew flirted with .400 and won the American League MVP. As a rookie 10 years earlier, he had won the Rookie of the Year Award. There are the 18 All-Star appearances, spanning from his rookie season through

## Batting Titles by the Year

| | |
|---|---|
| 1964 – Tony Oliva | 1975 – Rod Carew |
| 1965 – Tony Oliva | 1977 – Rod Carew |
| 1969 – Rod Carew | 1978 – Rod Carew |
| 1971 – Tony Oliva | 1989 – Kirby Puckett |
| 1972 – Rod Carew | 2006 – Joe Mauer |
| 1973 – Rod Carew | 2008 – Joe Mauer |
| 1974 – Rod Carew | 2009 – Joe Mauer |

*Rod Carew delivers a second-inning double against the Chicago White Sox in Bloomington, Minnesota, June 27, 1977, raising his batting average to .400. He finished the season with a .388 batting average. His .334 average with Minnesota is the highest in Twins history.*

1984 before he was left out of the game during his final season in 1985. And these things don't tell how great Carew really was.

Born on a train in Panama in 1945, Carew was named after the doctor who delivered him, Dr. Rodney Cline, as a token of appreciation. He moved to the United States when he was 15 years old, and three years later he signed with the Minnesota Twins.

By 1967, Carew had made his way to Metropolitan Stadium in Bloomington, Minnesota, and as a rookie he hit .292 and made his first All-Star Game. In his second season his average dipped to .273, but it would be the final time in a Twins uniform that Carew wouldn't hit at least .300 in a season.

Carew hit .332 in his third season with the Twins. That year would mark his first batting title and the start of 15 consecutive seasons in which he would hit at least .300.

Through the remainder of his eventual 12 seasons with the Twins, Carew turned himself into a legend. He won four consecutive batting titles, from 1972 to 1975, and then two more in a row when he took the honor in 1977 and 1978. Had it not been for George Brett topping him by two points in 1976, it would have been a remarkable seven straight titles for Carew to end his career in a Twins uniform.

After the 1978 season, Carew was traded to the California Angels for a group of four players. His tremendous career would continue as he was selected to six more All-Star Games, but he never won another batting title during his years spent on the West Coast.

Today, Carew stands as one of the greatest hitters in team history. He ranks first in batting average (.334) and triples (90), second in hits (2,085) and stolen bases (271), third in runs (950), and fourth in at-bats (6,235), doubles (305), and walks (613). Meanwhile, in baseball history only three players have won more batting titles (although Rogers Hornsby and Stan Musial have matched him): Ty Cobb (12), Tony Gwynn (8), and Honus Wagner (8), putting him in the company of baseball's elite.

Carew's No. 29 has been retired by both teams he played for, and a life-sized statue of him sits on the plaza at Target Field. At the age of 21 and as a rookie, the soft-spoken Rod Carew carried a big stick to the plate. Today, that big stick has been exchanged for one big legacy.

# 39 Twins Hall of Fame

Take a stroll up 7th Street in downtown Minneapolis, past the statue of Twins great Rod Carew and up toward his gate on the plaza of Target Field. As you near the entrance to the ballpark, turn yourself right and take a trip through the team's past with pennants featuring great players and personnel from the Minnesota Twins organization. These pennants make up the Twins Hall of Fame, and the wall as a whole is host to the faces of some of the most influential people in the team's history during their tenure in the state of Minnesota.

As the Twins began what would turn out to be their eighth consecutive losing season in 2000, team president Dave St. Peter was looking for a way to celebrate the great players in the team's history. Thus began the Twins Hall of Fame.

"[We wanted to] create a platform for the men and women who made this franchise what it is," St. Peter said. "We're pleased with the way it has evolved."

What evolved that year was an inaugural class of team greats. The team inducted Harmon Killebrew, Rod Carew, Tony Oliva, Kent Hrbek, and Kirby Puckett, three of their players in baseball's Hall of Fame located in Cooperstown, New York, and all of the players who have their numbers retired by the organization. Also inducted was Calvin Griffith, the man who brought the Washington Senators to Minnesota in 1961 and made the thought of a team Hall of Fame even possible some 40 years later.

That first class would be the largest, and since then no more than two people have been inducted in any season. Since its inception in

## Heading to Cooperstown

The Twins Hall of Fame will give you a good sense of the organization's greatest players and all-time most influential people. But to get a better sense of their best, and a good outlook on the best in the history of baseball, you have to travel east some 1,200 miles and 20 hours to Cooperstown, New York, home of the National Baseball Hall of Fame.

There is a lot to see at the Hall of Fame. The plaques, the players, and most of all, the artifacts, give fans a thorough look at the history of the sport. Through 50 seasons of existence in the state of Minnesota, there have been plenty of historic moments in Minnesota Twins history, and there are plenty of things to take a look at out east dealing with the team. Some things you'll see include:

- Batting gloves worn by seven-time batting champion and Twins Hall of Famer Rod Carew during his career with Minnesota.
- A program and tickets from the first regular season game played at the H.H.H. Metrodome on April 6, 1982, against the Seattle Mariners.
- The bat used by Twins Hall of Famer Kirby Puckett when he went 6-for-6 on August 30, 1987, to give him 10 consecutive hits for an American League record.
- A jersey worn by Minnesota native and Twins Hall of Famer Kent Hrbek near the end of his career during the 1993 season.
- The cleats worn by St. Paul native Paul Molitor on September 16, 1996, when he collected his 3,000[th] hit as a member of his hometown team.
- The bat used by catcher Joe Mauer in the final game of the 2006 season, when he became the first catcher in American League history to win the batting title.
- A ticket, ball, and third base from Game 163 played at the Metrodome on October 6, 2009. It was the final regular season game ever played at the Metrodome.

the first year of the decade, a combination of players, personalities, and management have all been incorporated.

Radio broadcaster Herb Carneal, who in the end would act as the voice of Twins baseball for 45 seasons, was inducted in 2001, and public address announcer Bob Casey, who announced the team's players in each of the first 44 seasons in Minnesota, was added two years later in 2003.

Management on the wall includes the team's second owner, Carl Pohlad (2005), whose family still owns the team today; Jim Rantz (2007), the team's director of the minor leagues, longest tenured employee, and the man responsible for finding Kirby Puckett; and George Brophy (2009), who was an original member of the organization when it moved to Minnesota in 1961 and was part of the front office until 1985.

There are five pitchers in the group. Jim Kaat, who spent 13 seasons with the Twins and won 189 games, was inducted first in 2001, and Bert Blyleven, who pitched half of his career in Minnesota and helped the team win a title in 1987, was added a year later in 2002. Since then, Frank Viola (2005), Rick Aguilera (2008), and Brad Radke (2009) have all been added, too.

Position players in the distinct group include outfielder Bob Allison (2003), who made two All-Star Game appearances as a member of the Twins; catcher Earl Battey (2004), who made four All-Star Games as a Twin; the team's first MVP award winner, Zoilo Versalles (2006); the third baseman from the 1987 championship team, Gary Gaetti (2007); and the shortstop of both championship teams in 1987 and 1991, Greg Gagne (2010).

And then there is the one manager. Tom Kelly—the man who won 1,140 games in 16 seasons at the helm in Minnesota, the man who helped the team win two championships, and the man who still acts as an assistant to the general manager—was inducted in 2002.

Before you head into the ballpark to watch what could be a few future members of the Twins Hall of Fame take the field, pause for just a second as you advance toward the gate and get to know the current members. These are some of the most influential people through the first half-century of Twins baseball.

# 40 The Closers

After throwing eight innings in Game 7 of the 1987 World Series, starter Frank Viola handed the ball over to the closer. Starter Kevin Tapani did the same thing in Game 2 of the 1991 World Series. It was also the closer who got the final out in Game 5 of the ALDS in 2002, moving the Twins to the second round.

The save became an official stat in 1969, and since then teams have paid top money for pitchers who can get the final three outs in a tight ballgame. In so many of the biggest games it's been the closer on the mound in the most critical situations.

There are five key closers in team history: Ron Davis, Jeff Reardon, Rick Aguilera, Eddie Guardado, and Joe Nathan. These five pitchers make up the top five on the team's all-time saves leader board; they're the only five closers in franchise history to have closed out at least 100 games, and they've ended some of the biggest games in the existence of Twins baseball.

Ron Davis spent his first four years of major league ball with the New York Yankees, but it wasn't until he came to Minnesota that he became a full-time closer. In 1982 Davis closed out 22 games for the Twins, and he never posted a total lower than that in his four full seasons in Minneapolis. When he was traded to the Chicago Cubs in August 1986, Davis had saved 108 ballgames for the Twins, and he'd never close out another game in his career.

The acquisition of Jeff Reardon prior to the 1987 season turned out to be huge. That year, Reardon closed out 31 games for the Twins and played a big role in helping the team to its first championship. With the Twins leading 4–2 in the top half of the ninth inning in Game 7 of the World Series, Reardon headed to the mound. A fly-out, pop-out, and ground-out later, and the Twins were the best in baseball. After that season, Reardon would put up great numbers for two more years in a Twins uniform; he saved 42 games in 1988 and then 31 more in 1989 before leaving as a free agent. Today the righty has the seventh most saves in baseball history, with 367, and 104 of them came as a Twin.

After the 1987 World Series, the Twins did some reshuffling, and one of the moves sent Viola to the New York Mets for an assortment of players. One of those players was pitcher Rick Aguilera. When he arrived in Minnesota, Aguilera had just seven career saves. In his first full season as a Twin in 1990, the then 28-year-old closed out 32 games. He'd spend a total of 11 seasons in Minnesota in two separate stays, and when all was said and done, he'd helped the team win the 1991 World Series and racked up 254 saves in a Twins uniform, which today remains a team record.

For Eddie Guardado, the nickname "Everyday Eddie" fit perfectly. In his two full seasons as the Twins' closer, he pitched what seemed like every day. Guardado was selected to the All-Star Game in both of his full seasons as the closer, and he closed out 45 games in 2002 and then 41 more in 2003 before moving on to Seattle. It was always interesting when the lefty was on the mound, and there is no better example than Game 5 of the 2002 American League Division Series. With his team up 5–1 in the game that would send the winner to the second round, Guardado allowed a three-run home run and a single before working out of the mess, helping the Twins to the ALCS.

When Guardado left via free agency following the 2003 season, the Twins were in search of a closer. On November 14, 2003, the team acquired Joe Nathan from the San Francisco Giants, and gave him a chance as the team's closer the following spring. It was a risk, of course. Nathan had one career save, and that had come in his rookie season. But the move couldn't have been any more brilliant.

Through his first six seasons as a Twin, Nathan had closed out 246 games, more than future Hall of Famer Mariano Rivera in that same span. The inaugural season at Target Field was supposed to mark the year Nathan would unseat Aguilera as the franchise's all-time saves leader, but Tommy John surgery in spring training delayed and possibly ended that chance.

From games in early April to critical late-season matchups, and even Game 7 of the World Series, it has been the closers in team history who have been handed the ball. These pitchers have been crucial, and even while making many games interesting, they've come through more times than not.

# 41 Playing the Nine

Sitting 27 games back of the Detroit Tigers in the division on September 22, 1968, Twins owner Calvin Griffith had an idea. The team had no opportunity to improve their seventh-place standing, and so Griffith arranged a plan for the versatile Cesar Tovar to play all nine positions in that day's game. It had been done just one time prior three years earlier when Bert Campaneris did it for the Kansas City A's.

Few players have ever played each position in one year or in their entire career, for that matter. But that night at Metropolitan Stadium, Tovar would turn the box score into a challenge for newspapers as the line next to his name would read "P-C-1B-2B-SS-3B-LF-CF-RF" by the time the game was over.

Sure, it was an odd feat, but if anybody could do it, Tovar was the guy. It was his ability to move around that earned him the nick-name "Mr. Versatility," and by the time his 12-year career was over, he had played more than 200 games as an outfielder, third baseman, and second baseman. He had never pitched before this day, however, and that one inning would be his only one on the mound through the remainder of his career.

As the lineups were announced, Bob Casey read out over the speakers, "Pitching, No. 12, Cesar Tovar." He was the starting pitcher, and to make the situation a bit more odd than it already was, the first batter of the game was Campaneris; the lone player to ever do what Tovar was about to. Tovar's one inning on the mound would go much better than Campaneris' did three seasons earlier. While Campaneris allowed one run on two walks and a hit, Tovar walked a batter and balked him to second, but no balls made it out of the infield, and he even struck out future Hall of Famer Reggie Jackson.

In the second inning Tovar put on the shin guards and chest protector as he headed behind the plate as the catcher. The crowd of 11,340 would get a laugh out of it, too; the equipment was too big for Tovar, and he couldn't crouch all the way down during his lone inning behind home plate. But the A's didn't score, and Tovar's jack-of-all-trades performance was just beginning.

Starting with the third inning, Tovar began his shift around the infield. He made a play at first base that inning and then headed to second base for the fourth inning, where he caught a pop-up. Nothing happened as he shifted to shortstop and third base during the fifth and sixth innings. For the final three innings, Tovar moved to the outfield, where he made three putouts.

When the day came to an end, Tovar had become just the second player to play each position, and he did it well. He finished the game with a scoreless inning on the mound and five putouts, one assist, and no errors in the field. At the plate, Tovar contributed to the team's 2–1 victory. He singled, walked, stole a base, and scored a run.

In the years since that game, the feat has been accomplished two more times as Scott Sheldon and Shane Halter both did it in 2000 for the Texas Rangers and Detroit Tigers, respectively.

Tovar died at the age of 54 from pancreatic cancer in 1994. Over his career, he hit .278 with 1,546 hits and stole 226 bases. Cesar Tovar was more than just a guy who could play anywhere on the diamond, but his career will forever be defined and remembered by that September day in 1968, when he played all nine positions and put himself into a unique space in baseball history.

# Tony Oliva

It was quite the first impression.

Signed out of Cuba as an amateur free agent in 1961, Tony Oliva burst onto the scene in a big way during his first full season with the club in 1964. That year he led the league in hits (217), runs (109), doubles (43), total bases (374), and batting average (.323). The incredible rookie season won him the first Rookie of the Year Award in team history, he made the All-Star Game, and he finished in the top five in MVP voting.

More impressive than his league-leading statistics that season were the facts behind them. He became the first player in American League history to win the batting title and collect 200 hits in a rookie season, and when he led the league with a .321 batting average the next year, he became the first player in baseball history to take home the honor in his first two major league seasons.

That rookie season was certainly something else, and his next seven years with the Twins would be equally superb. In the end, Oliva played 15 seasons in the league, so the fact that the number seven is mentioned can't be a good thing. It isn't to say that Oliva was bad in his final five seasons as a baseball player, but an injury would see his previously eye-popping numbers decline in those

*Tony Oliva crosses home plate after hitting Major League Baseball's first designated hitter home run at Oakland Coliseum on April 6, 1973. Greeting him are Steve Braun (4) and Rod Carew (29).*

final seasons, and in the end, they were enough to keep him out of baseball's Hall of Fame through his 15-year eligibility.

It was June 29, 1971, and the Twins were playing on the West Coast at Oakland Coliseum. As Oliva went after a line drive off the bat of Joe Rudi, he twisted his right knee, one that had already been repaired more than one time in the seasons before. At the time, he was hitting .375, and while he would still play on the injured knee through the season, winning his third batting title and making his eighth All-Star Game along the way, he would never be the same. Oliva had put forth a great career to that point, but the numbers, batting titles, and All-Star appearances would begin to disappear.

"I think the day will come when I get into the Hall of Fame. It bothers you sometimes. The only thing they have against me is I had a short career because I got hurt. I put in eight full years," Oliva told Bob Sansevere of the *Pioneer Press*. "The funny part is there are other people who got hurt who don't have my statistics. They had a short career, and they're in the Hall of Fame. I dominated that league for eight straight years. I know it was a short career, but other people had a short career, too."

And what a great short career it was for "Tony-O." By the time he called it quits after 15 seasons with the Twins, Oliva had collected 1,917 hits, blasted 220 home runs, scored 870 runs, and hit for a lifetime average of .304. And that was in eight great seasons and five less-than-stellar ones, comparatively.

To think what Oliva might have done, and how many mores seasons he might have played had he not battled injuries, isn't completely difficult. After diving for that ball in the summer of 1971, he would play in only 10 games during the following season. In 1973 the designated hitter role emerged in the American League, and it quite possibly kept Oliva's career alive. For the final four years of his career he would merely hit, and simply put, his numbers declined.

"People don't understand how hard the job is as a DH. If you don't produce that day, you don't think you're doing anything for the ballclub," Oliva told Sansevere. "If you play any other position, and you go 0-for-4, but you make a good play in the field, it's okay. If you only go 0-for-4 as a DH, you feel you didn't do anything."

In 1976 Oliva played in only 67 games. At the conclusion of that season, and at the age of 37, he called it a career. He never would make it to another Midsummer Classic or lead the league in hitting following that knee injury, and today his hopes of being enshrined in the Hall are in the hands of the Veterans Committee.

Hall of Famer or not, Oliva is one of the greatest players in Twins history, and nobody will ever wear his No. 6 again. While it'll forever be a mystery what those five final seasons might have resulted in had he been healthy, there is no doubting that Tony Oliva had his eight great seasons.

# Ballpark Battle

The Twins were four seasons removed from their second championship, and they were in the midst of what would turn out to be eight consecutive losing seasons. Having spent nearly 15 seasons indoors at the Metrodome, and with revenue dropping, the team first whispered the word *ballpark* that year in 1995.

"It was obviously very difficult. We first whispered the word *ballpark* in 1995 and didn't get it done until 2006," team president Dave St. Peter said when looking back on the process during the team's first season at Target Field. "There were multiple proposals of ideas and concepts. It was difficult on many levels, but as a franchise, we remained hopeful that a solution would emerge."

To say the process was difficult might be an understatement. Today the Twins sit in a new state-of-the-art ballpark across town from the Metrodome, with new revenue, and with an organization turned in a completely different direction. But it wasn't quite that simple. The ballpark battle would take more than a decade from the time the Twins first looked into moving outdoors, and that's the short story. Through those years, there were many proposals gone bad, and the team nearly hit rock bottom on several occasions as rumors of the Twins moving to North Carolina surfaced in one instance and contraction threatened in another.

By 1997, two years after the Twins first looked into the idea, a new ballpark was looking grim. Owner Carl Pohlad had saved the Twins by purchasing the team from Calvin Griffith in 1984, but now it was suddenly looking like he would be the reason they'd leave the state some two decades later. Don Beaver, a businessman from North Carolina, offered a reported $250 million for the team, and Pohlad appeared willing to sell. While many believed the sale idea was a bluff, talks for a referendum for a ballpark in North Carolina proceeded. The referendum would eventually be voted down, and Beaver and the idea of the Twins moving quickly disappeared.

Nevertheless, the fight for a new ballpark had gained no ground. Two years later, in 1999, the city of St. Paul attempted to lure the Twins across the river to its territory. That idea would fail, too, though, when voters rejected a proposal to increase the city's sales tax to help fund the construction of a new stadium.

In 2001 the Twins finally put together a winning performance on the field as they moved above .500 for the first time since the 1992 season. But with no progress toward a new ballpark after more than five years of discussions, the Twins were offered up for contraction. They would eventually survive, but the team's long-term future in the hands of the Pohlad family, and potentially the state, was in serious jeopardy.

Years after surviving contraction, and after the Twins made the playoffs in three consecutive seasons, the idea and proposals for a ballpark finally began to proceed.

On April 26, 2005, it was announced that the Twins and Hennepin County had agreed to a sales tax increase to help fund a portion of a new stadium. Several more hurdles remained, but the Twins had finally cleared the first one. One week later the Hennepin County Board approved the agreement, and shortly after that, a House committee signed off. The dream that at times had been a nightmare was finally proceeding, and only two more steps remained.

## Target Field Construction Timeline

The Minnesota Twins first whispered the word *ballpark* during the 1995 season, but it wasn't until a decade later, after the threat of contraction had subsided and after the Twins once again became relevant, that true progress was made.

April 25, 2005—The Twins and Hennepin County announce that they have agreed on a proposal to fund and construct a new ballpark in downtown Minneapolis.

May 21, 2006—After passing through the Minnesota House, the bill passes through the Minnesota Senate.

May 26, 2006—During an on-field ceremony at the Metrodome, Governor Tim Pawlenty signs the ballpark bill into action, and a new ballpark for the organization becomes an official reality.

August 30, 2007—The Twins officially break ground, with the help of players of both the past and present and other dignitaries, on a new ballpark.

September 15, 2008—Target Corporation and the Twins announce an exclusive 25-year partnership that includes naming rights to the new ballpark.

February 10, 2009—The Twins hire groundskeeper Larry DeVito.

August 24, 2009—At dusk, the Twins begin installing the grass at Target Field. The long process would be completed four days later.

December 23, 2010—Team employees go to work at the Metrodome for the last time. Afterward, the move across town to Target Field would begin.

January 4, 2010—Mortenson, the company that built the ballpark, hands the key to Target Field over to the Twins as they begin official business at their new home.

January 22, 2010—The city of Minneapolis officially renames a portion of 3rd Avenue North in downtown Minneapolis to "Twins Way."

April 2, 2010—In an exhibition game against the St. Louis Cardinals, the Minnesota Twins play at Target Field for the first time.

April 12, 2010—Nearly 15 years after mentioning the word *ballpark*, and five years after the Twins and Hennepin County first agreed on a deal, the first regular season game is played outdoors in Minneapolis at the new Target Field.

Those two steps would be critical ones. The bill would first head to the House, and if they approved, it would reach its final destination in the Senate. On May 21, 2006, Twins baseball would forever change. The House passed the bill on a 71–61 vote, and roughly six hours later the Senate voted to approve it by a narrow

34–32 vote. The battle had finally come to an end, and a new journey for the Twins and their fans was beginning.

"That was an incredibly historic night," St. Peter recalled. "It was a felling of tremendous relief, and there was a little disbelief that we actually got it done. At the time it culminated the end of one journey and started another."

Shortly after the bill passed, prior to a game on May 26, Governor Tim Pawlenty sat in a chair on the turf of the Metrodome and put the pen to the paper.

"Everybody's listened to enough speeches over the last 10 years," Pawlenty told the crowd before he penned his signature. "Let's sign this thing."

It was official, the Twins were moving outdoors.

"It really marked the dawn of a new era for Twins fans," St. Peter said of that night. "It signaled that we had finally solved as a community this challenge and were in a position to move forward."

On the March night when the bill passed, there was an oddity. Team legend Kirby Puckett had passed away just months prior, and as legislators changed their minds, the vote eventually settled on his great number.

"Kirby Puckett's number. How appropriate is that?" Bell said that night in reference to the final vote. "That's perfect. I didn't want 35. We got the 34 vote. Perfect."

Perfect indeed.

# 44 Frank Viola: Sweet Music

Oh, how sweet it was.

The man nicknamed "Sweet Music," partly because of his last name and partly because a sportswriter deemed that was the sound in the Metrodome after he pitched, Frank Viola took the mound on October 25, 1987, for the biggest game of his life—and in Minnesota Twins history to that point.

It was Game 7 of the 1987 World Series. The Twins had made one World Series appearance before, but that had been more than 20 years earlier, in 1965 when they lost in Game 7 to the Dodgers. This time the Twins had Viola on the mound, the man who had gone 17–10 with a 2.90 ERA during the regular season.

After a quick 1-2-3 first inning, Viola hit a bump in the second. He allowed three consecutive singles to St. Louis' Jim Lindeman, Willie McGee, and Tony Pena, and the Cardinals led 1–0. After retiring the next two batters, Viola would allow an RBI single to Steve Lake, and the Twins were down 2–0 early.

Two innings into the game, the sound wasn't very sweet at all. The Cardinals already had four hits, and they'd begin the third inning with the top of their lineup set to face Viola. But things were about to change on the mound, and in the end, the Twins would need no other pitcher than their closer.

Through the next six innings, Viola scattered two hits and allowed no more runs. He'd add six strikeouts to his line, and the end result was an eight-inning, two-run performance that would lead the Twins past St. Louis for their first championship in team history. On that October night, Viola took home the World Series MVP.

The next season the Twins would miss the playoffs, but it was no fault of Viola's. The former second-round pick would put up even better numbers than his 1987 season, winning 24 games while tossing more than 255 innings, including seven complete games. He'd win the Cy Young Award that season, which at the time made him the second player in team history to receive the honor.

In the spring of 1989 Viola made comments about his contract, and after spending more than half of that season in Minnesota, he was sent to the New York Mets on July 31 with the team receiving

*Frank Viola throws a first-inning pitch against the St. Louis Cardinals in Game 4 of the 1987 World Series. His Game 7 appearance—six strikeouts and two runs in eight innings to win the World Series—was the game of his career.*

Rick Aguilera and Kevin Tapani, two key components of the championship team two years later, along with two other players.

In the end, the team's draft pick from 1981 would spend eight seasons in Minneapolis, winning 112 games while throwing 1,772⅔ innings and striking out 1,214 hitters to place him fifth all-time in team history for each category.

There were a lot of great moments in Frank Viola's Twins career, and his success on the mound eventually landed him on the All-Metrodome Team. But there was no sweeter sound than that late-October night in 1987, when Viola was masterful for seven of his eight innings on the hill, guiding Minnesota to its first title.

On that night Viola allowed the Twins and their fans to hear a song for the first time in team history. As Viola and the team celebrated, the song "We Are the Champions" finally had a connection with Twins baseball, and it couldn't have gotten any sweeter.

 # Silver Bat x 14

The Twins had signed Tony Oliva as an amateur free agent prior to their first season in Minnesota in 1961. Now in his rookie season, it was 1964, and Oliva was preparing to make Twins history.

That year, Oliva became the first of five eventual Twins to take home the Rookie of the Year Award, and rightfully so. At the age of 25, Oliva led the league that season in runs, hits, and doubles. Oh, and batting average with his .323 mark. For the first time in team history, Minnesota had a winner of the American League batting title.

The next season, in 1965, as the Twins marched to their first World Series, Oliva collected the title again. This time he hit .321 and finished second in the MVP voting behind teammate Zoilo Versalles.

In 1966 Oliva would finish in second place, and it wouldn't be until two years later that the Twins saw the silver bat awarded at Metropolitan Stadium. The year Oliva had made his debut with the Twins, the team signed a kid named Rod Carew to a free agent contract. In 1967 he, too, broke into the league winning the Rookie of the Year Award.

Carew didn't win the batting title in his rookie season as Oliva had done, but the honor wasn't far off. In 1969, Carew's third season, he hit .332 and brought the honor back to Minnesota. It would be the start of a trend in which a Twin would win the award in eight of 10 seasons.

After Alex Johnson of the Angels won the award in 1970, Oliva hit .337 in 1971, the highest mark of his career, and took home his third and final silver bat. For the next four years the title stayed in Minnesota. Rod Carew strung together four straight seasons in which he led the league in hitting, and it never really was close. In three of the seasons Carew beat his closest opponent by at least 28 points.

It could have been seven consecutive titles for Carew, but in 1976, after having won the honor in four straight seasons, he fell to the Kansas City Royals' George Brett by just two points. The next season Carew would come back firing. He flirted with .400 for much of the season and eventually finished at .388, winning the MVP award to go along with a landslide victory over teammate Lyman Bostock and the rest of the league in the batting race.

In his final season with the Twins, Carew would win the title one more time. He would never again claim the honor after he left for California, but in his tenure with the Twins he set a high mark, winning seven silver bats in a span of 10 seasons; a feat that places him fourth all-time for the most batting titles won.

Following the team's first championship in 1987, Kirby Puckett was just 28 years old, and he was looking to become the first Twin in 10 seasons to win the batting title. That year, 1988, Puckett finished second to Wade Boggs, but the next year he'd hit .339, and after leading the league in hits for three consecutive years, he finally had a silver bat of his own.

It would be nearly two decades after that before the Twins would see a player collect the award again. Puckett had come close in 1992, and second baseman Chuck Knoblauch came close again in 1995, but following that, no Twin finished as high as second for the next 10 seasons.

Already a historic season for the Twins, Joe Mauer made more history on the final day of the 2006 season. With his .347 average, he knocked off Derek Jeter of the New York Yankees by three points, collecting his first batting title—the first won by an American League catcher in baseball history.

History-making would continue during the 2008 and 2009 seasons for Mauer. He won two more batting titles, matching the total won by all catchers in baseball history combined.

Through the first 50 seasons of baseball in Minnesota, the Twins have won 14 batting titles collectively, meaning nearly 30 percent of the silver bats awarded in the past half-century have been given to players from the Twins organization.

 **Target Field**

At the middle is a pitcher's mound. Four bases placed 90 feet apart surround it. There is dirt that makes up an infield, grass that makes up an outfield, and a warning track that encloses the diamond. This is a baseball field, and there are thousands of them all across the country.

For 28 seasons, the Twins played under the Teflon roof and on the AstroTurf of the Metrodome. It was a place that Twins fans tried their best to love and outsiders did all they could to mock and scoff at. After a near–three decade stay, it was time to move on. That's not to say there weren't memories created under the roof, because there were many, but baseball is meant for the great outdoors, and there is no better place for that than Minnesota.

## Target Field Facts

Cost to build: $545 million

Years of operation: 2010–present

Capacity: Seats: 39,504; Standing: 41,000

Dimensions: LF: 339 ft.; CF: 404 ft.; RF: 328 ft.

Ballpark Details: Overhang in right field is eight feet onto the warning track; Right-field wall is 23 feet tall (same as Metrodome baggy); Scoreboard is 57 feet tall and 101 feet wide; The original budget for Target Field was $390 million

Firsts: Game: April 12, 2010 (Twins 5, Red Sox 2); Hit: Marco Scutaro; Run: Denard Span; RBI: Michael Cuddyer; HR: Jason Kubel; Win: Carl Pavano; Save: Jon Rauch

It took over a decade before the dream became a reality. There were seemingly hundreds of discussions, legislation battles, threats of moving and contraction, and then finally on August 30, 2007, the gold shovels were brought out for a groundbreaking, and construction on an eventual $545 million, 21st century, state-of-the-art ballpark was underway.

After approximately two and a half years, the foundation of a new era in Twins baseball was complete. The organization and fans finally had a new home, which at one point in time seemed so far off and nothing but a dream. Sitting just beyond Target Center with right field open to the Minneapolis skyline, was Target Field, an anything-but-ordinary ballpark that surrounds your typical baseball field.

Quite possibly the greatest thing about the team's new home is the simplest thing: it's outdoors. Yes, that blue thing up above is the sky, that bright light is the sun, and that green stuff beneath the players is real, freshly cut grass. After decades of artificial touches, baseball in Minneapolis is back where it belongs—with nature and all of its elements.

The experience goes well beyond an outdoor atmosphere, of course. When you spend that much money and put forth that

*The $545 million Target Field returns Minnesota baseball to where it belongs: outside.* Photo courtesy Alex Halsted

much effort to complete such a big goal, it has to. All around the ballpark there are both big features and small touches that make Target Field unique to the state and unique to the organization.

All around, there is history. As you arrive on the plaza, there are statues to honor some of the greatest players in team history, pennants that make up the Twins Hall of Fame and all-time rosters, a Gold Glove that signifies the team's commitment to hustle and defense, and banners hanging from the outside of the ballpark to showcase each of the team's championships. And this is just the beginning.

As fans enter the ballpark, they do so by virtue of numbered gates. These aren't just random numbers, though, they're the greatest numbers ever placed on a Twins uniform. After walking through the gates, the flashback on the team's history continues. The retired numbers are again displayed on the administrative building down the left-field line, there are more pennants above left field to yet again honor the team's championships, and in center field stands a 46-foot-tall Minnie and Paul, the team's original logo that helps celebrate the best moments each game.

Restaurants and clubs fill the ballpark. There is Hrbek's, to honor the hometown kid who wore No. 14 for 14 seasons in Minnesota. There is the Town Ball Tavern that celebrates teams, players, and ballparks from Minnesota's Town Ball history, and there is a Twins Pub. For season-ticket holders and other fans willing to spend a few extra dollars, there are three clubs: the Metropolitan Club, the Legends Club, and the Champions Club. These areas pay homage to Twins greats, showcase the team's old home, and act as the home for the team's two championship trophies.

Pictures and words merely describe the team's newest home, but not much of either can completely illustrate the experience. Upon each trip you'll see something you didn't quite pick up in your last, and with natural elements combining with the game of baseball, who knows what could happen over the course of any nine-inning game?

One thing is for sure: the center of Target Field is a typical baseball field, and what you'll see as you surround that field in the team's new home is the game of baseball. With all of the amenities and historic touches aside, Target Field is a *ballpark*, and that is reason enough to head to a game in downtown Minneapolis.

# 47 Fireworks at Target Field

For nearly three of the team's first five decades in Minneapolis, there was no opportunity for unique experiences at the ballpark.

Playing under a roof, there was no chance you'd see any of Minnesota's nature, there were no flyovers before first pitch, and your best shot at seeing a fireworks show was watching home runs being launched into the home run porch in left field or the upper deck in right field.

As fans cheered on a July night during the team's inaugural season at Target Field, they did so not because superstar Joe Mauer was rounding the bases after a home run, and not because closer Jon Rauch was closing out a victory. The reason for the cheers that night had nothing to do with baseball.

It was the first-ever fireworks show at the team's new home, and the cheers stemmed from the lights at the ballpark slowly dimming and going out. With the exception of Minnie and Paul glowing red and blue in center field, the ballpark sat dark. A dark ballpark is a rare site, and for the first time in nearly 30 seasons, fans were taking in an experience meant for baseball.

How could it get any better? Baseball, America's pastime, coinciding with the country's Independence Day festivities.

While fireworks launched into the air on that first fireworks night at the Twins' new home, a sellout crowd remained seated and fell nearly silent. Already in that first season fans had seen a squirrel send third baseman Brendan Harris jumping into the air, and a kestrel making its home and eating moths on the right-field foul pole. But this was a new encounter. For a period of time, the final score and the events of that night's game held no significance. Several players and their families sat in foul territory outside of first base seemingly unnoticed by the crowd.

Going to a ballgame in Minneapolis is now more than an event, it's an experience. That sentiment became blatantly clear during the team's first season under the sky after having played under a Teflon roof for 28 years.

While the experience of attending a baseball game previously was judged solely on the outcome, fireworks on a warm summer night at Target Field can remind anyone that sometimes it's more than just a game. When fans leave a Twins game in the new era, there is now something much bigger than a final score; there are memories shared by friends, family, and a fan base that can last a lifetime.

## Talkin' Twins Baseball

In 1981 Terry Cashman wrote the popular song known by most as "Talkin' Baseball." Shortly after, he followed up with team-specific versions of the song, including one for the Minnesota Twins:

When the Senators stopped playin' ball
The Twin Cities got the call
Minnesota joined the American League
With Mele at the reins
The Twins made instant gains
In '65 they had the flag and an MVP

I'm talkin' baseball...
Allison and Perry
Twins Baseball...
Kitty Kaat and Jerry
Don Mincher and Mudcat comin' through
Jimmie Hall and Davey Boswell, too
Just like Tony...the Killer and Carew

Rod was Rookie of the Year
There was a Chance, no hitter here
Under Rig and Billy the Kid they won the West
But though Harmon kept on cloutin'
Tony's knees were givin' out
And he was never the same but he always came and gave his best

I'm talkin' baseball...
Roseboro and Uhlaender
Twins baseball...
Tovar, Reese, and Campbell
*(continued on following page)*

139

## Talkin' Twins Baseball (continued)

Perranoski and Darwin in the crew
Lyman Bostock, and Bert Blyleven, too
Just like Tony…the Killer and Carew

Talkin' baseball in Minnesota
Bernie Allen, Red Worthington
Kralick had a no-hit game
Danny Thompson what a shame
Hisle, Landreaux, Goltz, what can we say?
We love to watch 'em play
Well '96 is another year, and if the Twins can get their game in gear
T.K. will answer to the call
New names join the old
Another team unfolds
They're right at home in the Metrodome, so let's play ball

I'm talkin' baseball…
Aguilera is a starter
Twins baseball…
Kirby Puckett's not the part
Cordova, Meares, and Knoblauch comin' through
There's Molitor and David Hollins, too
Just like Tony…the Killer and Carew
There was Tony…the Killer and Carew

# 48 Torii Hunter

It's the game, or the play, on July 9, 2002, that captures every aspect of Torii Hunter best. Days earlier Hunter had become the first Twin since his predecessor, Kirby Puckett, to be voted into the All-Star Game as the starting center fielder. With two outs and slugger Barry Bonds up to the plate at Miller Park in Milwaukee, Wisconsin, Hunter did something he did on so many different occasions during his tenure with the Twins—he made the catch.

It wasn't just your typical catch; it was a catch that earned him the nickname "Spider-Man." It was the catch that really let baseball fans know who Torii Hunter was and what he stood for. It was the catch that had the biggest names in the baseball world talking. Most of all, though, it was the catch that captured the true essence of Hunter: his ability, his hustle, and his smile.

The catch consisted of Hunter jumping high into the air and reaching over the fence almost perfectly to rob Bonds of a home run. As Hunter ran toward the dugout, Bonds threw the soon-to-be 27-year-old over his shoulder, and the two players shared smiles that stretched from ear to ear. At that moment Hunter showed qualities that greatly resembled Puckett, and that certainly wasn't a bad thing.

It's a pretty tall task to play in the shadow of the greatest Minnesota Twin ever, but Hunter did about as well as anybody could have hoped for during his tenure with the Twins. Drafted with the team's first overall pick in the 1993 amateur draft, Hunter was a highly regarded prospect coming to the organization behind the future Hall of Famer in Puckett, who had been the hero of the 1991 World Series just two years earlier.

Hunter spent four full seasons in the minor leagues until he was called up for the first time in August 1997. He'd appear in just one game, making his major league debut as a pinch runner. The next season Hunter would play in a few more games for the Twins and had his first few at-bats. It was one year later, in 1999, though, that he would take over sacred ground at the Metrodome as the starting center fielder for the Twins.

In his first full season at the major league level Hunter did decently, but he struggled early on during the 2000 season and

*Torii Hunter's at-the-wall catch at the 2002 All-Star Game robbed Barry Bonds of a home run and displayed Hunter's ability and hustle. After the play, Bonds greeted Hunter and threw him over his shoulder.*

headed to Triple A where he hit .368 with 18 home runs, enough production to get him recalled later that season.

The next season the Twins would snap their eight-season losing streak, and Hunter was a big reason why. That year he broke out for

27 home runs and 92 RBIs, winning his first of an eventual seven Gold Gloves in a Twins uniform.

Over the next several years, Hunter became the face of the franchise and established himself as one of the game's best. In the field he kept making catches, and at the plate he kept improving. He reached the 20–home run mark in every full season but one after his breakthrough year, missing the mark only in 2005 when he broke his ankle attempting to make a catch at Fenway Park.

Hunter helped lead the Twins to the playoffs four times during his stay in Minneapolis, and before he left via free agency after the 2007 season, he had jumped into the top 10 in team history in nearly every major hitting category, including hits, home runs, RBIs, and runs scored, to name a few.

After a near-decade-long winning drought following their second championship, the Twins were desperately looking for a star to change things around. Torii Hunter became that player, and in the likeness of Puckett, he helped turn the team into a contender and once again made Twins baseball relevant.

# 49 Playoffs? Playoffs!

*"What's that? Ah…playoffs? Don't talk about—playoffs! You kidding me? Playoffs?"* —Coach Jim Mora

Yes, Mr. Mora, we're talking about playoffs. Each spring, every one of baseball's 30 teams start with a clean slate, tied atop their respective divisions. There is just one goal as the season begins each year: contend and make the playoffs. It's not an easy feat, to say the least, only eight teams—not even one-third of the league—advance into postseason play each year.

But that's the goal, and there is nothing better when it does happen.

For six months, about 24 weeks, and a total of 162 games (and in the Twins' case, sometimes 163 games) each year, there is professional baseball played in downtown Minneapolis and in 29 other cities around the country. There are highs and lows during this span, and both nail-biters and blowouts. Nothing compares to the playoffs, though. This is exclusive to a select few teams, and a select group of fans.

October in Minnesota can be cold, but for almost three decades, more than 50,000 fans crammed inside the Metrodome during this month. The result is somewhat magical. Fans are into the game's every pitch and every moment. The playoffs are do-or-die; win or go home. There is no "there's always tomorrow" talk, because at this point tomorrow in October there may be a trip down south for the players and months of wonderment for the fans as the focus shifts from the on-field production of the team to the hopes for next season.

As the national audience tunes in for these games, fans of teams sitting at home wonder what the feeling would be like in their city if these moments were to become reality, while fans in Minnesota wave the Homer Hankies as the broadcast goes live. The playoffs are about the excitement and about the dreams that both players and fans share together: the team piling up in the infield as baseball's champions at the conclusion of the World Series. After all, that is the ultimate goal, and only eight teams each fall have the opportunity to chase it.

You can watch on television, and it'll still be exciting. It's still *your* team, and it's still the *playoffs*. But at some point, you've got to head to Minnesota in October when the Twins are playing on the biggest stage possible. Don't take the chance and put the trip off until next year, because in baseball, you just never know when that might be.

While the 1990s started with a bang as the Twins won the World Series in 1991 for the second time, the next 10 seasons followed with underperforming efforts, and at that, no playoff appearances. In five of the final eight years of the first decade of the 2000s, the Twins turned things back around and pushed their way back into the most coveted games.

Nobody can predict when the Twins might hit a lull and miss the playoffs or when great moments will occur, and they do. If you're there, though, you certainly won't miss them. Win or lose, there is no experience like meaningful October baseball. From a ballpark filled with fans waving white hankies, to the players lined up down the base paths for introductions, to the first pitch with thousands of camera flashes, nothing compares.

There are no guarantees, but if you're in attendance for a playoff game, one thing can be assured: it'll be memorable, and as the crowd goes wild, chills will run through your body.

That's the playoffs, and nothing gets much better.

 **Fighting for .400**

Ted Williams wanted him to do it. Baseball fans did, too. And midway through the 1977 season, he was. Rod Carew was hitting above .400, one of the greatest, and today most untouchable numbers in baseball.

"I would love to see Rod Carew hit .400," Williams wrote in a 1977 article for *Sports Illustrated* before later writing, "You don't fluke into a .400 season. A lot of guys have lucked into .300, but there are no flash-in-the-pan .400s. Hitting a baseball—I've always said it—is the single most difficult thing to do in sports, and a .400 season is a magnificent achievement."

After collecting three hits in the first two games of the Twins' three-game series with the Chicago White Sox near the end of June that season, Carew entered the series finale approaching the mark that only Williams had finished a season at. It hadn't been done since 1941 when he hit .406, and so fans and the media were excited and glued in.

In that finale on June 26, 1977, a Met Stadium record crowd of 46,463 fans arrived at the ballpark to watch the first-place team and to see if Carew, although still relatively early in the season, could jump above the coveted batting average mark. The Twins won the game 19–12 in a slugfest, and right fielder Glenn Adams went 4-for-5 with a grand slam and eight RBIs. But it was Carew who drew the attention that day. He went 4-for-5, too, and his average moved to .403 through 69 games. Fans applauded him with multiple ovations.

"That was my most memorable day as a player," Rod Carew would tell the *Star Tribune* years later. "It wasn't my first day in the big leagues. It wasn't getting my first hit or my 3,000th. It was that Sunday in late June against the White Sox."

And on that day, the national spotlight turned to Rodney Cline Carew.

By the end of June, Carew was hitting .411, and he had hit .486 during the month to reach the mark. He stayed above .400 until exactly midway through the season, when he was sitting at .402 through the first 81 games.

The performance began putting him front-and-center across the country. He was featured, just Carew himself, on the cover of *Time* with the title "Baseball's Best Hitter," and then later he and Williams were featured on the cover of *Sports Illustrated* when the last man to hit .400 broke down his swing and his remarkable season.

During the 86th game of that 1977 season, Carew would go 1-for-5, and he dipped below .400 for the first time in 13 games. Through the month of July he hit *just* .306, and by the end of the month he was sitting at .383 with 57 games remaining in the season.

The feat was still possible, but it wouldn't be easy. The media followed Carew everywhere he went, and every sportswriter in every city wanted to do a story on him when he arrived. By August 26 his average had fallen to .374, and while it would climb in the final month of the season, Carew's quest for .400 would come up short. He led the league with 239 hits and had nearly 700 plate appearances, but when all was said and done, he was eight hits shy of reaching the seemingly untouchable milestone.

Since Carew flirted with .400 back in 1977, more than 30 seasons have passed, and few players have come close. In 1980 George Brett finished at .390, and in 1994 Tony Gwynn hit .394. But Brett appeared in 38 fewer games than Carew did that year and Gwynn 45 fewer, making their efforts, while still remarkable, just a bit less legendary than Carew's 1977 season.

It has been nearly 70 seasons since a player hit .400, and Williams was right when he called a .400 season a "magnificent achievement." During his 12-year tenure with the Twins, Carew won seven batting titles, and in that 1977 season he took home the MVP.

As Williams neared the end of his feature on Carew, he wrote, "For me, the .406 became a tag, despite all the other things I was proud to have accomplished in baseball."

Rod Carew might not have collected those eight hits that he needed, and his name might not sit in the .400 club, but the number .388 will forever hold a significant meaning in Twins history. It isn't .400, but it certainly is Carew's tag.

# 51 Justin Morneau

It is a notable day in Justin Morneau's history, and even Minnesota Twins history: July 31, 2004. It was the 2004 trade deadline, and the Twins had just moved their starting first baseman, a likeable guy who had called Minnesota home for parts of seven seasons, including four full ones. Fans loved Doug Mientkiewicz. They loved that he blew gum bubbles while batting, and his glove was nice, too. But there was a new kid on the way, a 23-year-old from New Westminster, Canada, who had some power.

Morneau would start at first base that day and for the remainder of the 2004 season. He hit 14 home runs after the Twins traded Mientkiewicz, and the next season he played his first full season with Minnesota, belting 22 home runs.

It was a good beginning for Morneau, but he was just getting started. In 2006 Morneau belted 34 home runs, becoming the first Twin since 1987 to surpass 30 home runs in a season. Along with his good friend Joe Mauer, Morneau helped the Twins to an improbable second-half run, and the Twins made the playoffs that year. The team wouldn't win any hardware, but Morneau took home plenty, becoming only the fourth player in team history at the time, and the first Canadian player in baseball history, to win the American League Most Valuable Player Award. He also joined Larry Walker as the only other Canadian to win the MVP.

Morneau and Mauer quickly became a two-headed monster in the heart of the Twins' lineup. The group earned the nickname "M & M Boys," and as Morneau continued to belt monstrous home runs into the upper deck at the Metrodome, he earned the title "Canadian Crusher" from many fans.

One year after putting up career numbers, Morneau hit 31 home runs, and he added 23 more in 2008 before the Twins handed him a contract extension. That off-season, he signed a six-year, $80 million deal that would keep him in a Twins uniform through at least 2013, well into the team's new era at Target Field.

Before reaching the age of 30, Morneau has already become one of the best players to hail from Canada, joining other notable players such as Ferguson Jenkins, a Hall of Fame pitcher, and

*Justin Morneau joined the Twins in 2004, and in 2006 became the first Canadian player in baseball history to win the American League MVP Award. That same year he hit 34 home runs.*

Walker, a guy who belted 383 home runs in his career. Since joining the starting lineup for an entire season in 2005, Morneau has hit fewer than 20 home runs in a season just once (when he missed half of the 2010 season), and he's on pace to reach 250 career home runs before his current deal expires with the Twins, if he can stay healthy and continue his production of years past.

With no upper deck in right field, Morneau now has a new playground across town in Minneapolis. His aim for home runs has become the direction of the Target Center and the plaza that stands in front of it. When the team opened a spot for Morneau back in 2004, fans knew his prospects were promising. Justin Morneau has gone above those expectations, and he has quickly become one of the best players in Minnesota Twins history.

 # No. No. No. No.

The feat isn't as prestigious as recording a perfect game, but pitching a no-hitter is still quite an accomplishment. Through baseball history, it's been done on average two times each season, and four pitchers in Minnesota Twins history have completed the feat.

There had been two no-hitters in Washington Senators history, but Jack Kralick threw the first no-hitter in Twins history during the team's second season in Minneapolis. On August 26, 1962, heading into the final inning, Kralick was tossing a perfect game against the Kansas City Athletics. With two outs to go, Kralick would walk George Alusik to ruin his chance at a perfect game, and he eventually settled for a 1–0 victory and the team's first no-hitter.

Five years later Dean Chance took the mound against the Cleveland Indians. He had thrown a five-inning perfect game earlier in the month, but by major league rule, a game must be nine innings for the feat to be official. On this day, the Indians would score, and they scored first. But because the run came on two walks, an error and a wild pitch, the no-hitter was still intact. The Twins would win the game 2–1, Chance recorded the team's second no-hitter, and the Twins wouldn't see one of their own toss another one until some 27 years later.

On that day, April 27, 1994, Scott Erickson would take the mound at the Metrodome and would eventually pitch one of the most unexpected no-hitters in both Twins and possibly even baseball history. Erickson was a guy who allowed a lot of hits. In fact, he'd led the league in hits allowed during the previous 1993 season. What made the feat more improbable was his 7.48 ERA that he had when he entered the game. In that game against the Milwaukee Brewers, Erickson would walk four hitters and hit another, but he never once allowed a hit on his way to recording the first no-hitter in Metrodome history.

Eric Milton would toss the second and final no-hitter in Metrodome history. At the time he was in only his second season at the major league level and was still just 24 years old. On September 11, 1999, Milton took the mound against the Anaheim Angels. He walked the second batter of the game and walked another batter in the third inning, but from that point on Milton would allow no more base runners, striking out 13 hitters along the way to a 7–0 victory and the team's fourth and final no-hitter in the first 50 years of Twins baseball in Minnesota.

There have been some close calls along the way. The most notable one was the near perfect game by Scott Baker. On August 31, 2007, Baker was moving quickly through the Kansas City Royals' lineup. Through eight innings he had tossed a perfect game. In the ninth inning Baker walked catcher John Buck to lead off the inning, but he still had a no-hitter, and he retired the next batter. Needing two more outs to become the fifth Twin to toss a no-hitter, Baker surrendered a single to longtime Twins nemesis Mike

Sweeney. He would still record the complete game and shutout, but the game would go down in team history as nothing more than a 5–0 victory over a division rival.

Two teams in Major League Baseball, the New York Mets and the San Diego Padres, have never received a no-hitter from one of their pitchers, and despite a drought of almost three decades without any Minnesota pitcher completing the feat, the Twins have four no-hitters credited to their team history, including three in front of the home crowd. Now, if only they could get that first perfect game.

# 53 Attend TwinsFest

At this point, spring training is still weeks away, and the regular season still sits more than two months later on the calendar. It's the final weekend of the first month of the year, and the Super Bowl normally follows the next Sunday. But if you head to the Metrodome on these final days of January, it's baseball season, even if none of the players have taken the field.

The Minnesota Twins might be long gone from the Metrodome (in reality just one season, but they're never headed back), but in the midst of the cold Minnesota winter, you can still see them down on the same field where Kirby Puckett once made that catch and where Dan Gladden once scampered home. This three-day event actually marks the only time fans can once again draw the connection from the Dome Dog experience to the baseball one, and the only time fans can slouch back in those blue chairs and relive the memories, or nightmares, from the 28-season existence of Twins baseball under the roof. (That is, of course, if the Metrodome is open. In 2011 TwinsFest was moved to the National Sports Center in Blaine, Minnesota, while the Metrodome roof was being repaired.)

As the doors open on each of the three days, fans push into the ballpark, running, right after they spin through the turnstiles. They aren't trying to get the best seat in general admission, though. Instead, fans run for the different sections where players—past, present, and future—sign autographs and smile for the camera.

This is TwinsFest, and there is no better signal that baseball is on the horizon.

Two years removed from their first championship, the Twins put together what today is one of the largest team-run fan festivals in professional sports. Since its inception in 1989, TwinsFest has drawn thousands of fans and raised more than $4 million for charities and programs supported by the Twins Community Fund.

There are two primary draws at this mid-winter event: autographs and collectibles. While players ranging from Ben Revere to Joe Mauer to Harmon Killebrew sign autographs for fans of all ages, one of the premier collectible shows sits on the outfield turf, where things ranging from cards to sports memorabilia are sold.

But there is so much more than autographs and collectibles.

While kids take part in a home run derby in the same spot where Greg Gagne fielded grounders and at the same ballpark where the home run derby first came into existence during the 1985 All-Star Game, adults sit in the stands down the left-field line, listening to personnel and players talk about the roster and the upcoming season.

Out near the center-field warning track, people bellow the National Anthem, hoping they'll make the cut to sing it at Target Field in the upcoming season. Down the right-field line, others sit on the television set and pretend they are a major league broadcaster.

One of the greatest sections of the event is history. You could go to Cooperstown, New York, or you could head to the Metrodome on this weekend and see things such as Hall of Fame plaques and artifacts from huge moments. And when else can you stand inches away from the trophies the team brought home nearly two decades ago as baseball's world champions?

Outside it may be snowing, and the Twins may have moved across town to their new outdoor ballpark, but for three days of the year the Metrodome becomes home once again. There is no better time to see some of the biggest icons in team history or to stand down on the turf and dream of those special moments in 1987 and 1991.

And maybe you'll make some new memories at the old stadium the team has left behind.

 ## Secrets of the Trade

It's so easy to sign a free agent, making a trade can oftentimes be quick and simple, and if a player isn't cutting it with his production, you can just go ahead and drop him. What's so hard about being a general manager? It may be that easy to do those things in the ever-so-popular fantasy baseball that many fans participate in each season, but in reality, building a roster, especially a competitive one, is difficult. Fans question every move and scowl when their favorite team doesn't make a trade for or sign that one particular player, but making a deal is much more complicated than clicking a few buttons on the computer.

"One of the key aspects of pulling a deal together is finding the right match. Many times we may have interest in a player from another organization, but if we don't have players at positions they are looking for, it is difficult to match up," said Twins assistant general manager Rob Antony of the complexities in making a trade. "Secondly, the other club must be as motivated to make a deal as you are. If not, they will want to be overwhelmed, and that is when you pay too much and make a poor deal."

## Player Profile: Francisco Liriano

*A mirror image to ace Johan Santana*, thought many in 2006. As Francisco Liriano made his way to Minnesota that season, he brought with him a high-speed fastball, a nasty change-up, and a left arm that reminded many of the team's Cy Young winner.

What Liriano did on the mound that year only reinforced those thoughts. At 22 years old, Liriano entered the rotation on May 19, and before he hit a bump in August, he had gone 12–3 with a 2.16 ERA. The bump that he hit that summer was a big one, though. Liriano had hurt his arm, and in November of that year he was on the operating table undergoing Tommy John surgery.

During that rookie season, Liriano was twice named Rookie of the Month and was in discussion for both the Rookie of the Year and Cy Young Award before his season abruptly ended. Liriano missed the 2007 season as he recovered, but he has slowly worked his way back into form in recent seasons, and back to the nasty pitcher fans watched emerge back in 2006.

Over the years, there have undoubtedly been deals that in the end that have favored the other team, and that's because every deal a team makes can't be a gem. With the trades that may not have turned out as planned have come several trades that ended as one-sided steals for the Twins. One of those deals came in 2003, when general manager Terry Ryan and his front office made a deal with the San Francisco Giants.

"A large majority of the credit for the Twins getting Joe Nathan in that trade goes to former assistant GM Wayne Krivsky," Antony said. "He was in charge of scouting the National League, and he believed that Nathan had the stuff and the makeup to be a closer."

The deal came on November 14, 2003, as the Twins sent catcher A.J. Pierzynski to the Giants in return for Nathan and pitchers Francisco Liriano and Boof Bonser. Nathan had accumulated just one save to that point in his career, but the Twins had done the scouting to believe he could be successful. In his first season he was an All-Star, and he soon became one of the league's highly regarded closers. Another part of the deal, Liriano, would soon shine, too.

"We had a few of our area scouts at the time, Sean Johnson, Mark Wilson, and Lee MacPhail, who saw Liriano in Instructional League with the Giants and had big future numbers on him," Antony recalled of getting Liriano in the deal. "They projected that he would be a very good prospect and were right. It was a combination of good scouting and getting a player who had a lot of injuries early in his career. There was enough uncertainty on the Giants' part that they were willing to include him."

## The Memorable Deals

Over the team's first 50 seasons of existence, there have been only three long-tenured general managers. Nonetheless, there have been several memorable deals made over the five decades, and those bold moves have helped launch the Minnesota Twins to both division titles and championships.

May 2, 1963—The Twins acquire pitcher Jim Perry from the Cleveland Indians for pitcher Jack Kralick.

June 15, 1964—The Twins acquire Jim "Mudcat" Grant from the Cleveland Indians for pitcher Lee Stange and third baseman George Banks.

February 3, 1987—The Twins acquire catcher Tom Nieto and closer Jeff Reardon from the Montreal Expos for Al Cardwood, Yorkis Perez, Jeff Reed, and Neal Heaton.

July 31, 1989—The Twins acquire pitchers Rick Aguilera, Kevin Tapani, David West, and Jack Savage from the New York Mets for pitcher Frank Viola.

February 6, 1998—The Twins acquire outfielder Brian Buchanan, shortstop Cristian Guzman, and pitchers Eric Milton and Danny Mota from the New York Yankees for second baseman Chuck Knoblauch.

November 14, 2003—The Twins acquire starting pitchers Boof Bonser, Francisco Liriano, and closer Joe Nathan from the San Francisco Giants for catcher A.J. Pierzynski.

November 28, 2007—The Twins acquire outfielders Delmon Young and Jason Pridie and infielder Brendan Harris from the Tampa Bay Rays for pitchers Matt Garza and Eduardo Morlan and shortstop Jason Bartlett.

After debuting in 2005, Liriano would win 12 of his 16 starts in 2006 while posting a 2.16 ERA as a rookie. Eventually he'd miss time because of Tommy John surgery, but he has nonetheless been a productive pitcher during his tenure with the team. To obtain these commodities, the Twins were forced to give up a player that had been key to their previous success. The Twins liked Pierzynski, and while things didn't work in San Francisco, making the deal a huge win for the Twins, it wasn't easy to let him go.

"When we traded A.J. Pierzynski to the Giants, it wasn't because we didn't like him or didn't think he was a very good player. We had Joe Mauer coming, and we thought he was ready for the big leagues. Thus we were trading a commodity to fill other needs because we had an able replacement," Antony recalled. "For whatever reason, things didn't pan out with the Giants for Pierzynski, but he was certainly a main cog in the White Sox winning the 2005 World Series.

"That was a good old-fashioned baseball trade, where both clubs got talent. Ours was projected, and theirs was a proven commodity."

In that case, the projected talent eventually outperformed the proven talent that the Twins shipped to the West Coast. But it doesn't always work that way. Sometimes the other team gets the better end, and trades are always made for different reasons.

"There have been other such trades, such as when we had to trade Scott Erickson and Kevin Tapani for prospects, knowing that we needed to move their salaries because the team was losing money and not going anywhere," Antony concluded. "Fans might not always understand, but general managers have an obligation and responsibility to their owners to make such moves when they have a chance to cut their losses."

And win or lose when making a deal, getting to that finish line is never easy.

# 55 Enter Enemy Territory

For almost three decades, the reason to head on the road to watch the Minnesota Twins was simply to see the team play outdoors. Now back under the sky at Target Field, fans don't need to get in the car and drive to see the Twins play baseball in its natural state. But that doesn't mean a road trip isn't a good thing, or that there aren't good reasons to head around the Midwest or even beyond to catch the Twins in action in other cities.

Heading on the road can be an adventure. Thrust into an opposing team's ballpark, away from the friendly confines of the home fans and next to fans that despise your team can be challenging. Your cheers will feel great if the Twins win, but if they lose you'll be forced to sulk down in your seat and hope that the home crowd doesn't give it all right back to you. Watching a game on the road allows you to root a little harder, but fall a little further if they come up short.

Chicago and Detroit offer two of the most intense matchups. Since the beginning of the 21st century, the team's biggest competitors have been the White Sox and Tigers, as the two teams have either placed second to the Twins or won the division in eight of those years. Standing 414 miles from Minneapolis, U.S. Cellular Field in Chicago offers an experience from one of the older ballparks in the division. Only two decades old, U.S. Cellular Field is far from a classic, but it was one of the final ballparks built before the ballpark boom started in the 1990s and 2000s. Meanwhile, Comerica Park stands 691 miles from Target Field. It doesn't have the history of the old Tiger Stadium, but Comerica Park offers a nice experience in downtown Detroit and a Monument Park that includes statues to showcase the team's history.

Heading to the two other cities that make up the remainder of the American League Central offers a chance to see two additional modern ballparks. In Kansas City, there is Kauffman Stadium, which sits 439 miles from Minneapolis. After its recent renovations in 2009, the ballpark known simply at "The K" offers a new experience. While it was built nearly 40 years ago and stands as the sixth oldest ballpark in baseball, Kaufman Stadium still offers a unique atmosphere. Heading in the other direction to Cleveland, about 753 miles away, you'll find Progressive Field, which many people still refer to as "The Jake." The home of the Indians has been named the best ballpark in baseball, and like the other ballparks in the division, it's a must see. Even when the Royals and Indians are down, as they have been in recent seasons, the ballpark experience in their cities remains premier.

And who could forget the National League? If you want to watch baseball in not just a different ballpark and city, but also in a completely separate manner, head to Milwaukee as the Twins take on the Brewers in the Border Battle. Miller Park, which stands 337 miles from Target Field and is the closest major league ballpark around, offers a guaranteed game with its retractable roof and is nice and new, having opened in 2001. This is the closest place to see the pitchers take some hacks, to see the team bunt to manufacture runs in the National League style of baseball, and to watch a matchup between two interleague rivals.

With Target Field and a new outdoor atmosphere in downtown Minneapolis, the need for a road trip isn't as strong as it used to be. That isn't to say the trip isn't worth it, though. There is nothing greater than cheering on the Twins in another team's ballpark, especially if they come out in front.

# Minnie and Paul

Minnie, meet Paul.

Paul, meet Minnie.

After the Minneapolis Lakers bolted from Minnesota for Los Angeles in 1960 because of poor attendance, much of the blame was placed on the people of St. Paul for not supporting the team. So as the Washington Senators made the move to Minnesota the next year in 1961, owner Calvin Griffith was looking to unite the two cities. His primary goals were to make sure fans didn't see the club as just a Minneapolis team and to make sure those located in St. Paul were included.

The first proposed name for the state's new baseball team was Twin Cities Twins, but after the league deemed it to be too generic, Griffith settled for the title Minnesota Twins. There was no city name included in the team's new title, making the Twins the first franchise in any professional sport to ever be named after the state in which they played rather than the city.

Shortly after they picked up their new title, the Twins commissioned freelance creative writer and illustrator Ray Barton to come up with a sketch for the team. What Barton drew for just $15 was a picture of two baseball players shaking hands over a river. He figured the logo would appear on cups at Metropolitan Stadium. To his surprise, the sketch would become the team's official logo, and it remained part of the team through their first 50 seasons in the state.

"It represents the Minnesota Twins," Twins historian Clyde Doepner said after Barton passed away in 2010. "I think the word *tradition* comes up. It goes back to '61. When you think of

*The Minnie and Paul sign that stands in Target Field's center field symbolizes the friendly union between the Twins' two hometown cities.* Photo courtesy Alex Halsted

Killebrew, Carew, even when you think of Puckett, you think of that logo."

The guys in the logo weren't just any baseball players, though, and it wasn't just any river. Initially the players in the sketch wore the letters "MT" on their sleeves, standing for Minnesota Twins. But that was soon changed. One player eventually wore an "M," standing for Minneapolis, and the other "StP," standing for St. Paul. The players represented the Twin Cities, and as they shook hands over the Mississippi River that divides the two cities, they showed unity and a connection to the state's new team.

"[The logo] uniquely links the Twin Cities of Minneapolis and St. Paul with the entire state in a united effort behind Major League Baseball," Griffith said when the design was unveiled on November 26, 1960.

Griffith was right. The two cities had finally been united after having argued over many issues in years prior. They supported the local team, and the Twins became highly regarded not just in the state, but all across the Upper Midwest.

A half-century after Minnie and Paul first shook hands on the bridge over the Mississippi River, the image still remains as an immense aspect of the organization. A 46-foot sign of that very logo now stands in Target Field's center field. And as a player hits a home run or as the Twins win a game, Minnie and Paul shake hands once again to signify all of Twins Territory coming together to support one team.

Minnie and Paul have become good friends.

# Johan Santana

Being connected to Hall of Famer Roberto Clemente can't be a bad thing.

On December 13, 1999, the Minnesota Twins made one of their best transactions in franchise history. With the first overall pick in the Rule 5 Draft, the team would eventually land 20-year-old Johan Santana, previously of the Houston Astros.

Each December the Rule 5 Draft takes place with the goal of preventing teams from stockpiling young talent in the minor league

*Arguably the best Rule 5 selection in baseball history, Johan Santana won two Cy Young Awards while a Twin before he was traded to the New York Mets in 2007.*

system when some teams would be willing to put the players on their major league roster. There are rules, of course: to be selected, a player must not be on the team's 40-man roster and must have been in the organization for four or five years, depending if he was originally signed at the age of 19 or earlier.

Signed by the Astros in 1995, and left off the 40-man roster leading up to the Rule 5 Draft in 1999, Santana was available to be taken, and the Twins agreed to a deal with the Florida Marlins; they would select pitcher Jared Camp, who the Marlins coveted, and the Marlins would take Santana. After the draft, the sides would swap picks, in the end leaving the Twins with Santana and an additional $50,000. Little did anybody know at the time, Santana would become arguably the best Rule 5 selection in baseball history, rivaled only by the Pittsburgh Pirates' selection of baseball great Roberto Clemente in 1954.

Santana's first season in Minneapolis wasn't the best, but as a stipulation, he needed to remain on the Twins' major league roster for the entire season or be offered back to Houston. So the Twins kept him, and all but five of his 30 appearances were out of the bullpen. At the age of 21, Santana posted an ERA of 6.49 in his first major league season.

In 2002 the Twins had Santana start the season at Triple A, where he worked with pitching coach Bobby Cuellar on a change-up. Cuellar was the same guy who had worked with Pedro Martinez as his pitching coach in 1997, and years later he'd gain praise for Santana's improvement.

After making nine starts in the minors, posting a 3.14 ERA and striking out 75 hitters in fewer than 50 innings of work, the team recalled Santana. Half of his appearances that year were as a starting pitcher, and Santana ended the season with a 2.99 ERA. The next season he made a few more starts, and he continued to post a higher strikeout total than his total number of innings pitched.

When the Twins inserted Santana into the rotation from day one in 2004, he had spent two consecutive seasons splitting time between the bullpen and the rotation. On April 6, 2004, Santana would start against the Cleveland Indians, and from that point forward he never again pitched out of the bullpen, instead establishing himself as one of the game's best starting pitchers.

In his first full season as a starting pitcher, Santana won 20 games, fueled primarily by a second-half run in which the lefty won 12 consecutive decisions from his last July start to his final regular season start in September. He posted a 2.61 ERA and struck out 265 hitters, both of which led the American League and helped him earn his first (and the team's third) Cy Young Award.

Santana would post solid numbers again the next season, but finished third in the Cy Young voting. In 2006 he went 15–2 over the final three months of the season, playing a crucial part in one of the most improbable comebacks in baseball history. That year, the Venezuelan native earned the Pitcher's Triple Crown, joining a group of Hall of Famers including Cy Young, Walter Johnson, Lefty Grove, and Bob Feller, after leading the American League in ERA, wins, and strikeouts. He would also win his second and final Cy Young Award with the Twins, becoming the only player in team history to win the honor twice.

Following the 2007 season, the Twins traded Santana to the New York Mets in fear that they wouldn't retain him during free agency the following year. In his eight seasons with the Twins, he put forth several gusty performances. A total of 26 times he struck out 11 or more hitters in a game, including a 17-strikeout performance in one of his final starts in Minnesota.

From a Rule 5 Draft selection whom the Astros didn't care to protect and nearly nobody had ever heard of, Johan Santana established himself in Minnesota, becoming one of the greatest players to ever wear the team's uniform.

# 58 Out at First!

The Series carried with it a lot of big moments and memories when all was said and done. Kirby's home run and catch and Morris' 10-inning shutout to clinch the championship were all legendary. But there was one play that October that is equally as memorable. Twins fans remember it with admiration, and the play brings back less pleasant memories for fans of the Braves.

On October 20, 1991, the Twins and Braves took the field at the Metrodome after the Twins had won the first game of the Series the previous night. After Chili Davis homered in the first inning, the Braves got one back with one lone run in the second inning. Then they threatened again in the third.

David Justice should have been striding from the on-deck circle to the batter's box with two outs. There should have been two runners on for him. And he should have had a chance to tie a game that only two teams have a shot to reach each season. It's *should have* because he never did make it there. What kept Justice from stepping to the plate was one of the most memorable plays in World Series history.

"Out," shouted first-base ump Drew Coble.

Just like that, a crowd of 55,145 fans roared with approval, the Braves protested, and pitcher Kevin Tapani had worked out of a threat.

For one dugout, the call was admired, for the other it was despised.

With Lonnie Smith on base and with two outs in the inning, center fielder Ron Gant had singled to left field, and Smith advanced to third base on the play. First and third with two outs and a chance to tie things up was the scenario for the Braves. At least it was until Gant rounded first base. Left fielder Dan Gladden had thrown the ball in, and pitcher Tapani caught and fired it to Kent Hrbek at first to nab Gant and the Braves' chance to even the score.

Countless times each season a player nudges a runner at the base, but this wasn't quite the same. For one, it was on the biggest stage possible. And when shown in slow motion, it appeared to some as if the 253-pound Hrbek had put a wrestling move on the 172-pound Gant to lift him off the base to record the out. But Coble had made the decision.

"His momentum was carrying toward the first-base dugout," Coble said after the game as he explained the call. "When he did that, he began to switch feet. He tried to pick up one foot and bring the other one down. That just carried him more to the first-base dugout. Hrbek took the throw low and tried to tag him as his feet were coming up, too. As he did that, he just went over the top of him."

After the inning-ending call, players from the Braves moved up onto the field, manager Bobby Cox rushed to first base, and Gant vociferously argued. It was all to no avail. Coble had made up his mind. Gant was out, the inning was over, and the momentum had remained with the Twins.

After the game, Hrbek kept it simple, saying, "He fell on top of me. He pushed me over. That's the end of the story."

Gant meanwhile wasn't so pleased with Hrbek's explanation of the play. "It doesn't matter what he said," Gant told reporters. "It was so obvious. He pushed me. Everyone on TV and in the stadium knew I was on the base. I didn't know you could push a guy off the base."

Push or not, Gant was ruled out. The Braves would eventually tie the game, but because of that call in the third inning that night, nobody will ever know how that World Series may have been changed had Justice stepped to the plate with two on and two out in the third inning. The Twins won by one run and eventually took the Series by one game.

"If you can get the edge and help him off the bag, so be it," Braves third baseman Terry Pendleton said after the game. "This is a game, and you're trying to win."

And because of Hrbek's "T-Rex Tag," that's exactly what the Twins did.

# Visit the Minor Leagues

Some say the Minnesota Twins are homegrown. Some say they're small-market. Whichever it may be, their operating style has been a pretty solid way of building a successful franchise in Minnesota.

Since 1961, when they signed Tony Oliva to a minor league contract and sent him through the minors; to 1964, when they did the same with Rod Carew; to the championship teams in 1987 and 1991, when homegrown talents such as Kirby Puckett, Kent Hrbek, and Frank Viola led them to victory; to the late 1990s, when at the major league level the team struggled, but at the minor league level the organization developed the likes of Torii Hunter, Brad Radke, and Michael Cuddyer, the Twins have consistently built from within.

## Minnesota Twins Minor League Affiliates

| Location | Team | Class |
|---|---|---|
| Rochester, New York | Red Wings | Triple A |
| New Britain, Connecticut | Rock Cats | Double A |
| Fort Myers, Florida | Miracle | High A |
| Beloit, Wisconsin | Snappers | Low A |
| Elizabethton, Tennessee | Elizabethton Twins | Rookie |
| Fort Myers, Florida | GCL Twins | Rookie |
| Dominican Republic | DSL Twins | Rookie |

## More on the Minors

When Seth Stohs started SethSpeaks.net back in 2003, the minor leagues were an afterthought for most fans, and the coverage was far from illustrious. Fans became familiar with players when they arrived at the Metrodome and when they reached the professional level.

There was some coverage in various publications, but nowhere to be found was the daily analysis of the minor league affiliates and the players rising to stardom. Fans didn't pay close attention to the draft, there weren't bunches of top prospect lists, and even general coverage was hard to come by.

"Back in the early part of even this decade, people really knew very little about the minor leagues," Stohs said. "There was *Baseball America* and some in *Baseball Weekly*, but there was very little daily content and such."

So Stohs started blogging. He did interviews with various minor league players, he covered all parts of the minor league system, and slowly but surely, his blog became a top destination for fans looking for coverage on the Minnesota Twins below the surface.

"When I first started blogging on the Twins' minor leagues, I would get a few comments here and there about players. Today the majority of the questions I get from readers are relative to the minor leagues and various prospects," Stohs said of his blog. "I think that's great as more fans understand the economics of the game and that the teams, like the Twins, who put an emphasis on the minor leagues and player development are those that can best maintain success."

As information on the organization's young players becomes more coveted, Stohs' blog becomes more popular. Today he sells a yearly prospect handbook with information on every player in the system, and that's just part of the extensive coverage available.

"There is, and will continue to be, a lot of talent coming through the Twins' minor league system," Stohs concluded. "And it is fun to gain knowledge of the future Twins before they become household names."

Thousands of fans think so, too, and the interest is continuing to grow.

What if someone told you that you could have seen Puckett develop into one of the team's great players, or that you could have watched Joe Mauer develop the skills needed to win three AL batting titles more than any other catcher in baseball history?

You'd probably answer that you would have liked to do that. With seven different minor league locations connected with Twins baseball, the opportunities to watch young players still exist. Twins baseball lies all across the country, and even internationally, allowing fans from all regions a chance to stay well connected.

The Twins may have moved outdoors to Target Field, and in their first season in their new ballpark their payroll may have reached an all-time high, but that doesn't mean their longtime philosophy and dependence on the minor league system will soon change.

"Even with the increased revenues thanks to Target Field, the Twins will continue to be wise with their funds. They will continue to run their business intelligently, and that means they will put restrictions on salary," said minor league blogger Seth Stohs. "Sure, they will be able to maintain or add a few more big-money players, but they will still need to supplement those players with inexpensive players, and that means they will need to continue to depend upon their minor league system."

And if you make the trip to one of these ballparks, you can see those prospects.

Some of the affiliate locations might just be a short trip away, while others might be a bit longer. If the opportunity arises, stop by and take in some minor league action. Who knows? Maybe you'll see the next big star before he hits the field in Minnesota. And if not, at least you can see baseball from a new perspective and watch a group of young aspiring players fulfill a childhood dream of playing professional baseball.

 **Those Piranhas!**

It was just Ozzie being Ozzie.

The talkative, creative, and witty manager of the Chicago White Sox has an admiration for the Minnesota Twins, so much so that you'd think he, and not Ron Gardenhire, was their manager. He has shared his admiration for their superstars, Joe Mauer and Justin Morneau; he has talked about the way the Twins run their organization; and most notably, he once drew a connection between their short and speedy players and piranhas, small fish with sharp teeth.

"This team beats you so many ways," said Ozzie Guillen during the 2006 season. "You wake up, they look like little piranhas.... All of a sudden, you wake up; you ain't got no meat—all those little piranhas. A blooper here, a blooper there, beat out a ground ball, then the first baseman hits a home run. Then they're up by four. How the [heck] are they up by four? Then you're down four with that pitching staff, that bullpen? Sit down and look at the lineup. Those little piranhas."

At the time, Guillen was referring to the top and bottom part of the team's lineup that consisted of four players who never hit for much power, but would reach base, then steal and score on the big blows from the heart of the lineup. It was infielders Luis Castillo, Nick Punto, and Jason Bartlett, and outfielder Jason Tyner who Guillen was praising, and the nickname stuck.

It actually fit the group perfectly, but it was rare to hear players outside of Mauer, Morneau, and Torii Hunter get so much praise. During that season, the four players tabbed as piranhas hit just six home runs collectively, but they combined to steal 56 bases, and they scored 230 of the team's 801 runs, all while hitting .299 as a group.

Over the course of the next few years, even while some of the players from the group disappeared, the moniker stayed. The Twins continued to play "small ball," and they continued to put scrappy players on the field, watching new players join the pool of players Ozzie Guillen had named.

During that 2006 season, the Twins did just as Guillen explained, they bit their way to a division title, pulling into first place in the American League Central on the final day of the season after having gnawed away at their previously large deficit for several months.

More so than a moniker for a select group of players, the term became a marketing tool. There were T-shirts sold with parts of the quote surrounded by little fish that represented rival teams, there were clothing pins given away by the team, and a commercial even appeared with Punto and Bartlett swimming underwater.

It may have just been Ozzie being Ozzie on that August day in 2006, but his remarks were the root of a long-term trend in Twins Territory. The team's speedsters embraced the nickname, and both the organization and fans continued to make use of it several years later.

# Enjoy Family Time

At a young age, it's a difficult concept. We struggle to throw the ball and catch it, and standing at the plate and holding the bat seems anomalous, too. Once we connect our minds to these concepts, baseball sticks. We stand in the front yard throwing the ball around the lawn, and the weeknight evenings or weekend afternoons asking—sometimes begging—to play catch.

As we get older, we start trying to make the ball do funny things, and we pretend—sometimes on the lawn and sometimes at an actual ballfield—that we're the big stars making the big plays and turning the big dreams into some sort of mystical reality. Eventually it turns into a competitive game; the catch sessions in the yard come less frequently, and sometimes the glove is put to rest for years. But hooked from a young age, the passion and magic of baseball forever remains.

## Attend Batting Practice

Getting a ball at a professional baseball game is no easy feat. The chances of catching a foul ball or a home run during the game are minimal at best, and even then you have to hold on as the ball crashes into your hands. The best way to take home a souvenir is by arriving at the ballpark early to attend batting practice.

At Target Field you won't see the hometown team, but as the gates open for most games, the opposing team stands on the field for batting practice and blasts ball after ball into the cheap seats. Batting practice is your best chance to get up close, and your best chance to watch the greatest baseball players in the world show off their talents.

And if you're lucky, you might take home an official baseball.

Baseball is America's pastime. It's a connection between fathers and sons and a gateway to something we sometimes wish would last just a bit longer: family time.

For generations, baseball has been a family game. Ken Griffey Sr. and Ken Griffey Jr. played together at the professional level. Guys like Bobby Bonds and Barry Bonds, Bob Boone and his sons Bret and Aaron, blended generations on the diamond. In Twins history, there has been a father-son combination on one occasion. After Sal Butera put on the uniform during the 1980s, his son Drew made his debut on April 9, 2010, with Minnesota.

No matter how infrequent those days of catch may become over the years or how far into the past baseball may seem, a chance to once again make that connection or put yourself back into those moments is just a trip to the ballpark away. Sitting at a ballpark can bring back memories, no matter how distant they might be.

There is more than just the game experience when a family takes a trip to the ballpark. There is the journey itself, and the amazement in seeing the players up close. As the game begins, there are the explanations for why the crowd is booing an opposing player and what the things on the scoreboard mean. These are the connections that come only through baseball. All attention might not always be on the game, maybe at times it's the hot dog or the screaming fans, but these moments show how much more baseball can be than just a competitive game.

And the opportunity holds no limit. Whether young or old, a trip to the ballpark can be both meaningful and memorable. Don't put the trip off; you don't want to miss out. In life, you never know when it might be too late to make the expedition, and when all is said and done, this isn't an experience you should wish you *could* have had, it's one you want to look back on and say you *did* have.

Baseball is a magical game, and for as many memories that are made on the field each season, just as many can be made off of it. The opportunities to make these connections may not last forever, but the memories that are made through these experiences certainly will.

# 62 Calvin Griffith

In Washington, he's the man who first took baseball away; in Minnesota, he's the man who brought Major League Baseball to the state. In one city, he became a villain and a guy who broke his promise; in another, he became the hero fans had long been waiting for. His name is Calvin Griffith, and he is both the first owner of the Minnesota Twins and the primary reason a book can be written about a baseball franchise in the state 50 years after he made his move.

Growing up, his name was Calvin Robertson. Because of financial difficulty, Calvin moved to Washington, D.C., to live with his uncle, Clark Griffith, when he was 11 years old, and from there he became known as Calvin Griffith. Through his childhood, Griffith was the batboy and mascot for the Washington Senators, the team his uncle owned. He worked his way up in the organization as he got older, and when his Uncle Clark passed away in 1955, the team was left in Calvin's hands.

It was October 26, 1960, when the announcement was made; Griffith had decided to relocate the Senators to the state of Minnesota. The following spring, a team known as the Twins took the field at Metropolitan Stadium for the first time. Having a big-league team in the state had been a dream for years, and thanks to Griffith, that vision had finally been turned into a reality.

Things went well early on for Griffith. The team excelled, making it to their first World Series as early as the 1965 season, and during the first decade in Minnesota, the Twins were near the top of the league in attendance twice and were in the top five each year. But over time there was fallout. The product on the field eventually worsened, and with it, the crowds lessened. Griffith also liked to talk—about players, managers, and one time, about race.

"Black people don't go to ballgames, but they'll fill up a wrassling ring and put up such a chant they'll scare you to death," Griffith said at an event in 1978. "We came [to Minnesota] because you've got good, hard-working white people here."

Griffith would backtrack on those comments, claiming he was taken out of context. But the damage of that quote was done immediately, and it was major. One of the team's great stars, Rod Carew, made it clear he would no longer play for Griffith, and by 1979, he was in California playing for the Angels. Over time, Griffith and Carew smoothed things out, and when Carew was elected to the Hall of Fame, Griffith was the first person to hear from Carew.

What also hurt Griffith, and what many believe eventually forced him to sell the team, were his old-school principles. He was always bargaining for every last penny during negotiations, even with the team's first Hall of Famer, Harmon Killebrew.

*Lauded as a hero for bringing baseball to Minnesota, owner Calvin Griffith was also known for pinching pennies and an outspoken demeanor.* Photo courtesy Minnesota Twins

"We were $500 apart, and I wasn't going to let $500 stand between us and me getting to spring training," Killebrew told ESPN about his contract negotiations with Griffith during his career. "I ended up signing the contract. I told him that if that $500 meant that much, I'd go ahead and sign the contract."

After the start of free agency, the Twins began to falter, and in 1982 Griffith had a fire sale, moving all his highly paid players along the way. That year the team lost a franchise record 102 games, and following the 1984 season, Griffith sold the team to Carl Pohlad for $36 million. For 72 years the Griffith family had owned the team that played in either Washington or Minnesota, but the tenure had come to an end.

The Twins never did win a championship under Griffith, but he was essential in the titles they did win in both 1987 and 1991. Sure, he was the reason they were playing with the words *Minnesota* and *Twins* across their chests during those seasons, but there was another reason. Several key players from those teams, including guys like Bert Blyleven, Gary Gaetti, Frank Viola, Kent Hrbek, and Kirby Puckett, were all added to the team under Griffith's watch.

Griffith passed away at the age of 87 in 1999. His legacy with the franchise has carried on, as he was inducted in the inaugural class of the team's Hall of Fame in 2000 and has a statue in his honor at the team's new home at Target Field. Griffith did many things during his life, but baseball and the Minnesota Twins defined the biggest moments.

"It was the greatest thrill I ever had in my life—bringing baseball to Minnesota," Griffith said years after he sold the team. "Everybody there was so joyful."

And because of Griffith, that joy still remains as fans watch professional baseball in the state of Minnesota some 50 years after he made his move.

 **Attend the Twins Caravan**

While baseball sits still with no on-field action, with few transactions in the dead part of the off-season, and while snow falls and the temperatures dip to numbers below zero, fans wish it were spring and Opening Day for both the weather's sake and for the return of baseball, and players and personalities from the Minnesota Twins organization travel.

They don't just travel across the city of Minneapolis and St. Paul; they travel all across Twins Territory. They travel across the state lines to North Dakota, South Dakota, and Iowa. It's the annual Winter Caravan, and stops include places such as Rochester, Minnesota; Fargo, North Dakota; Sioux Falls, South Dakota; and Mason City, Iowa. And those are only a small percentage of the caravan's destinations each off-season.

In all, the team makes around 50 stops each winter, and it's been doing it every year since the team moved to the Midwest and to Minnesota back in 1961. The caravan is the longest-tenured and one of the biggest team caravans in professional sports, and it's a big part of the team's effort to reach fans of all ages and of all locations across the Upper Midwest.

"It's just super for us to come out and see everybody in their Twins stuff, fired up about Minnesota Twins baseball," manager Ron Gardenhire said at one of the stops in Fargo, North Dakota, during the 2009 tour. "That's what it's all about for us and why we do it. We come out here on Caravan to say thank you for the fans' support and what they mean to us. Our organization, more so than any other organization in all of professional sports, I think, understands what our fan base means to us, and that's why we try to get out and see them."

With games stretching into several states and cities across the Midwest through both radio and television, Twins Territory truly does span hundreds of miles in every direction from the team's downtown Minneapolis home. Each year there is one opportunity in which the players you watch and the team you follow all season potentially come to you and your city, or maybe one close in proximity.

They head in groups, oftentimes with players or former players, a coach, and some sort of announcing personality. And in addition to heading in every direction from Target Field, they depart to several types of places. From schools to care centers to community centers, the Twins reach all kinds of destinations on their caravan, and every type of fan who can possibly follow the team.

It may be January, and baseball may seem far from reality, but attending one of the many stops is the best way to get back in the swing of things. Many of the events open to the community include a dinner, a video, a question-and-answer session with the stars of the show, and autograph-signings.

You could always stay at home and shovel the snow, and wait until spring to purchase a ticket, head to the ballpark, and see the players there. Or, you could let the snow pile up, get back into the baseball groove, and see the personalities in a way that is hardly possible in any of the other 364 days each year.

It's totally your call, but the latter certainly tends to be the big hit.

## 64 Kitty Kaat

Reflexes like a Kaat is one way to put it.

The man nicknamed "Kitty" was one of the best defenders of his position in the history of baseball. During his 13 seasons as a member of the Twins, the southpaw pitcher Jim Kaat won 12 Gold Gloves, and throughout his entire 25-year career, he won a total of 16. When he retired, Kaat held the mark for the most Gold Gloves won, and he still sits near the top of the list, although pitcher Greg Maddux passed him years later by winning the award 18 times during his career.

There is no doubt that Kaat was a prolific defender over the course of his lengthy career, but what some people occasionally forget is that he was just as smooth on the rubber.

Signed as an amateur free agent in 1957 by the Washington Senators, Kaat pitched in two seasons on the East Coast before the team moved to the Midwest and became the Twins in 1961. In that inaugural season of Twins baseball, Kaat posted a 3.90 ERA but went 9–17. It would be the one and only season in his tenure with the Twins in which Kaat wouldn't put a double-digit number in the win column.

Over the course of his next 12 seasons in Minnesota, all of which were played at Metropolitan Stadium, Kaat won at least 10 games. During the course of his entire career, he won 20 games in three different seasons, and he reached at least 15 wins in eight seasons.

It was 1965 when Kaat first pitched on the big stage. After going 18–11 with a 2.83 ERA during the regular season, the Twins won the pennant and reached the World Series for the first time. Going up against the Los Angeles Dodgers, Kaat was handed the challenge of facing Sandy Koufax—not just once or even twice, but three times during the seven-game World Series.

After the Twins won the first game, Kaat took the mound on October 7, 1965, at Met Stadium. That day he tossed a gem. Kaat went the distance against the Dodgers, scattering seven hits and allowing just one run as the Twins took a 2–0 series lead with a 5–1 victory. Koufax would win the other two games, though, and his team eventually took the championship in seven games, too.

The next year the Twins didn't live up to expectations as they fell off and finished second. The end result wasn't any fault of Kaat's, though. In fact, Kitty put forth the best season of his career. He went 25–13 that year with a 2.75 ERA while starting 41 games and tossing an incredible 304⅔ innings for the season. That 1966 season would mark the final time that only one Cy Young Award was given out in all of baseball (instead of one for each league as it stands today), and unfortunately for Kaat, the award was given to Koufax, who somehow topped him in each of his American League–leading categories. Kaat was, however, named the Sporting News Pitcher of the Year, and his 25 victories remain a single-season team record through the first 50 seasons of Twins baseball.

*Pitcher Jim Kaat won 12 Gold Gloves in his 13 years with the Twins. Over the course of his 25-year career, he won the honor a total of 16 times, placing him second to Greg Maddux for total Gold Gloves.*

After that season, Kaat would spend six and a half more years with the Twins before the Chicago White Sox claimed him off waivers during the 1973 season. By the time he called it quits after 25 years in the major leagues, Kaat had won 283 games and made three All-Star Games in addition to his tremendous Gold Glove totals.

When his career was over, Kaat spent time as a baseball broadcaster and became one of the game's best behind the microphone, too, being nominated for seven Emmy Awards, though today his legacy still is tied to his achievements with his leather and what he did on the mound.

Jim Kaat won 189 games as a Minnesota Twin, 40 more than the next closest pitcher, his 12 Gold Gloves during his stay in

Minnesota are five more than the next closest Twin, and his 283 career victories place him eighth all-time among left-handed pitchers in baseball history, making him not just one of the best southpaws in team history, but in baseball history.

# 65 Back-to-Back-to-Back-to-Back

It had been done just two times prior, and it has been accomplished just four times since. Not just four home runs in one inning, but four home runs by four consecutive batters in one inning. On that spring day at Municipal Stadium in Kansas City the Minnesota Twins went back-to-back-to-back-to-back, crushing three home runs off one pitcher and one off another to win an extra-inning ballgame.

Saturday, May 2, 1964. Rookie Tony Oliva had already homered earlier in the game, and slugger Harmon Killebrew had done the same. Despite their efforts, the Twins headed to extras tied at three apiece with the then Kansas City Athletics.

After an uneventful 10th inning, the teams headed to the 11th still tied. Due up for the Twins to lead off the second extra frame was the two-hitter Oliva. Pitcher Dan Pfister had worked a quick 1-2-3 10th inning, but Oliva worked the count to 3–2 before launching a shot into the right-field porch for his second home run of the day, to give the Twins a 4–3 lead.

No big deal. One home run and a one-run lead for the Twins, but still a manageable game for the home Athletics, and not by any means an incredible feat for baseball history. To the plate stepped Bob Allison, and he, too, worked the count full, then launched a second consecutive home run over the fence.

Back-to-back.

Jimmie Hall stepped up to the plate next, and after watching three straight pitches out of the zone, he grooved Pfister's fourth pitch, finally a pitch in the strike zone, over the right-field fence.

Back-to-back-to-back.

The A's yanked Pfister and called upon rookie Vern Handrahan, who had never faced Killebrew, to limit the damage. He would end the inning, but not before Killebrew pushed the Twins further ahead and into the record books. One pitch is all Handrahan threw to "Killer." That ball landed over the left-field fence.

Back-to-back-to-back-to-back.

It didn't take long. Tied at 3–3 in extra innings, the Twins had launched four different pitches over the fence in a matter of minutes to gain a 7–3 victory. On that day the Twins became just the third team to accomplish the feat, and today they remain the only team out of seven to ever do it in extra innings.

Four 1964 All-Stars, four pitches, four home runs. The four players would combine for 138 home runs that season, including 25 by Hall, 32 each by Oliva and Allison, and a career-high 49 by

## Player Profile: Bob Allison

He wasn't incredibly fast, and he never hit for a great average, but Bob Allison was a powerful outfielder and became one of the great power hitters in Minnesota Twins history. After making his debut for the Washington Senators in 1958, Allison was an original member of the Twins when they moved to Minnesota in 1961, and he burst onto the scene in a big way.

In the team's inaugural season Allison hit 29 home runs. He would reach the 20–home run mark five consecutive seasons, and during his 10-year tenure with the Twins, he hit 20 home runs seven different times.

Home runs played a role in Allison's biggest moments as a Twin. On July 18, 1962, he combined with Harmon Killebrew to become the first pair to hit grand slams in the same inning, and on May 2, 1964, he combined with Killebrew, Tony Oliva, and Jimmie Hall to hit back-to-back-to-back-to-back home runs.

Allison hit 211 home runs as a Twin, good for fourth on the team's all-time list.

Killebrew. But on no other occasion did the group, or any other group in team history for that matter, combine for four home runs in a row. That is a feat in baseball's record books just seven times, and one of them has the name Minnesota Twins right next to it.

 ## From Press Row

From the first time we see professional athletes take the field, we dream of one day doing the same. The players become idols, and the dream becomes a goal. For many, the dream in the end stays just that, but what still remains after that realization sets in are different opportunities to still be involved with the game. It's the view from press row, and it's a spot most fans would love to own.

As Opening Day 2010 approached, sportswriter Kirk Hardcastle from the *Globe Gazette*, a newspaper based out of Mason City, Iowa, crossed his fingers with the hope of securing a rare opportunity to sit in a major league press box. He had been in a press box before, but as a fan he couldn't wait to do it again.

"We knew that a lot of newspapers in Minnesota would probably want credentials as well, so there was excitement that we received passes in the first place," Hardcastle said. "Once we got into the stadium, and I found my spot in the press box, the first three innings or so were just spent looking around at the beautiful park from my seat in the press box. I admit that I didn't really pay too much attention to the game."

For most fans, that mindset and initial lack of attention to the action would be similar. But for Joe Christensen, who covers the Minnesota Twins on a regular basis from press row for the *Minneapolis Star Tribune*, taking in a baseball game from press row has become a regular routine. Covering baseball for a living seems like a luxury, but even though it would be a tremendous experience for any big fan, the job isn't as simple as sitting in a seat and watching the ballgame. It includes tight schedules and long hours that often go unnoticed by fans.

"The part that surprises my friends is the long hours. If a game starts at 7:00 PM, I'm typically in the press box by 2:30. By then, I've done several hours of prepping and reading, maybe made a few phone calls and written something for my blog," said Christensen. "The clubhouse opens at 3:30, and you have to have a game plan, knowing what questions you want to ask certain players for your pregame notebook. Gardy [manager Ron Gardenhire] meets the media at about 5:00 PM. He provides great information and talks fast, so it takes a while to transcribe those sessions from my recorder and then sift through the important stuff for my pregame blog and notebook."

All that work goes into covering the team before the game even begins. By the time first pitch rolls around later in the evening, Christensen and many other writers have already logged between four and five hours' worth of getting quotes and setting up their stories for later in the night. Then things get underway. Even with the start of the real action, the job doesn't become easier. Writers have little time to sit back and enjoy the game, instead spending the game taking notes and putting together the framework of a story for the early editions.

"I try to file my notebook by 6:30, allowing time for a quick bite and a few innings to sit and watch the game without distractions. By the third or fourth inning, it's time to start forming the framework of the game story, writing details about the early innings, which may or may not make it into the first edition," Christensen said of the in-game job. "I need to send a story by 9:45 for our out-of-state editions, whether the game is finished or not, so sometimes it will have a feature angle about the starting pitcher. Our goal is to get those readers the score, but it takes a lot of teamwork with the copy desk because those papers are on the press by 10:15, I believe."

When those papers hit the press, the job doesn't slow down. Beat writers rush to the clubhouse at the conclusion of each game to retrieve the reaction from both players and coaches that will help enhance the story and provide an additional angle for readers.

"I have time to get reaction from Gardy and the players before resubmitting my story by 11:30 for metro editions. The goal is to tell the readers a story that's relevant, even if they know the score or the main details," Christensen said. "What can we tell them that they didn't know when the cameras turned off? When the Twins play extra innings or are out on the West Coast, the deadline crunch can be crazy, but it's all pretty exhilarating."

Pretty exciting and pretty exhausting, too. After writers finish their final copy with quotes and additional details, the night comes to an end. The next night they do it all over again, telling a story from the seats most fans would love to relax in.

"It's a great vantage point—behind home plate and about half-way up the grandstand," Christensen concluded. "We get all the sights and sounds, but we have a comfortable work environment to help meet the deadlines.

"I never take it for granted because I know fans would pay good money for the seats teams give us in the press box."

# 67 Baseball at the Mall

It may be just a faded plaque that resembles home plate, and a red chair hanging from a wall beyond an amusement park, but those two features located at the Mall of America in Bloomington, Minnesota, have a story—and a connection to Minnesota Twins baseball.

There are thousands of malls across the country, and many of them have the same thing you can find at this $650 million mall. Store after store after store sell jerseys ranging from Denard Span to Joe Mauer. You can find pictures of the team's first ballpark, Metropolitan Stadium, or you can get one of the Metrodome, or even the team's newest home, Target Field. Autographed memorabilia ranging from baseballs to bats seem to be somewhere on each floor, and you can even watch the team's games at one of the many restaurants.

A lot of those same things can likely be done in one of the several other malls across Twins Territory. But this isn't just another mall. Aside from being the largest mall in North America in terms of retail space, it has a distinct connection to the history of Minnesota baseball.

After opening in 1956, Metropolitan Stadium hosted the Minneapolis Millers, a Triple A minor league ballclub, for five seasons. When the Washington Senators became the Minnesota Twins in 1961, it became their home. For the next 21 seasons, the Twins would play at "The Met." Over the years, they played in a World Series, hosted an All-Star Game, and created many memories in the great outdoors of Minnesota.

The Twins moved to the Metrodome in 1982, and eventually Metropolitan Stadium disappeared. In 1992, after the team had already won two championships in their new indoor home, the Mall of America opened to the public. Its location: the grounds that once saw Hall of Famers roam the outfield and scoop up grounders in the infield.

Yes, The Met had become The Mall.

Even with all the stores, a part of Minnesota Twins history has remained. On the ground near the entrance to the amusement park is a plaque symbolizing the location of home plate some three decades ago. Above on the far wall, if you look very closely, you can see a red chair hanging seemingly in midair. This chair marks the exact location and height of Harmon Killebrew's 520-foot blast on June 3, 1967, the longest home run of both his career and in Twins history, a blast that landed several rows into the upper deck in right field at Metropolitan Stadium.

With a roller coaster and the surroundings of hundreds of stores, it can be hard. But if you close your eyes and imagine, you might just see it. This mall and this location were once the home of many great moments. At one point in time, all-time greats such as Killebrew, Rod Carew, and Tony Oliva stepped up near this plate on a warm Minnesota summer night. Never could fans have been so close, even if the stadium is long gone.

# 68 Killebrew's No. 500

It was August 10, 1971, and slugger Harmon Killebrew entered the night game at Metropolitan Stadium with 12 home runs on the season. This in itself wasn't any feat; Killebrew had ended a total of seven previous seasons in Minnesota with more than 40 home runs in a single year. But that 12th home run was a big one, and the one that would follow on this August night would be bigger—in fact, it was one of the biggest home runs in his illustrious career.

Its distance wasn't anything magnificent. It certainly didn't come close to his 520-foot blast that he launched into right field at The Met during the 1967 season. This home run would be measured at 385 feet from home plate, and it landed in the left-field pavilion. What was so big about this 13th home run of the 1971 season was where it placed Killebrew in baseball history. That night, with that blast, Killer became just the 10th player to collect 500 home runs in a career, at the time joining the likes of Babe Ruth,

Willie Mays, Hank Aaron, Mickey Mantle, Jimmie Foxx, Ted Williams, Eddie Mathews, Mel Ott, and Ernie Banks.

Entering the season with 487 home runs through the first 17 years of his eventual Hall of Fame career, Killebrew blasted 10 home runs through the first two and a half months of the season. On June 22, he hit his 11th home run. It wouldn't be until more than one month later, on July 25, that Killebrew hit that 12th home run, pushing himself to 499 career home runs and within reach of one of baseball's great milestones.

With the pressure to reach that big milestone on his shoulders, Killebrew took the field on this August night in Bloomington, Minnesota, still one home run shy of joining this select club. It had been 16 days since his previous home run, but with two outs in the bottom half of the first inning, with a count of one ball and no strikes, Killebrew took the Baltimore Orioles' Mike Cuellar's pitch and sent it into the seats.

Carneal called it out on the radio as the crowd rose to their feet and Killebrew rounded the bases. At 35 years old, Killebrew had accomplished something few players had ever done and something few have done since. As Tony Oliva stepped to the plate, the crowd continued with its ovation, prompting the quiet and reserved Killebrew to step out from the dugout and lift his cap to the fans.

After waiting several weeks to reach the landmark, the first great slugger in team history wouldn't wait long before his next home run. In the sixth inning with the Twins trailing 3–1, Killebrew launched his 501st home run to even the score. The moment would mark the 32nd time that Killebrew homered twice in a single game, and when his career was all said and done, he had done it 45 times.

There would be another 72 home runs in Killebrew's career after this day, the 13th home run was far from his longest, and the Twins would eventually lose in extra-innings that night to the Orioles. But with that home run on that night, Harmon Killebrew did something few have ever done. Reaching the 500–home run club is an exclusive event, and in front of the home crowd, he had placed himself with baseball's elite.

 ## Zoilo Versalles

That year he led the league in plate appearances, runs, doubles, and triples on his way to the first Most Valuable Player Award in Minnesota Twins history, and what today some statisticians say is the most undeserving MVP Award ever handed out.

Zoilo Versalles did a lot right during that 1965 season. His Gold Glove defense up the middle helped solidify the infield. He missed just two games. But he struck out a league-high 122 times, and some say his batting average, which stood at .273 and wasn't in the top 10, made other players, including his teammate Tony Oliva, more deserving of the honor.

Versalles' teammates, and many others, would respectfully disagree.

While Versalles put forth the best year of his career that season, the Twins won a franchise-high 102 games and eventually lost in seven games to the Los Angeles Dodgers in the World Series. Despite not winning the title that season, Versalles was a big reason why the series went to the final game. He hit a three-run home run in the first game, and overall led the team with eight hits and a .286 batting average for the series.

It was a career-best year for Versalles, the Cuban-born shortstop that the team had been waiting on. In his first four years in Minnesota, after his two years with the Washington Senators before they moved to the Midwest, Versalles was often injured and often complaining. But in that 1965 season, he played and finally

*Shortstop Zoilo Versalles leaps over Yankee Bill Skowron after tagging him out at second base and fires to first to complete a double play in a 1961 game while Twin Billy Martin looks on. Versalles won the MVP in 1965 and was awarded two Gold Gloves in his 12-year career.*

reached his potential. In the end, he received 19 of the 20 MVP votes, making him not just the winner of the award, but a near-unanimous selection.

To see how much Versalles meant to the team that year, you don't need to look past his production during the following 1966 season. After his breakout year, and after he helped the Twins make it to the World Series for the first time in team history, expectations were high. This time, though, Versalles dropped off. He played in 27 fewer games, scored 53 fewer runs, and his previous league-leading double and triple totals were cut in half. The Twins missed his defense on the field, his slowed production hurt at the plate, and the team won 13 fewer games and finished second.

That poor season would be the beginning of the end for the man nicknamed "Zorro" by teammates. After falling off following his career-best season, he hit just .200 in 1967, and he was shipped to the Dodgers following that season. In the years after his departure Versalles bounced around to a few more teams before heading to Japan for one year in 1972 and calling it a career at just 32 years old.

When his baseball career was over, Versalles returned to Minneapolis, but life didn't get much easier. He had never learned English, and baseball was what he had known best. Eventually, Versalles was forced to sell his MVP trophy, his All-Star rings, and his Gold Glove award. He died at the age of 55.

Zorro may have been a one-year wonder, but what a wonderful one season he did have. When all was said and done, Versalles had led the Minnesota Twins to the big stage for the first time in franchise history, and he became the first player in team history to be honored as the league's best player.

# 70 By the Numbers

Baseball is a numbers game.

Everywhere you look, there are numbers. The line score is composed of the number of runs scored in a ballgame. There are stats and more stats that are a collection of numbers: hits, home runs, and strikeouts, to name a few. How much money a player earns is one *big* number. How many fans attend each game is another number. Even the way we identify a player is, you guessed it, by the number he wears on his uniform.

So often in the sports world, we hear a number and can instantly put a name behind it. No. 42. Jackie Robinson. No. 23. Michael Jordan. In Minnesota, that is no different. In fact, there are six numbers that mean so much to the history of the Twins, they've been retired, commonly represented, and can be easily recited.

When fans hear No. 3, No. 6, No. 14, No. 28, No. 29, and No. 34, some think of the gates that make up the entrances to Target Field, and some think of the numbers they once saw hanging in the upper deck at the Metrodome or currently see down the left-field line at the team's new ballpark. These are the great numbers in team history, the five that no player will ever don again.

When the Twins moved to Minnesota in 1961, Harmon Killebrew was already wearing No. 3, and when the team retired it in May 1975, it meant that no other player would put it on again. Killebrew hit 475 of his 573 home runs as a Twin, and he is the one and only player to ever wear No. 3 in Minnesota.

As a rookie in 1964, Tony Oliva wore No. 6, but there had been four players who had put the number on prior to his arrival: Billy Consolo (1961), Ted Lepcio (1961), Jim Snyder (1962), and Vic Wertz (1963). When Oliva's career ended, he wore the number as a coach from 1986 to 1991, before the Twins retired it in July of 1991.

Before Kent Hrbek put on No. 14 for 14 seasons with the Twins, it was worn by five different players: Pedro Ramos (1961), manager Sam Mele (1961–1967), Danny Monzon (1972–1973), Glenn Borgmann (1974–1979), and Pete Mackanin (1980–1981). The team guaranteed that he would be the final player to wear No. 14 when they retired it one year following his retirement in August 1995.

Number 28 has proven to be a popular one in Twins history; 14 players have worn it over the years, but no one wore it longer than Bert Blyleven. To commemorate his induction into the Hall of Fame, the team retired the number in his honor in 2011.

Six players donned No. 29 in the early years of the team's existence in Minnesota, but each wore it only briefly before Rod Carew scooped it up for the final time. The players were Julio Becquer (1961), Fred Lasher (1963), Wally Post (1963), Chuck Nieson (1964), Mel Nelson (1965), and George Mitterwald (1966). Carew would wear it for his rookie season in 1967 through his final year with the team 12 years later, and the Twins retired it in 1987.

And then there is No. 34. It needs no introduction; fans of the Minnesota Twins know that Kirby Puckett wore No. 34. But even this number has a background. Nine different players wore Puckett's number before he put it on in 1984. Nobody would ever wear it after his career abruptly ended in 1996, though; the Twins retired it just one year later.

The lowest number ever worn by a player in Twins history was No. 0, and that was put on just once when Junior Ortiz wore it in 1990. The highest number worn by a player was No. 77, and Tony Batista wore that in 2006. While Batista takes the honor of wearing the highest number by a player in team history, the highest number ever handed out by the team was actually in 2008, when Riccardo Ingram joined the team as a coach late in the season and wore No. 81.

In a game full of numbers, the history of numbers worn by Twins players runs deep. Six players have showcased their talents and meant so much to the franchise during their careers with the team that they have their numbers stored away and honored. The only question is, what number will be put to rest next?

# 71 Stealing Home in 1969

"And you can't be afraid of being thrown out," manager Billy Martin told Rod Carew during spring training prior to that 1969 season, "because that's going to happen occasionally. You have to do it recklessly."

Carew had never done it before in his first two major league seasons, and he had done it just once in the minors, but his manager was encouraging him to act upon his advice, and the two spent hours practicing his technique. What Martin wanted Carew to do was be more aggressive on the base paths by using his speed, and he didn't just mean stealing second and third base. He wanted Rod Carew to steal home.

"All I knew about stealing home was that Jackie Robinson had done it so spectacularly," Carew said of the increasingly rare act. "I remember seeing newspaper photos of him, with a big hook slide and a lot of dust around home plate and the catcher lunging at him."

But there Carew was, standing at third base during the fifth inning of the second regular season game in the 1969 season. With the Twins and Royals tied 2–2, Carew prepared himself. He slowly took his lead and then watched Roger Nelson of Kansas City pitch to Harmon Killebrew. The first pitch had passed, and Carew was ready to make his move on the next.

"I signaled that I wanted to go. Martin and Nettles [actually Killebrew] got the message. When Spider went into his windmill act again, I took off," wrote Carew in his autobiography titled *Carew*. "When Nelson saw what was happening and finally untangled himself, he threw high, and I slid home safely. It was my first steal of home in the major leagues. I couldn't wait to try it again."

Ten days later he would. This time knuckleballer Hoyt Wilhelm was on the mound during the seventh inning of a game with the California Angels. Carew gave Martin the sign, a tap on his belt buckle, that he was going for it, and he thought hitter Harmon Killebrew knew he was coming, too. But Killebrew nearly swung, and Carew nearly acted as the ball.

"Wilhelm started into the windup. I went. I was coming down the line, and I was amazed to see that Harmon was preparing to hit the pitch: if he swung, I'd end up a double down the left-field line," wrote Carew. "Suddenly out of the corner of his eye he saw me, and he held back in the nick of time. I came sliding in and beat the knuckleball home. It proved to be the winning run of the game."

It was the second of two times that Carew would steal home when the Killer stood at the plate, and the Twins' PR guy had some fun with the danger of completing such a task by writing a one-line poem: "Here lies Rod Carew, lined to left by Killebrew."

Eleven days later Carew stole home for the third time in April, and two weeks later he did it yet again. In June he stole home twice more, and his total now stood at six for the season. He would get number seven on July 16, when he swiped home off of pitcher Jerry Nyman of Chicago. It was getting more difficult now. Opposing pitchers were paying more attention and throwing differently with Carew at third.

"It was getting harder and harder to go now," Carew wrote of the increasing difficulty. "Everyone was watching me when I got to third. Pitchers were taking a stretch now instead of winding up."

Ty Cobb had stolen home eight times in 1912, and Carew stood just one shy of the record in August. But his chances were running dry until suddenly came a shot to make his move. It would prove to be his last real shot at the record.

"Against Seattle I had the opportunity to go for No. 8, the record. Skip Lockwood, a right-hander, was pitching. I got a great jump on him, and I slid by the plate as the ball popped into the catcher's mitt," Carew recalled of the play at the plate that day. "But the umpire called me out. I couldn't believe it. [Jerry McNertney] was catching, and he couldn't believe the call either (he didn't tell me that until the next day). I think the umpire's vision was blocked, so he automatically gave me the thumb.

"That was my last good chance to steal home in 1969."

Carew never did get that eighth steal in 1969, but he would pick up another eight through the remainder of his career and finished with 17 overall. Manager Billy Martin told him to be reckless, and he was. Rod Carew scampered home seven times during that 1969 season, turning the act of stealing home into something of an art. And few have ever done it so beautifully.

# 72 Attend Opening Day

There is anticipation. There is excitement. There is navy and red. There are lines. It's Opening Day, so most of all, there is baseball. It may be just one game, and there may be 161 that follow it over the course of the next six months, but something makes this one day of the year great. It isn't a game to make the playoffs or decide some title, but even the worst teams in the league wait months for it. It's like Christmas in the spring for baseball fans, and it's an event that must be attended.

After a champion is crowned each fall, all 30 teams in the league look ahead to the next season. Into the winter there are meetings filled with free agent signings and trades. The first months of the New Year are slow, and the national focus shifts to other things. Mid-February and the month of March bring baseball back into focus with spring training, but it isn't until the first week of April that baseball returns to the forefront.

It's Opening Day. While spring brings with it new life, it also brings a new baseball season. Every team starts with a clean slate. The best team from the previous season sits on the same pedestal as the worst. There are no wins and no losses in the standings, and each team in the league shares the same vision and dream of reaching the World Series and bringing a title home to their fans and to their city.

As fans are ushered into their home ballpark on this day each year, their faces are filled with smiles, and their minds with great expectations for the team they are about to watch. The smell of hot dogs and peanuts fills the air for the first time, and fans watch the players shag batting practice fly balls on the freshly cut grass and

## Buy a Scorecard

For 100 pennies, or 10 dimes, or four quarters, or one dollar, you can get your hands on a scorecard at Target Field. It's well worth the minimal price. Not only will you get the form you need to keep score, you'll also receive notes on both the opponent and your own Minnesota Twins.

After teaming up with *GameDay* in 2009, the scorecard is now a foldable publication containing write-ups from local writers to give fans a better outlook on the series and game. Inside is an overall outlook of the teams, a preview of the matchup, statistical analysis, and a short feature story.

Keeping score is one of the best ways to immerse yourself into the game, and when it's all over, it's a great way to remember the day. But even if you aren't into keeping score, a scorecard in Minnesota provides more than its title and is a must-have.

recently dragged infield. Even those not at the ballpark—the kids who sit in classrooms at school, the adults who can't escape work, or others who just can't make it to the much anticipated event—wear Twins gear with agitation and pride.

The best moment comes shortly before first pitch. You'll catch it in the playoffs, but during the next 24 weeks or so of baseball, the routine becomes much more basic. The rosters are announced, and the players form a line down each base path. After fans rise and greet their team with ovations, the American flag spreads across the outfield, the National Anthem is sung, and planes fly above.

What follows is just one pitch, but it marks the beginning of a new season and a fresh start for the players, team, and fan base. What happened the previous year, winning record or losing record, playoffs or no playoffs, is put to rest. There will be thousands of pitches to follow, many wins and hopefully less losses, but Opening Day marks the return of America's pastime.

You can head to the ballpark for months to follow this event and you'll likely see a similar product on the field. But there are few regular season experiences quite like Opening Day. If you want to see a new type of excitement, fans filling the ballpark with the colors of the

Minnesota Twins, and possibly the beginning of something special, then the place to be for that first home game is at the ballpark.

# 73 Ron Gardenhire

Consistently consistent is one way to put it.

Drafted in the sixth round by the New York Mets in 1979, Ron Gardenhire played only five seasons in the major leagues. In only two of those seasons did Gardenhire play in more than 27 games, and his career batting average stood at just .232 when all was said and done.

But there was one characteristic that Gardenhire carried well on the field. It alone won't send any player to an All-Star Game or Hall of Fame, but it can play a role in success, and in the long run, it's what has allowed the man known as "Gardy" to remain in baseball as a coach for more than two decades following the conclusion of his on-field career. Gardenhire is a leader, and today he's one of the highest-regarded managers in professional baseball.

After his playing career came to an end following the 1987 season, Gardenhire became a part of the Twins organization. For three seasons, from 1988 to 1990, he led two different minor league teams and helped guide them to two first-place finishes and one second-place finish. Following the 1990 season, *Baseball America* named Gardenhire the Best Managerial Prospect, and the next season he was in Minnesota as a member of Tom Kelly's coaching staff.

As the third-base coach, Gardenhire earned a World Series ring when the team won their second championship in his first year during the 1991 season. For the next 11 seasons, Gardenhire would remain, until on October 12, 2001, shortly following the team's first winning season since 1992, a spot opened.

That day, Kelly suddenly and surprisingly announced his resignation, and the Twins now needed to find a replacement for the man who had guided them to their only two championships. Quickly, the rumored frontrunners became Minnesota native and Hall of Famer Paul Molitor, as well as the longtime third-base coach.

On January 4, 2002, the Twins made their decision.

"He has proven that he is the best person for this position because of his hard work, loyalty, and familiarity with the Minnesota Twins since he came to the organization in 1987," GM Terry Ryan said that day.

## "You're Outta Here!"

When Tom Kelly resigned following the 2001 season, he left the team in the hands of then third-base coach Ron Gardenhire. The general philosophy remained the same, Gardenhire operated the team in nearly the same fashion, and the foundation that Kelly had put in place years earlier went unchanged, too.

The results showed on the field. With his style, Kelly led the Twins to two titles during the 1987 and 1991 seasons. In his first season as manager, Gardenhire led the Twins to a division title, and through his first nine years at the helm, the Twins had made the playoffs six times.

In that sense, the two managers shared the same style. But while Kelly was quiet and reserved, Gardenhire has been much more vociferous, and Major League Baseball has plenty of his checks to prove it.

As the manager of the Twins for 16 seasons, Kelly was ejected just five times for an average of one ejection every three seasons. He was never tossed more than one time in any season at the helm, and even went seven straight seasons during his tenure as the leader without heading to the clubhouse early.

Gardenhire meanwhile has been a different story. In his nine seasons as the leader of the Twins, Gardy has been ejected a total of 54 times. He has been tossed as many as eight times in a single season (which happened in both 2006 and 2007), and in seven seasons he has either tied or surpassed Kelly's entire career total.

Their overall success with playoff appearances may make them similar, but there has been one key distinction between the two: Gardenhire has heard the phrase "You're Outta Here" much more frequently.

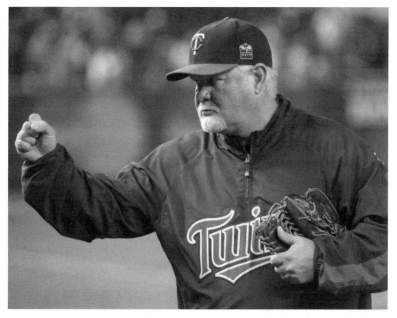

*Ron Gardenhire has been in the Twins organization since his playing career ended in 1985. As manager since 2002, he has led the team to the playoffs six times and was named the American League Manager of the Year in 2010.*

He was referring to Gardenhire, and on April 1, 2002, in Kansas City, Gardy had moved to the bench as the Twins played under the gloomy threat of contraction.

"We all know that contraction is out there," Gardenhire said when he was introduced. "But I can't do anything about that. All I can do is go and get this team ready for spring training."

And he did just that and much more. That year the Twins made the playoffs for the first time since they won it all in 1991, and then something happened. Gardenhire led them to another divisional title in 2003, and then a third consecutive one in 2004.

By the end of the first decade of the 2000s, Gardenhire had managed the Twins for eight seasons, and the team made the playoffs in five of them. But there was no recognition for him, at least not in the form of an award. Five times during those years, Gardenhire placed as the runner-up for the American League Manager of the

Year. In 2010 Gardenhire was finally rewarded for his work. Despite losing their All-Star closer for the season during spring training, and their All-Star first baseman at mid-season, the Twins did what they had done in the past under Gardenhire: they pushed on and won 94 games. At the end of the season Gardy was named the American League Manager of the Year, joining former mentor Tom Kelly as the only other manager in team history to receive the honor.

What Gardenhire did in that span goes beyond making the play-offs. In those final years of the first decade, the Twins never had a payroll higher than 18th in baseball, yet they consistently competed.

On the field in the 1980s, Ron Gardenhire never established himself as one of the game's elite. He was a role player, but his biggest strength has followed him into the dugout. Today Gardy is not just one of the team's greatest managers ever, he is currently one of the best in baseball.

# 74 Living in Luxury

You can't spend more than $14,000 on season tickets? That's okay.

The majority of fans can't shell out the big bucks to sit in the extra-wide green chairs with extra padding that bring with them an extraordinary view. Everybody would love to sit right behind home plate and right behind catcher Joe Mauer. It makes you feel part of the game. You can hear the conversations at home plate, you can listen to manager Ron Gardenhire and hear what he says when he gets tossed from the game, and even if you can't spend thousands of dollars, you can still sit there.

They call it the Champion's Club, and it's the most expensive and most exclusive section at the new home of the Minnesota Twins. Inside, the team houses its two championship trophies and a collection of World Series rings. On average, the seats cost season-ticket holders $175 for each home game, but some seats in the section cost ticket holders $275 for every one of the team's 81 regular season home games. It is quite a price, and for most, it is far from economical. But for one day and one game, even if it means attending one game instead of a couple, it's an experience well worth taking in.

How often can you sit at field level and be right up with the players? When else can you be front and center where the television camera points for each pitch? And where else can you see the team's most prized possessions and receive the best amenities a fan can be given? The answer to all of these questions is only when you're in the Champion's Club, making it the best destination for the biggest Twins fans.

Holding a ticket to watch a game from this exclusive location grants you access to many perks beyond watching the ballgame. Fans in the Champion's Club gain access to a sit-down dining area that features displays commemorating the 1987 and 1991 seasons, upscale concession areas, and even some complimentary food and drink. Heck, the area even includes a viewing window for fans to watch the players take some swings in the cage and warm up indoors. It's like sitting in first-class on an airplane, but instead of sitting behind the pilot while zooming through the sky, you're sitting behind the ump and some of the best baseball players in the world.

The tickets are not sold individually, and the primary way of getting your hands on these seats and a one-of-a-kind experience may be by spending thousands of dollars for access throughout the entire season, but there is one other way. Each game, a small number of tickets for this section become available from ticket resellers on the Internet. It may still be more costly than a standing-room-only pass, but for one day, the price is worth the experience.

Finally, you can experience a game from first-class.

# 75 5-4-3, Triple Play!

The triple play is one of the rarest acts in baseball. The reason isn't because it's particularly hard to turn, but for any team to have a chance to make the odd play, things must occur in an almost perfect sequence with at least two runners reaching base, most commonly first and second, and a ball generally needing to be hit at someone on the left side of the infield. Nonetheless, the Minnesota Twins have turned one on numerous occasions in team history, including an unfathomable two times in one game.

Scott Erickson took the mound on that July 17, 1990, summer evening against the Boston Red Sox at Fenway Park. He would pitch well, allowing just four hits and one unearned run over six innings before John Candelaria relieved him for the final two innings.

Scoreless into the bottom half of the fourth inning, Wade Boggs reached base with a leadoff walk, and Jody Reed doubled to right field, pushing Boggs to third base. Carlos Quintana walked to load the bases, and with nobody out in the inning, Erickson was facing an uphill battle. Up to the plate stepped former Twin Tom Brunansky, a guy who had played seven seasons in Minnesota, including one as a member of the world championship team in 1987. Brunansky hit a ball down the third-base line, and Twins' third baseman Gary Gaetti fielded it, stepped on third base, and threw the ball to second baseman Al Newman, who turned and fired to first baseman Kent Hrbek to end the middle-inning threat with a 5-4-3 inning-ending triple play.

One triple play was odd enough, but the Twins weren't done. Boston entered the eighth inning leading 1–0, and shortstop Tim Naehring doubled to left field to lead off the inning. Boggs would reach base again with a walk, and with runners on first and second base and nobody out, the triple play opportunity again came to life. Second baseman Reed hit a grounder down the third-base line, and in the exact same sequence as the play four innings earlier, the Twins turned a 5-4-3 triple play to end the threat.

Minnesota would never score that day, as Red Sox pitcher Tom Bolton tossed eight scoreless innings and former Twin Jeff Reardon, who had played in Minneapolis the season before, closed the door for the save. But the talk after the game was about the two triple plays, and rightfully so. The feat the Twins accomplished that day had never occurred in baseball history, and it still hasn't in the two decades since. No two teams have ever combined for two triple plays in a single game, let alone one team doing it.

Interestingly enough, the Twins have recorded multiple triple plays on the same day but in different years. The first came on August 8, 1983, and five years later the Twins would pull off another one in 1988.

The combination between Gaetti and Hrbek turned out to be natural. The second triple play on that summer day in 1990 marked the sixth and final time each player would complete the feat in their Twins' career, meaning they've been involved in over half of the triple plays in team history. The next closest any player is to their implausible feat is two, with Newman, Steve Lombardozzi, and Rich Rollins all tied for that feat.

Turning one triple play in a game is no easy task, and turning two is mind-boggling. But in Twins history, that rare feat is reality, and something only one team in baseball history can claim to have accomplished.

# 76 Roof Deck and Overhang

There are good seats everywhere you look at Target Field. You could sit behind home plate and see the ballpark from the same perspective as catcher Joe Mauer, or you could sit in the left-field bleachers and feel like you're back in the old days. Seating down both the first- and third-base lines offers a nice perspective, and even the upper deck seats are significantly better than anything the Metrodome offered during the team's near three-decade stay.

But there are two locations at Target Field that offer an experience like no other. You can't get it all at Wrigley Field, Fenway Park, or Yankee Stadium, and even newer, more modern ballparks such as PNC Park and Busch Stadium don't offer this opportunity. It has nothing to do with the food you can enjoy in these seats or some other special service, it's all about the uniqueness. The distinctiveness of taking a ballgame in from these seats is matchless.

At Wrigley Field there are the rooftop seats across the road just beyond the ballpark, and at Fenway Park in Boston there are seats above the Green Monster. That's about the closest you can get to the Roof Deck that sits in the left-field corner in downtown Minneapolis.

If you're a fan who wants to see and keep track of every pitch, this probably isn't the best place to be for the game. But that doesn't mean you can't see the action. There are seats, about 120 of them, where you can see the field, and railings along the side allow fans to look down on the field, too. It's just that you can't follow the game as intently as you could in one of those green seats down below. The view is unmatched, though. There is the skyline, and there is something special about watching the game of baseball from up above. And if it gets cold come fall, and maybe even late October, this deck is home to the lone fireplace in baseball.

"It is a cross between the Monster seats [at] Fenway Park and the roof decks literally across the street from Wrigley Field," Twins president Dave St. Peter told the *Star Tribune* during the building's inaugural season. "It's not about bearing down on every single pitch. It's about being part of the atmosphere, probably having a couple of cold ones and taking in the scenes and sights and sounds of Target Field."

There is another exclusive place to take in the sights and sounds at the ballpark, and this particular quirk doesn't resemble anything else in any of the other 29 major league cities or parks. If you've always dreamed of being on the field during a game, this is probably the closest you'll ever be able to get. Head over to right field, and as Michael Cuddyer heads back to the warning track, you can hang eight and a half feet over both him and the field.

Just imagine: Justin Morneau drives a ball to deep right field. As the opposing right fielder goes back, thinking he has a play on the warning track, the ball bounces into the overhang and into your glove. Meanwhile, down below the player looks up at the limestone with disgust as you look at your new souvenir. Of course, the same thing could happen when the Twins are in the field, and you'll be hassled and booed until you either throw the ball back onto the field or tuck it away and wait for the fans to turn their focus to the next hitter.

While there are undoubtedly a few tucked away around the ballpark, it's hard to find a bad seat at Target Field. It's equally as difficult to get an opportunity to watch the game from up above or over the field. But it's a must. And as you look out at the Minneapolis skyline on a summer night or catch the ball on the warning track during the game, it'll be a moment unattainable anywhere else.

# 77 The Men in Charge

Scout. Analyze. Execute. Repeat.

The process, and therefore the job, never slows down. There is no break, and even when the season ends and the off-season arrives, things keep on progressing and keep on moving. If anything, no baseball just means more work, and the job is far from easy. The good signings and the good trades bring praise from fans, writers, and analysts. Then there are the inevitable less-than-stellar moves. They happen because every move can't possibly be a good one, and no matter how many good moves are made, the poor ones are scrutinized and sometimes remembered equally, if not more so, than the best ones.

Welcome to the front office, and in particular, the seat of the general manager.

Fans love to act as the man in charge, but in reality there have been less than a handful of general managers in team history. After Howard Fox stood in the position for just one year after it became an official front-office role, Andy MacPhail led the team from 1985 to 1994, building two championship teams along the way. Terry Ryan took over from there and led the team back into contention during the early 2000s before he resigned in 2007 and current GM Bill Smith took over. Thousands of armchair GMs span the Upper Midwest, voicing their opinions on the best signings, call-ups, trades, and various other roster moves they feel the team should make. But the real job is a bit harder and certainly more complicated and time-consuming.

"The toughest part of the job for all of us is the time we must dedicate to the job. You can't work in this business if you don't have passion for the game," Twins assistant general manager Rob Antony said of the difficulties. "Unfortunately this does take all of us away from our families and causes us to miss some things that we would like to attend. We all must have understanding families. That can be difficult, but it is part of the job."

Also part of the job is working on different tasks at different times. From the lowest level of the minor leagues up to the team that calls Target Field home, every player and every move is kept track of. The chore goes well beyond the general manager, though. To build a successful roster and organization as the Twins have done in recent years, a collective effort by the front office is key, and so, too, is communication.

"Both the GM and assistant GM travel throughout the system to see all our minor league affiliates so we have a good idea of what we have coming. Along with that come the reports we have to write on all our players, as well as opposing pitchers that we see," Antony said of the collective effort. "We are in daily contact with the director of minor leagues Jim Rantz, director of baseball operations Brad Steil, VP of player development Mike Radcliff, special assistant to the GM and former GM Terry Ryan, minor league field coordinator Joel Lepel, as well various scouts and minor league field staff. We believe communication is of the utmost importance for the system we use."

It may seem as though the off-season would be the key time for the front office with the exception of the trade deadline in the middle of each summer, but the schedule is full throughout the entire regular season, too. In addition to minor league visits, the general manager and the rest of the front office spend time evaluating the organization's needs and players, as well as those from other teams around the league.

"During the season, a lot of time is spent keeping track of transactions and checking scouting reports on players who may be on waivers or available. We are also constantly evaluating our own team and discussing possible moves to improve the club," Antony said when describing the in-season process. "There is probably less conversation with other clubs than fans may believe, but when there are possible deals to be made, there is a lot of legwork necessary. We have to check with our scouts and get verbal reports on players, and contracts must be analyzed to make sure you know exactly what commitments come with each player."

And then comes the off-season. As players leave, the front office looks to replace them either with players inside of the organization or ones from the trade or free agent market. Some players under team control go through a lengthy arbitration process, and the biggest key is looking for ways to upgrade the roster for the upcoming season with the hope of constructing a championship-caliber team.

"The off-season is primarily about evaluating potential free agents and getting contracts done. The more arbitration-eligible players, the more work there is to be done in the off-season," Antony said. "A lot of time also goes into the winter meetings and preparing for spring training in Fort Myers, Florida."

It's a time-consuming and neverending job, and every move is watched closely and sometimes scrutinized. There is no way to make every fan happy, and there isn't much time to reflect, even after a successful season. But for as difficult as the position may be, being a general manager or a member of the front office can be very rewarding.

"The most rewarding aspect of the job is when the team on the field is successful. We are in the business of winning baseball games and providing our fans with a quality product," Antony concluded. "It is also very gratifying for everyone in the organization when we draft a player, develop him in our minor leagues and he graduates to the big leagues and becomes a good major league player. What makes it doubly satisfying is when that player is also a good person who becomes a productive member of our community. It is always rewarding to look at the core of our roster and see our homegrown talent."

# 78 One Game, Six Hits x 2

There have been plenty of five-hit games in Minnesota Twins history, but there are only two occasions in the team's first 50 seasons of existence in which a player has collected six hits, and the feat has been accomplished by the same player, both during the team's two different championship seasons.

During his storied career, Kirby Puckett did a lot of things. He made the historic catch and hit the historic walk-off home run in Game 6 of the 1991 World Series. He mentored Torii Hunter as a youngster, a player who would become the next big star for the franchise. He was also the lone guy in Twins history to ever reach base six times in one game by hitting his way on—and he did it twice.

Like many of baseball's rare feats, a six-hit game is no easy achievement. First, a player has to step to the plate at least six times, which means the rest of the team must hit, as well. Secondly, in addition to stepping into the batter's box six times, a player can't be walked or hit by a pitch, or one of those crucial at-bats will go by the wayside and scrap the chance at the accomplishment. And finally, a player has to be on fire and just a little bit lucky.

The day was August 30, 1987, and the Twins were in a slump. They had lost seven of their previous eight games entering the series with the Milwaukee Brewers, dropping out of first place in the division along the way.

Puckett singled in the first inning, and he collected his second hit with a solo home run in the third. After starter Frank Viola surrendered a three-run home run in the fourth inning, Puckett led off the fifth by collecting his third hit, a single that would be the start of a three-run inning for the Twins. Puckett again would lead off in the sixth inning, and this time he doubled. Already with four hits, Puckett doubled in the eighth inning to up his hit total to five. There was just one more inning left for that sixth hit, and that little bit of luck would need to come into play. It did. In the ninth inning with two outs, Greg Gagne struck out, but a passed ball allowed him to reach base safely, and it brought Puckett to the plate looking for one more hit. He'd get the hit; in fact, it would be a two-run home run.

That season, Puckett would go on to lead the league in hits, and the team would go on to win its first championship.

Puckett would collect six hits on one other occasion during his career, but it wasn't quite the same as his first six-hit game. The game went 11 innings, and that final hit came in his seventh at-bat and in the final frame of extra innings. Nonetheless, he did do it. On that day, May 23, 1991, Puckett singled five times and tripled once, picking up six hits in a game for the second time in team history, and for the final time in the first 50 years of baseball in Minnesota.

There were other close calls in Puckett's career and over the course of the first five decades of Twins baseball in Minnesota. Kirby himself had four five-hit games, and the team's hometown hero most recently came close. In that game Joe Mauer had already gone 5-for-5 with a double, a home run, and three singles. Scheduled to hit in the eighth inning for the sixth time, Mauer was pinch hit for, leaving Kirby Puckett as the only player in team history to hit safely six times in one game, with maybe just a little bit of luck on his side.

 **Field of Dreams**

"If you build it, he will come."

They built it, all right, and fans of all ages and geographic locations have since visited in droves. The outfield is a cornfield, but what stands before it is a baseball field. That field was built in just four days by Universal Studios in 1988 on a farm just outside of Dyersville, Iowa, a small, quaint town just 244 miles from Target Field in Minneapolis, Minnesota, for the movie *Field of Dreams* that hit screens in 1989.

> *John Kinsella:* Is this heaven?
> *Ray Kinsella:* It's Iowa.
> *John:* Iowa? I could have sworn this was heaven.
> *Ray:* Is there a heaven?
> *John:* Oh yeah, it's the place where dreams come true.
> *Ray:* Maybe this is heaven.

The movie, like baseball so often does, brings to life the dream of Ray Kinsella as he listens to the voice telling him to build the field and in the end plays catch with his father, John. It's one of the biggest baseball movies of all-time, and it remains popular several decades after it first debuted. Equally as popular, and equally as magical, is the field that remains in that small town in Iowa.

It's *the* Field of Dreams.

On that very place where one of the biggest baseball movies ever was filmed, and in the very same spot where that dream came true, if only fictionally, is the baseball field surrounded by a cornfield. Each year more than 65,000 people visit, and since it became a tourist attraction more than 20 years ago, more than 1 million people have stepped foot on that field. That includes Twins great Kirby Puckett.

"One day after his retirement, we went to Dyersville, Iowa, to the location of the Field of Dreams," Twins president Dave St. Peter recalled when talking about some of his greatest memories. "Spending the day with Kirby and Bob Casey was a pretty memorable day."

That field was the place where Puckett could hit one last home run after his career tragically ended, and it's the same place where fans of all ages can emerge from the cornfield like Shoeless Joe Jackson did, and for a moment at least, turn that fantasy into a reality and make dreams come true.

The farm, the house, and the field are all memorable, and they're all located on the same lot right in that small town in Iowa and right in Twins Territory. To some, the Field of Dreams is a piece of living sports memorabilia, and to others it represents something much greater.

"We are the caretakers of a living piece of sports memorabilia," owner Becky Lansing once said of the land. "This is an organic, living, breathing piece of memorabilia."

It's a place where an award-winning film was created, a place where baseball fans can go to envision their own dreams, and a place where fathers and sons and families can go to play their own special game of catch.

It may just be Iowa, but to some, that field really is heaven.

# 80 Clyde the Collector

To some, Clyde Doepner is a history teacher. To others, he's a driving instructor. To most, both the Minnesota Twins organization and their fans, he's Clyde the Collector. He's a man with more Twins memorabilia and knowledge of the organization than most could ever dream of, and today he has switched from collector to curator as the team's official historian.

Baseball has long been in Doepner's blood, and for that matter, so too has collecting. He was the youngest boy on his block growing up, but because he was big for his age, he says he was accepted as an equal. From his early childhood, Clyde dug antiques out of a family shed, barn, and an old fruit cellar and learned about them. Each summer day he'd play baseball for hours, and his favorite hobby was collecting baseball cards—and of course, attending baseball games.

"Each summer my Uncle Russ took me to several doubleheaders between the St. Paul Saints and the Minneapolis Millers," Doepner recalled. "They would play a morning game in one town and then the afternoon game across the river in the opposing stadium."

Then one year those teams disappeared, and one big new one arrived.

"Nineteen sixty-one was a significant year for me as a lover of baseball. I still remember the moment I heard that the Washington Senators were moving to Minnesota and changing their name to the Minnesota Twins," Doepner said while thinking back to that day. "My father and I attended the first game on April 21, 1961, and I still have a pennant, program, and ticket stub from that game."

Those three items are now just a very small portion of more than 7,000 total artifacts in his collection. That inaugural game back in 1961 sparked something new in Doepner's life; a new type of history to research and teach, a new calling in life, and a chance to years later live a dream of one day being connected with the Twins organization in a unique way.

In 1966 Doepner, along with other high school baseball coaches from around the state, received a letter from the Twins with a free season pass for the upcoming season included. The next weekend as the Twins faced off against the New York Yankees, he arrived at Metropolitan Stadium early to seek out owner Calvin Griffith and thank him for the gift.

"Upon entering Cal's office, he looked up and almost barked, 'What do you want?' I replied that I just wanted to say thanks for the free season pass," Doepner recalled of the conversation with Griffith. "Cal asked, 'What free season pass?' I told him that I was referring to the free season pass I had received because I was a head baseball coach. He then said, 'Okay, but what's wrong with you?' Puzzled, I asked, 'What do you mean?' Calvin replied that he had given those passes away for some time and I was the first person to ever say thanks. I just stated, 'I was brought up to say thanks.'"

Little did Doepner know at the time, that short message and his eventual conversation with Griffith would jumpstart his opportunities to get close to the team and eventually have a chance to immensely build his collection. Griffith told his secretary to write Doepner's name down, and as they arrived in Griffith's box, he told him, "When you come to a game, you don't have to sit out there (motioning to the cheap seats) with those thankless sons-of-guns, you can sit here."

In the years after, Doepner created a relationship with Calvin and his brother Billy. It gave him exclusive access to the players and the team, and when the Twins moved from Met Stadium to the Metrodome in 1982, Doepner struck gold.

"That relationship gave me an in when the Twins moved out of the Met after the 1981 season and tossed so many valuable items that they had brought with them from Washington or accumulated during their years at the Met," Doepner said. "It was my mega leap in collecting the history of the Minnesota Twins."

His next leap would come in 2009 as the Twins neared the beginning of a new era with their new ballpark, Target Field. Looking to preserve the team's history and bring it to the forefront, the organization extended its hand to Doepner, offering him the opportunity to become Clyde the Curator.

"I could argue he's been the unofficial curator for a long, long time," Twins president Dave St. Peter told the *Minneapolis Star Tribune* of Doepner. "He's the most curious man I've ever met…always looking for that little morsel, that diamond in the rough, so to speak, in terms of history."

What Doepner has brought to the team, along with his complete knowledge of team history, is a collection that includes thousands of baseball cards dating as far back as 1961, thousands of documents; programs; yearbooks from each season; auto-graphed baseballs; bats; uniforms; shoes; hats; pennants; buttons;

## Clyde's Collecting Tips

Whether you're looking to go big in collecting the way Clyde Doepner has, by building the biggest Minnesota Twins collection ever, or if you just want to put together a set of items to retain your memories and share with the next generation, it's never too late to get started.

"When starting a collection, don't look at the item in [terms of] what it might be worth someday in resale, but look at it as a reminder of the experience. Collect for your love of the game. Pick a favorite player, one who is a great role model and someone whom you identify with," Doepner said. "Maybe you want to collect pennants or baseball cards. Or maybe you are someone who just wants to buy a ticket and enjoy the game, letting the experience 'live' in your heart and memory, creating a magic moment that will last forever."

As Doepner mentions, there are different reasons to collect. Some do it to make money, but true collectors save items to share and tell a story. At one point, Doepner himself was just a beginner, and if you follow some of his tips, you, too, could one day be known as the Collector.

- If you buy something claiming to be "game-used," make sure it has an MLB hologram.
- Keep your ticket stub; it is proof that you attended the game.
- Purchase a scorecard, a program, or a yearbook, and you'll get a closer connection to the game.
- Purchase items that are dated, such as a pennant or a commemorative baseball.
- Take advantage of promotional giveaways—they are worth the wait.
- Attend TwinsFest and the Summer Autograph Party for in-person autographs.

bobbleheads; things such as game-used items from Kirby Puckett, Harmon Killebrew, and other team greats; and so much more.

You'll never find these items on the market, though, and Clyde Doepner is finally living his dream.

"I never collected…to sell my collection," Doepner concluded. "I've collected as the historian that I am, always looking, always researching, and displaying part of it, whenever the chance came up.

"I had a dream that someday the Twins would have a new stadium and I would be the curator. Dreams do come true!"

 **Small Market**

The Minnesota Twins have long done things differently than most. Like most other teams, they have limited assets to work with, but unlike most other teams, they've managed to compete regardless. Through the draft, with scouting, and by developing their minor league system, the Twins have consistently contended in the American League Central.

Small market is what they call it.

"I have contended for years that the key to our organization is our ownership. When Carl Pohlad was running the club until passing away in January of 2009, he hired good people and let them do their jobs," said assistant general manager Rob Antony. "He understood limitations, and when we were struggling just to break even and we did not have the payroll flexibility that other clubs had, Mr. Pohlad didn't have unrealistic expectations. He was as competitive as anybody, but he didn't try to place unfair blame on his president, general manager, manager, or others in charge."

The men who Pohlad put in charge developed a system to succeed with limited funds, and while that system has fit into the small-market scheme, the results have been far from tiny. Sitting at 27 out of 30 teams in payroll during the 2002 season, the Twins won the division. They did it again the next year sitting at 18th, and then again for a third consecutive season in 2004 sitting at 19th in the payroll standings. Through the first decade of the 2000s, the Twins won the American League Central five times, and not once were they higher than 18th in the league with their total payroll.

Regardless of payroll, the Twins won, and they won consistently. Year after year a competitive team took the field in

Minneapolis, and for the most part, the Twins found themselves in the thick of things even when they failed to make the postseason. The keys for the Twins were scouting young players and building from within.

"We have primarily developed our own players, and we do things in the minor league system the same way as we do in the big leagues," said Antony, "which makes for an easier transition when young players get to the majors."

A large portion of the team's players at the major league level have done things the same way through their entire professional career, and that's because the Twins have prided themselves on building through the draft. In 2001 they selected Joe Mauer; the next year they picked up Denard Span; in 2003 they picked up Scott Baker; and then they got Trevor Plouffe next. The list goes on

## Player Profile: Jim Rantz

He's been there since day one.

After signing a contract with the Washington Senators in 1960, Jim Rantz played for the Twins in the minor leagues for four seasons after they moved to Minnesota in 1961. Through his minor league career, Rantz went 22–16 with a 3.64 ERA, but following the 1965 season, he ended his playing career and joined the Twins in the front office.

For the first four years on the business side, Rantz was the team's assistant public relations director. After that, he joined the team's minor league and scouting department, and he has been there ever since. Under Rantz, the Twins have been named the Organization of the Year on multiple occasions, and their success as a small-market team has become coveted around Major League Baseball.

The biggest year for Rantz, and his biggest move, came in 1981, when he was watching his son play. That day, Rantz also saw a young man named Kirby Puckett, and heeding his advice months later, the Twins selected him with the third pick in the draft.

He never stepped foot on the field in Minneapolis as a player, but Rantz has been connected with the organization for each of their first 50 seasons in existence, and his role has been vital.

and on, and year after year, the Twins have selected players who shortly after have made their way to Minneapolis.

"Our starting staff, with Scott Baker, Nick Blackburn, Brian Duensing, and Kevin Slowey, were all drafted and developed by the Twins," said Antony of the team's roster during the 2010 season. "Add in relievers Jesse Crain, Jose Mijares, and Jeff Manship, as well as position players Joe Mauer, Justin Morneau, Danny Valencia, Jason Kubel, Denard Span, and Michael Cuddyer, and that's a fairly impressive list of players."

Equally as impressive have been the results. Multiple players from that list have turned into the league's best as All-Star-caliber athletes, and many others have been cornerstone pieces on multiple division title teams. It may all be part of the small-market way, but with their philosophy and success on the field, the Twins' style has become coveted around the major leagues. It has become the Twins Way.

"To win a title, a lot of things gotta go right for a club, whether it's in a big market or a small market," said Reds general manager Walt Jocketty in 2010. "There's no exact science to this, so you have to have a plan, stick with a plan, and hope it works."

The Twins have found their plan, and so far it has worked just fine.

## 2010: Déjà Vu

New stadium. Increased payroll. Updated roster. Same result.

As the Minnesota Twins entered their 50th season of baseball in the state of Minnesota, they made the move from indoor baseball at the Metrodome back to the great outdoors with the opening of the long-awaited Target Field. The dawn of a new era in Minneapolis provided new funding that allowed for free agent moves never before possible, and for the long-term extension of hometown hero Joe Mauer.

The year 2010 had years before been marked as "the year" for the Twins. In addition to kicking off a new era with the outdoor ballpark, several players were also now seasoned with years of playing time in the majors. The general consensus among both fans and players was that a division title would be nice, but nowhere near satisfying. The Twins had made the playoffs four times since that magical 2002 season when they avoided contraction, but not once since then had they advanced past the first round. Now the idea of a World Series appearance was up for open discussion.

At 6–2 on April 12, the Twins pulled into first place in the division. It wouldn't be until the final week of June that they would fall into second place. For most of July, with the exception of four days, the Twins stayed behind the Detroit Tigers and Chicago White Sox. But as had been the case with the Twins in the years since the memorable second half in 2006, they were primed for a second-half run.

On July 24, the Twins won the first game of what would eventually be an eight-game winning streak. By August 10, they were in first place, and the White Sox had emerged as their biggest competitor. When the Twins left Chicago two days after moving into first, they did so with a one-game edge in the division. The next week the White Sox arrived in Minnesota, and the season's defining moment was on the horizon.

With a three-game lead in the division, the key for the Twins entering the series was to keep Chicago from moving any closer. With his team trailing 6–5 in the bottom half of the 10th inning, Jim Thome stepped to the plate with one runner on base. Against his former team, Thome launched the pitch into deep right field, helping the Twins to a walk-off win and providing momentum for the final weeks remaining in the season.

Thome was a big part of the entire 2010 campaign for Minnesota. The left-handed slugger launched 25 home runs on the

## Player Profile: Jim Thome

Through the first 19 years of his career, Jim Thome played for two of the Twins' division rivals: the Cleveland Indians and the Chicago White Sox. In that period Thome became a big nemesis for the team. He hit 57 home runs against the Twins, and only one team, the Detroit Tigers, felt his wrath more in that department.

But as the 2010 season and a new era in Twins baseball approached, Thome sat unsigned in the free agent market. For a mere $1.5 million (plus incentives) investment, the Twins picked up their longtime nemesis, and what fans saw was a future Hall of Famer solidify himself amongst baseball's all-time greats.

On July 3 at Target Field, Thome hit home run No. 573 of his career, tying Twins great Harmon Killebrew. Later that day he hit home run No. 574 to pass the Hall of Famer and move into 10th place all-time on baseball's home run list. Thome's quest for 600 continued throughout the season, and by the time the 2010 season came to an end, Thome had moved himself to eighth all-time on the home run list.

Signing Thome took one of the team's biggest foes off the market, but what fans saw that year was a Hall of Fame slugger make history and help propel the team to the playoffs along the way.

*Jim Thome rounds the bases after hitting a home run against the Cleveland Indians in September 2010. By the end of the season, he had 589 home runs, placing him eighth on the all-time home run list.*

season and moved into eighth place all-time with 589 career home runs. In front of the home crowd he passed former Twins slugger Harmon Killebrew on the vaunted list, and with his blast that nailed the top of the flagpole in right field at Target Field, he set the bar high for future home runs at the team's new home.

What made Thome so valuable was that he had provided this production in the place of Justin Morneau, who in early July suffered a concussion that put him on the shelf for the remainder of the season. Injuries played a large part in the team's season. Joe Nathan never stepped foot on the field during the regular season after being forced to undergo Tommy John surgery, and Morneau played just half of the season.

Nevertheless, the season went on, and as the Twins had often done under Ron Gardenhire previously, new players stepped in and stepped up, and the team marched forward.

On September 14, the Twins arrived in Chicago for the final time, holding onto a six-game lead in the division. With just more than two weeks remaining on the season, it was far from over. The White Sox could move within striking distance if they could somehow take down the Twins. Behind Francisco Liriano, Brian Duensing, and Carl Pavano, the three pitchers who had aided the team on their second-half resurgence, the Twins swept the White Sox and left town with the division nearly locked up.

One week after they had arrived in Chicago, the Twins became the first team in baseball to clinch the playoffs. The team had gone 45–18 in the second half to that point on September 21, and for the sixth time in nine seasons under manager Ron Gardenhire, the Twins were the American League Central Division champions.

In a new environment, and without two All-Stars, the Twins fought for 94 victories. They went 53–28 at Target Field, posting the best home record in the American League while proving the home-field advantage outside of the Metrodome could be just as great. But the job was far from done. Up against the New York Yankees, the Twins couldn't be satisfied with another first-round exit.

For five innings during the postseason, things seemed perfect. Liriano, the pitcher who had bounced back so perfectly from Tommy John surgery during the regular season, was rolling, and the Twins provided him with an early lead. The Yankees took the lead in the sixth inning, and after the Twins tied it up in the bottom half, they took it back again in the next. The Yankees won that game and the following two. For a second consecutive season, the Twins had marched to the playoffs, only to be swept away by New York.

The year 2010 will long be remembered in Twins Territory, despite the disappointment that saw the team's hard work go for naught. From Opening Day, when the team's legends and fighter planes helped christen a new era of Twins baseball, to the mustache that helped lead the team to victory on the mound, to the victory in New York against Mariano Rivera and the one in Minnesota against Chicago, and to that champagne that once again filled the home clubhouse in Minneapolis, the Minnesota Twins put forth another memorable season to close out the first half-century of their existence in the state.

For now, however, the quest for a third trophy continues into the future.

# Bobbleheads

Who would have thought that a three-pound, 7½-inch giveaway could be so big?

As the Twins moved toward an eighth consecutive losing record in the summer of 2000, their average attendance had dipped to 12,000 fans per game, and the interest level in the team was slowly dropping as the season wore on. But the Twins had the next big thing sitting in their pocket, and when the giveaway day arrived in June that season, there was finally a mad rush at the gates of the Metrodome.

"The response to the first giveaway was overwhelming, with fans lined up around the block to get one of the five thousand dolls," said Patrick Klinger, the Twins' vice president of marketing who started the craze. "Much of the demand was fueled by a front-page article that appeared in the *Star Tribune* that morning that quoted a well-known baseball memorabilia expert saying the bobbleheads might be worth up to $100 immediately on eBay."

It was the start of the bobblehead craze. While only a ceramic, hand-painted figurine with a bouncy head that fit its name, the bobblehead quickly became one of the most sought-after giveaways. On that particular day, when the Twins handed out the first bobblehead in team history, the little figure shaking his head was Hall of Famer Harmon Killebrew, and the fans loved it, lining up outside of the stadium early in the morning for the night game. On the field the Twins were still attempting to break through, but off it they were successful in creating a new full-blown phenomenon.

"We thought the bobbleheads would be successful, but never imagined the incredible phenomenon they would become," Klinger said. "When the first bobblehead was given away in June 2000, the five thousand dolls were gone in five minutes, causing many angry fans but also stoking the fires of demand. As a result, we increased the number of bobbleheads given away during future promotions from 5,000 to 10,000 and instituted security measures designed to prevent fans from getting more than one doll each."

The prototype had arrived on Klinger's desk the previous season in 1999. What he received from Alexander Global Promotions based out of Bellevue, Washington, was a Willie Mays doll that the San Francisco Giants were giving away that year as they closed Candlestick Park. The lack of a sponsor prevented the Twins from moving forward with the promotion that season, and the Giants ultimately gave away the first bobbleheads. But while the Giants were first, the Twins did it the biggest, giving away four different dolls in 2000 and creating a huge sensation along the way.

"Though bobbleheads had been around for decades, they had not been given away at the ballpark for many years. Though the prototype was rough, we saw potential in the item as a promotion that would drive ticket sales," Klinger said. "A lack of a sponsor prevented us from offering bobbleheads in 1999, but Mountain Dew stepped forward in 2000, and four were given away: Killebrew, Hrbek, Puckett, and Oliva."

It was that lineup—the one consisting of some of the team's all-time greats—that created the most enthusiasm and biggest crowds during that 2000 season. While the Twins finished in last place in attendance that year with just more than 1 million fans, nearly 85,000 fans who entered the gates during that season did so on the four dates in which the Twins handed out bobbleheads.

"We wanted to bring back nostalgic promotions that hadn't been done in a few years," Klinger said near the end of the 2000 season. "I think we were shocked and amazed. We expected big things out of the promotion, but I don't think we realized it would be as big as it became."

What it would become is a national craze in sports venues all across the country and all across the sports scene. While the Twins didn't break through their losing stretch until the next season, the bobblehead craze pushed the Twins into the spotlight in 2000.

# 84 17 Strikeouts

August 19, 2007, was your typical Sunday afternoon baseball game. The Twins had catcher Joe Mauer in the lineup as the designated hitter because he'd caught the previous night. In the series finale with the Texas Rangers, the Twins sent their two-time Cy Young Award winner to the mound in Johan Santana.

That day Minnesota right fielder Michael Cuddyer would belt a solo home run in the second inning, and the team would collect just four hits and never score again. On a typical day that would lead to an "L" in the standings, but this wasn't an ordinary day, and that one run from one bad pitch would win the Twins a ballgame.

Santana started the game by getting second baseman Ian Kinsler to ground out. He struck out the next two hitters to end the first inning, and then struck out the side in the Rangers' half of the second inning. In the third inning Santana K'd two more hitters, and one-third of the way through the game he had already sat down seven Texas hitters.

Through the middle three innings Santana would strike out four more batters, and he allowed his first hit of the game when Sammy Sosa singled in the fifth inning. Kicking off the seventh inning, Santana's strikeout total was up to 11, and although that number was solid, it still was nothing extraordinary.

The seventh inning began with two strikeouts by Santana, and after he allowed his second hit of the game, this time a double for Sosa, he ended the inning with yet another strikeout. The lefty strolled to the mound in the eighth inning and struck out three more hitters to push his total to a solid 17. Having thrown 112 pitches, Santana's day was over, and his chance at 20 was not meant to be.

Closer Joe Nathan recorded two more strikeouts in the ninth inning, and in the end the Twins had put away a total of 19 Rangers via strikeout, setting a new team record for the most strikeouts in a game. Santana struck out every Texas hitter at least one time, and their lone two hits were scattered and both allowed to Sosa.

It may have been just another ordinary day at the ballpark when the first pitch was thrown, but when all was said and done, the crowd of 36,353 had seen one of the most dominant pitching performances in team history.

# Sacred Streets

New York City has Broadway and Wall Street. Chicago has Michigan Avenue and Lake Shore Drive. Los Angeles has Hollywood Boulevard and Melrose Avenue. New Orleans has Bourbon Street. Boston has Newbury Street.

You get the point. All across the country, big cities have big streets that are commonly known. They're almost landmarks with people stopping to take pictures along the way.

Minnesota has some too. Someone from another part of the country may have never heard of them, but if you're a Minnesota Twins fan, you've got to check them out. These streets are landmarks because they mark the location of some of the greatest moments in team history.

The Twins street sign tour is actually as easy as one, two, three.

## Killebrew Drive

His career wasn't even over, and they were already renaming a street after him. After the Twins moved to Minnesota and to Metropolitan Stadium in 1961, Harmon Killebrew played 12 seasons at the team's new home before they renamed 83rd Street in Bloomington, Minnesota, to Killebrew Drive in April 1973.

Today that street marks the home of the Mall of America, but there is a much greater significance behind it. Killebrew Drive is the place where the Twins played the 1965 World Series, and it's where Killebrew hit many of his 573 career home runs. That street marks the old stomping grounds for the team—Metropolitan Stadium.

The ballpark may be long gone with a shopping center in its place, but marking the location of the team's early years and early memories is a street named after the first great slugger in Twins history.

## Kirby Puckett Place

For 12 seasons, center fielder Kirby Puckett made memories in a Twins uniform, and most commonly at one primary location. Two seasons after the Twins made the move to the Metrodome in 1982, Puckett made his mark as a major leaguer, making his debut at 24 years old during the 1984 season.

It would take a few seasons, but starting in 1986 with his 31 home runs and his first All-Star Game appearance, Puckett became a recognizable face throughout baseball. The year was 1987 when Puckett made his first big mark on the franchise and state, and then in 1991, he turned himself into a trademark.

There was the trademark catch, followed by the trademark home run. Puckett did them both, and he did it on the biggest stage possible during the 1991 World Series. He became the icon of Twins baseball.

When his career suddenly ended in 1996 from glaucoma, the Twins asked the city of Minneapolis to rename the portion of Chicago Avenue in front of the Metrodome to Kirby Puckett Place in his honor. They did, and in the years following it became the pregame destination for fans.

This address, team president Dave St. Peter once said, "is one of the greatest addresses in sports." Behind it sits the H.H.H. Metrodome, the place that Hall of Famer Kirby Puckett once roamed, and the location of the greatest memories in team history.

## Twins Way

A new era in Twins baseball, kick-started by their move across town to the outdoor Target Field, meant a move from the sacred street they once renamed, and a change on the letterhead, too.

Prior to the inaugural season in 2010, the Twins applied for a portion of Third Avenue in front of the new ballpark, to be renamed Twins Way.

"We've been blessed with signature addresses in the past—from Killebrew Drive to Puckett Place," St. Peter said the day the Twins unveiled the street sign. "In many ways I think Twins Way says it all. People around Major League Baseball talk about the Twins' Way and it's the way we do things on the field."

Marking their desire for "doing the little things right," the team's new address also marks the beginning of something new for the franchise, and the place it hopes can soon be called the home of many memories—just as its old addresses are.

 **Gary Gaetti**

Gary Gaetti sure did like debuts.

When he was 23 years old, Gaetti made his major league debut with the Minnesota Twins near the end of the season. It was September 20, 1981, and in his first at-bat, he homered. The next year the Twins debuted in the Metrodome, and in the inaugural game, Gaetti smashed two home runs. Finally, when the Twins reached the postseason in 1987, he homered twice more in his first two postseason at-bats, at the time becoming the first and only player to ever do so; although Evan Longoria became the second player to complete the feat in 2008.

Gaetti's first full season with the Twins was during the 1982 season, and as he established himself as a solid fielder, he pushed John Castino to second base. At first base the Twins had a rookie in Kent Hrbek, and the two became friends during Gaetti's 10-year stay in Minnesota.

*Gary Gaetti watches the ball sail off his bat for a home run against the Detroit Tigers in Game 1 of the 1987 ALCS, contributing to his being awarded the MVP for the series.*

"He had the guts, and every night he wanted to go out there and kick the other team's butt," Hrbek said years after their playing careers were over. "And I liked that."

Over the first years of his career, Gaetti hit for more power than the team had seen from a third baseman since Harmon Killebrew. During that first full season, he smashed 25 home runs, and in three of his first four seasons he hit at least 20.

It was 1986 when Gaetti broke out, though, and for a string of three consecutive seasons, he turned into one of the best third basemen in baseball. That season, the man called "the Rat" by teammates, quite possibly for the mustache he wore on his face, hit .287 with 34 home runs and 108 RBIs, and he won his first of an eventual four Gold Gloves as a member of the Twins organization.

The 1987 season may have seen Gaetti's numbers dip just a bit, but his glove work remained just as strong, and in the end it turned out to be quite possibly his best season during his 20-year career. He hit .257 that season with 31 home runs and 109 RBIs. His regular season numbers were solid, but it was the postseason where he truly made his mark. In the ALCS against the Detroit Tigers, Gaetti hit two home runs and drove in five to collect the series MVP Award. Then in the World Series he collected four extra-base hits, scored four runs, and made the final out in Game 7 as the Twins won their first championship in team history.

Gaetti's numbers would fall after the 1988 season, but he continued to hit for power. After the 1990 season Gaetti signed with the California Angels during free agency, and through the remainder of his career he would play for a total of five other teams not named Minnesota. When he retired after the 2000 season, Gaetti had hit 360 career home runs and made two All-Star Games.

In the 2007 season the Twins honored Gaetti 20 years after he fielded that final out of the 1987 World Series by placing him in the Twins Hall of Fame. During his tenure with the Twins, Gaetti racked up numbers that today have him placed highly on the team leaderboard. He ranks fifth on the Twins' all-time list in RBIs (758), and he ranks sixth in doubles (252), games (1,361), at-bats (4,989), hits (1,276), home runs (201), and total bases (2,181).

After being inducted on that August afternoon at the Metrodome, Gaetti threw out the first pitch in a new fashion; he threw the ball from third base over to Kent Hrbek just as he had done two decades previously. After the throw, the two embraced in the middle of the infield just as they had done after that championship.

From his power to his glove work to that final out of the World Series, Gaetti will forever be remembered by Twins fans. Maybe most of all, though, fans will remember that mustache that years ago graced his face.

# Hitting for the Cycle

Single. Double. Triple. Home run.

Through the first 50 years of baseball in Minnesota, only 10 players have ever collected all four of those things in a single game. Never has a Twin done it in order, though; that feat has been accomplished only 14 times in the history of baseball.

After moving to Minnesota in 1961, the Twins didn't get their first cycle until May 20, 1970, when Rod Carew did it for the first time in team history at Municipal Stadium in Kansas City. In the first inning, Carew singled. He then led off the third inning with a home run, doubled in the fifth, and tripled in his final at-bat in the eighth inning. That season Carew went on to hit .366, his second-best batting average during his long 19-year career.

Through the next decade, five more Twins would add their names to the list with Cesar Tovar, Larry Hisle, Lyman Bostock, Mike Cubbage, and Gary Ward reaching the bases necessary to be mentioned.

It was August 1, 1986, when Kirby Puckett did it. That night at the Metrodome Puckett led off the game with a triple, later scoring the first of 10 Twins runs in an eventual victory. After flying out in his second at-bat, Puckett doubled in the fifth and then singled in the sixth. Just as Carew had done some 16 years earlier,

Puckett stepped to the plate in the eighth inning for his last at-bat needing that one perfect hit to become the seventh player in team history to complete the feat. Puckett needed a home run, and he got it. It would be the first cycle in the history of the Metrodome, and the team wouldn't see another one for more than two decades.

Carlos Gomez had come to Minnesota the previous off-season in the Johan Santana trade. The young center fielder had a lot of speed and a lot of hype surrounding him. That night, on May 7, 2008, in Chicago, he showed why. Leading off the first inning, Gomez homered. After striking out in the third inning, he followed in order with a triple and double through the middle innings. Only fittingly for the speedster, Gomez singled to lead off the ninth inning, bouncing a ball up the middle that the pitcher couldn't field. That night, the Twins got their first cycle in 22 seasons, and what Gomez accomplished was rare—he collected one of only three reverse cycles since 1956, picking up the needed hits in the opposite order.

After having waited two decades to see another cycle after Puckett did it, the Twins kept doing it. Following the cycle by Gomez in 2008, the team saw two players do it in a two-month span before the Metrodome closed after 28 years of use.

As Jason Kubel stepped to the plate on April 17, 2009, he had already collected a single, double, and triple through the first seven innings. With the Twins trailing by two runs to the Los Angeles Angels, they had loaded the bases for Kubel in the eighth. He would launch the pitch into the air, warranting this response from announcer Dick Bremer.

"A high blast to right field. Up, back, gone…a grand slam for Kubel, and the cycle is complete!"

The Twins had scored seven runs in that eighth inning for the comeback victory, and Kubel had the ninth cycle in team history. It wouldn't be the final one in the Metrodome's history, though, that accomplishment would go to Michael Cuddyer when he did it just over one month later.

With 10 cycles in a 50-year span, the Twins are in the top one-third in baseball history for cycles by a team. Five have come on the road, and five others have come in front of the home fans at Metropolitan Stadium and under the roof of the Metrodome. Some who have accomplished the feat have been Twins greats, and some haven't. With its unpredictability, it's anybody's guess who'll do it next.

# 88 The All-Star Games

Imagine an outfield of Willie Stargell, Hank Aaron, and Willie Mays in Minnesota, with additional outfielders including Roberto Clemente and Frank Robinson on the bench. If you were on hand at Metropolitan Stadium on July 13, 1965, then you don't need any such imagination. There, a lineup with these very players trotted out onto the field in Minnesota as the Minnesota Twins hosted the All-Star Game for the first time in franchise history.

Looking back, it should have been an easier victory for the National League. They put one of the best lineups in All-Star Game history on the field for that Midsummer Classic ballgame, and a small sample of their pitchers included Don Drysdale, Bob Gibson, Sandy Koufax, and starting pitcher Juan Marichal. The team included 11 future Hall of Famers, and while the American League roster included five Hall of Fame players, the National League was, to say the least, a dominant group.

With the game in Minnesota, it was only fitting that the Twins were represented with a large number of All-Star-caliber players. Their six players included starters Harmon Killebrew and Earl Battey, bench players Jimmie Hall, Tony Oliva, and Zoilo Versalles, as well as pitcher Mudcat Grant. This home All-Star Game featured more players from the Twins than any other All-Star event in the team's first 50 seasons of baseball in the state.

The game itself featured five home runs, including one by Mays to lead off the game. With the National League leading 6–5 in the ninth inning, and with Oliva on second base, Killebrew struck out, and the American League fell. It didn't matter, though, it was just an All-Star Game, and the crowd of 46,706 fans had seen a collection of the greatest players in the game take the field together.

It would be 20 years before another compilation of the game's best players took the field together in Minnesota. This time at the Metrodome, a group of players, including the likes of Ozzie Smith, Tony Gwynn, Nolan Ryan, George Brett, Rickey Henderson, and Eddie Murray, stepped onto the turf. The game also featured home-town heroes Dave Winfield and Jack Morris, and pitcher Bert Blyleven took the mound as a representative of the Cleveland Indians. This time around the Twins weren't nearly as well represented as they were when they played host to their first All-Star Game; only outfielder Tom Brunansky made the cut.

The game saw the National League win 6–1, but the bigger story during these days in Minneapolis was the home run derby. Players had long participated in home run contests, but this 1985 event marked the first year Major League Baseball would acknowledge it, and the home run derby was officially born. Twin Tom Brunansky tied for second place with four home runs in the event, but it was Dave Parker of the Cincinnati Reds who took home the first crown with his six home runs at the Dome.

Through the first half-century of Twins baseball, the game's best players have been hosted in Minnesota on two separate occasions. The games have included numerous Hall of Famers, and fans have been witness to the best that baseball has to offer. With a new ballpark in downtown Minneapolis, the team is again set to host a legendary group of players. Come 2014, according to early reports, fans will be sitting under the stars for the Midsummer Classic, watching players launch home runs onto the plaza in the same city the tradition first began.

And who knows? Maybe this time the American League will take home a victory.

## 5th Street Murals

Baseball in itself is an art. The way a player stands in the batter's box and the way he swings at a pitch is art. The way a pitcher delivers the ball to home plate is art. The way coaches communicate with players in the field and the way catchers communicate with their pitchers on the mound is an art. With so many parts of America's pastime being its own unique style of art, combining the ballpark experience with art only makes sense.

When the Minnesota Twins began putting together their new home across town from the Metrodome, they carefully thought of little touches that could make Target Field unique to the state of Minnesota. They held an art contest in 2008, and the result was three murals on the left-field side of the ballpark facing 5th Street.

Artist Craig David, along with his artist assistants Mary Aguilar, David Cubus, and Robert Sutherland, won the contest with their proposal of murals to be constructed in porcelain and stone.

"The selection committee pre-chose the subject matter for the murals," said David. "I related that content to my experiences and local history, and then made the most compelling, beautiful, and thought-provoking pictures possible."

The three murals that face the rail transit on the backside of the ballpark represent a range of history in Minnesota. One shows the complex relationship between the natural world and humanity,

*Artist Craig David designed three murals on the left-field side of Target Field facing 5th Street. The artwork shows the deep connection between Minnesota and baseball.* Photo courtesy Alex Halsted

another offers a perspective on the history of the transit system in the Twin Cities, and a third one relates to baseball itself, with things such as Lexington Park and Nicollet Field, the old homes of the St. Paul Saints and Minneapolis Millers, being one of many primary focuses.

"Those who see the murals, in a sense possess them," David said. "Their experience is what the murals become in their hearts and minds, a kind of iconography that is different for every individual."

The symbolism of the 5th Street murals goes deeper than what is shown in each picture, the artwork builds a connection between all types of visitors to the ballpark, and they allow each person to put their own stories behind the images, whether they can relate to the history shown in them or not.

"For some, the game is all-important. For others, they take away an experience of another sort," David mentioned. "What is rewarding for me is that the ballpark, including the art, truly belongs to the people."

From the Hall of Fame statues on the plaza, to the pennant flags above the home run porch, history is a prominent part of going to a game at Target Field. The artwork is yet another aspect of the ballpark experience, and it's something many can relate to, baseball fan or not.

# 90 The Music Man (and Woman)

Right there in Twins Territory, in Mason City, Iowa, is the home of Meredith Wilson, also known as the Music Man. If you head north to the epicenter of Twins Territory, also known as Target Field, you'll find another music man, and his name is Kevin Dutcher.

Back in 1999 Dutcher, who moved to the Twin Cities in 1984, noticed the music playing in the background during a Minnesota Twins game at the Metrodome. He mentioned the fact to his friend and Twins employee Jim Cunningham, and the rest is history.

"While attending a Twins game in 1999, I noticed songs playing between innings. Obviously someone was pushing the buttons to make that happen, so I mentioned to my friend Jim Cunningham—who has been the 'Minister of Fun' for the Twins since the mid-'90s—that if that position ever opened up, I'd like a crack at it," Dutcher recalled of his conversation that day. "The following winter the position was vacated, and they interviewed three people, all of whom knew people who worked there."

Dutcher got the job, mainly because his sound-design history, he believes, and for the past 11 seasons and for more than 850 games, he has been the guy pushing the buttons to ignite the crowd in critical moments and lighten the mood when times haven't been so great. For every home game each season, Dutcher sits in the booth and plays music. The job isn't quite that simple, though. It involves hours of planning prior to each home game, and even the smallest details are taken into consideration.

"We have a production meeting every game day that starts two and a half hours prior to the first pitch. There we discuss all of the elements of the pregame at length, and I determine what kinds of musical beds are needed," Dutcher said of the pregame preparation. "Once we've discussed the pregame, we launch into a discussion of the in-game elements. Every announcement, game, and video is preplanned and covered so that it will all run as smoothly as possible."

When the action begins, the real test does, too. Any particular situation can call for a different type of music and a quick decision from Dutcher. Over the years, Dutcher has learned that you can never have enough music, and his large collection of songs has him covered for nearly every potential scenario.

"Once the game starts, I always try to have a few pieces of music ready to go at any moment, depending on the situation. I have three computers, two of which have thousands of cues that I've edited, including the players' walk-up music and songs for just about any conceivable scenario," Dutcher said. "The third has my library—30,000 songs that I've brought in from home—everything I could ever imagine possibly playing at the park. And if all goes well, the last major thing that I do every night is crank up U2's 'Beautiful Day'!"

While Dutcher is the modern-day Music Man in Twins Territory, he isn't the only part of the production at Target Field. For the past 12 seasons, organist Sue Nelson has been behind the organ providing an old-time baseball feel to complement the recorded audio. Nelson plays among the fans in the Twins Pub behind Section 213, and in addition to being a one-of-a-kind musician, she's one of the team's biggest cheerleaders and fans.

"Sue is a tremendous organist and a sports fanatic. Her home is decorated with Twins and Wild paraphernalia, and she is passionate about her teams. She loves the Twins, and after every game one can gauge the team's performance by the bounce, or lack thereof, in Sue's step," Dutcher said of Nelson. "She is extremely social and is a great ambassador for the team. I think her passion for the Twins is reflected in her music; you can hear her playing

## Walk-Up Music

Walk-up music at one point in time was for the most part selected by Kevin Dutcher. That changed over time. Players slowly became more enamored with the music played when they stepped to the plate for each at-bat, and as they started providing input, walk-up music slowly evolved.

"When I started out in 2000, the player walk-up music was in its nascent stages. A few of the players selected what they wanted to hear, most of them were happy to let me choose something that got the crowd revved up," Dutcher said. "That led to some fun and enduring choices, like Cristian Guzman's music, which was just a tune I found on an obscure Latin dance music CD. Soon more and more players got into it, and a few—Jacque Jones and David Ortiz—had three to four songs that they changed up with great regularity whenever they went into a slump."

Today the majority of players pick their own music, and Dutcher has the system figured out, receiving a list from each player prior to the start of the season.

"Nowadays I've got it down to a science," Dutcher said of the process. "I give the players a form during spring training that they fill out, stating what walk-up song or songs they want. I also give them a chance to throw in some requests for tunes to be mixed into batting practice."

getting more animated as the game gets exciting. And if we're losing, you can almost feel her fingers urging on the team as her organ resounds throughout the stadium."

For every home game each season, music plays an integral role at the ballpark. From the sound of "We're Gonna Win, Twins" that accompanies the team on the field each night, to the organ urging the team on, music is constantly filling the air in downtown Minneapolis, and it stems from the fingers of Kevin Dutcher and Sue Nelson, two people who live for music.

"When I was a 12-year-old kid thinking about what I'd be when I grew up, if someone had told me that one day I'd be the music director for the Minnesota Twins, that I'd get paid to come to the stadium every game and crank music for 40,000 people, I think my head would have exploded," Dutcher concluded.

"I'm glad nobody did."

# 91 "The Sky Is Falling!"

For 28 seasons the Twins played under the Teflon roof of the Metrodome. During that near three-decade stay, the roof was a savior for the team. It kept snow away when it was time for baseball, it kept fans dry when the storms rolled in, and even throughout the cold nights during the playoffs, it kept fans at a comfortable temperature as they sat in the blue seats indoors. But that doesn't mean the roof was always perfect.

Through the years, the roof caused many awkward moments on the field. There was Dave Kingman's pop-up that went up and never came down, David Ortiz once hit a blast headed for the upper deck in right field until it met a speaker before reaching its destination, and on countless other occasions, players lost the ball in the white roof. But even the quirky plays don't quite compare to the moments when the roof itself became the story.

On three different occasions over the years the Twins played there (and once in 2010 after they had moved to Target Field), the roof of the Metrodome collapsed. It hadn't even been inflated one month, and no games had ever been played, when on November 19, 1981, the rapid accumulation of more than one foot of snow caved the Teflon roof in for the first time. One year later, on December 30, 1982, snow caused it to collapse again. But there was only one time in which a collapse caused a postponement. On April 14, 1983, a tear in the roof caused by snow forced the Twins to postpone their matchup with the California Angels. That postponement was the only one during the team's tenure at the Metrodome caused by weather or the roof.

It must have been something about the Angels, because on April 26, 1986, they were back in Minnesota again as the opponents. It was dark, gloomy, and stormy in downtown Minneapolis, but fans and players gathered inside the dry Metrodome, safe from the weather elements. Despite bad sightlines and no opportunity to enjoy Minnesota's nature, nights like this were enough to remind any fan about the one good perk about playing under a permanent white roof.

Through the first seven and a half innings, all was fine. The score was perfect with the Twins leading 6–1, and while the thunder struck and the lightning flashed outdoors, the 31,966 fans in attendance stayed dry. Then, all of a sudden, it wasn't so dry.

Winds gusted at 60 mph, the thunder struck louder than before, and suddenly the lightning wasn't shielded. The rain poured down into the upper deck in right field, and as fans ran from their seats, the Angels ran from the field for the dugout. The roof had torn open, the lights were swaying, and the innings remaining in the game seemed to be in doubt.

The game did resume, though. After a nine-minute delay, the teams retook the field despite the tear and how badly the Twins were about to be hit by the storm.

Still leading by five runs with three outs remaining, starter Frank Viola allowed a leadoff double and then a two-run home run. Ron Davis was summoned from the bullpen, and he quickly allowed a single and two-run home run, too. He'd retire two of the next three batters while mixing in a walk to Reggie Jackson, but needing only one more out, the Twins still led by one run. At least they did until Wally Joyner stepped to the plate and hit the third two-run home run of the inning to give the Angels a 7–6 lead and an eventual victory.

It was the fourth and final time the Twins would encounter a problem with the roof. Over the course of the remaining 23 seasons at the Metrodome after that wet night in 1986, there would be no other roof collapse or tear. For the most part, the Teflon roof upheld its role as the team's protector and made the Metrodome useful. But for at least one night during the team's long stay, some fans got a taste of outdoor baseball.

 **Dan Gladden**

*"And the pitch to Larkin. Swung on, a high fly ball into left-center, the run will score, the ball will bounce for a single, and the Minnesota Twins are the champions of the world!"* —Vin Scully, 1991 World Series

At the end of spring training in 1987, the Minnesota Twins made a trade to acquire a 29-year-old outfielder by the name of Dan Gladden. That year Gladden played in 121 regular season games and every playoff game as the Twins won their first championship in team history.

Signed as an amateur free agent after college in 1979, Gladden played four seasons with the San Francisco Giants before the Twins traded Jose Dominguez, Ray Velasquez, and eventually Bryan Hickerson for him during that spring day on March 31, 1987. In his first year in Minnesota, he hit just shy of .250 with eight home runs and 38 RBIs.

Gladden never was a flashy player during his five-year stay with the Twins. They acquired him before that championship season with the idea of his being their starting left fielder and leadoff hitter. The Twins also hoped he would add some fire to the club, and he certainly did during his tenure with the team—both on and off the field.

During Game 1 of the 1987 World Series, Gladden launched a grand slam to cap off a seven-run fourth inning for the Twins. They would never look back in that game and eventually won the title with Gladden hitting .290 over the course of the seven-game series.

*Dan Gladden celebrates as he heads home on teammate Gene Larkin's single in the 10th inning of Game 7 to win the 1991 World Series.*

When his career was over, Gladden would tell *Sports Illustrated*, "I was somebody who played like it was his last game every day. I expected that type of effort out of my teammates, and sometimes I didn't see it."

One of those occasions came in July 1988, when teammate Steve Lombardozzi was pulled for a pinch-hitter and marched to the clubhouse for the remainder of the game. Gladden let Lombardozzi know after the game how he felt about his departure from the bench, and the next day when he showed up at Gladden's apartment, punches were thrown. It was Gladden who got the punches in, though; Lombardozzi would show up for the next game with the bruises to prove it.

In his final season with the Twins, Gladden played in 126 regular season games and hit .247 with six home runs and 52 RBIs. He would again play in every playoff game that year, and had it not been for him on that October 27, 1991, night, Twins history could have been different.

Jack Morris had just completed his 10th consecutive shutout inning, and leading off the bottom half of the inning in Game 7 of the 1991 World Series was Gladden. As he swung, his bat broke, and the ball softly dropped into left field for a bloop hit. Like he always did, Gladden hustled and reached second base for a leadoff double. While Gene Larkin lofted a hit into left-center later that inning and while Vin Scully made the call on the radio, Gladden threw his arms into the air and crossed home plate; lifting the Twins to their second championship in team history.

After playing two seasons with the Detroit Tigers following that memorable moment, Gladden won a title with the Yomiuri Giants of Japan before calling it quits. He would bounce around as a scout for a few years, and in 2000 "the Dazzle Man" returned to Minnesota. As a broadcaster, Gladden continues to be a part of team history as he makes calls of his own. To date, there have been none as big as the one Gladden was involved in on that fall night back in 1991.

# 93 Get to Know 'Em

"How can you not like the Twins? It's anti-American not to like a team that beats the odds. It's simply unpatriotic not to like a team that sticks it to the big guys," wrote John Donovan in *Sports Illustrated* during the 2002 season. "They're scrappy! They're fun! They're underdogs!

"Just one question. Who the heck are these guys?"

That was a common question around the league during that 2002 season. As the Twins entered the campaign having posted a losing record in eight of the previous nine seasons and on the brink of extinction following the threat of contraction the previous off-season, their roster was full of players few had ever heard of. Fans around the league couldn't have named the team's rookie manager or many of his players. Heck, the hometown fans were still familiarizing themselves with the guys gracing the turf at the Metrodome.

The previous year in 2001 the team started the "Get to Know 'Em," campaign, which helped reenergize the fan base.

"The campaign was brought to life by local ad firm Hunt Adkins," said Twins vice president of marketing Patrick Klinger. "The brilliant creative combined with a fast start by the team in 2001 captured the sporting public's attention and helped reinvigorate the Twins brand."

There was still a lot to get to know in 2002. Only one offensive player was over the age of 30, and that was utility guy Denny Hocking, who was better known for representing the Twins in the players' union that year than he was for his production at the plate. A 26-year-old Torii Hunter and Jacque Jones (27 years old) were in the outfield, Luis Rivas (22) and Cristian Guzman (24) manned the middle infield, and A.J. Pierzynski (25) crouched behind home plate as the team's catcher. And that was just a start.

On the mound, Johan Santana (23) officially entered the rotation that season, Michael Cuddyer (23) was still a mere bench player, and David Ortiz (26) was just breaking out. Meanwhile, corner infielders Doug Mientkiewicz (28) and Corey Koskie (29) were considered team veterans. The Twins, with an average age under 27 years, were young and unheard of.

No matter how much anybody knew about the Twins, and no matter how much respect they were getting from their counterparts around the league, they were ready to pounce. The league would quickly become familiar with the young players. By May 2 that year, the Twins were sitting in first place, and with the exception of one lone day at the end of that month, the Twins were in first place for the rest of that season.

By the time the 2002 season had come to an end, the Twins had fought off the threat of contraction, Torii Hunter had started in the All-Star Game, the Twins had won 94 ballgames, and for the first time since 1991, they were headed to the playoffs after winning the American League Central by 13½ games over the second-place Chicago White Sox.

In the playoffs the Twins continued to let their names be known. They beat the Oakland Athletics in five games during the ALDS, and the national spotlight was on them as they faced off against the Anaheim Angels in the second round. Every magazine and every newspaper was telling the story of the unknown. Players whom most had never heard of were now part of a great underdog story.

By the next year, the slogan needed updating. It was no longer "Get to Know 'Em." Fans of the team, and fans of baseball spread across the country had become familiar with the small-market Minnesota Twins. So the team tweaked the slogan accordingly.

"Gotta See 'Em," read advertisements during the following 2003 season.

That group of unknown players would become the group that helped turn around the organization, and the team that some say helped save baseball.

They went from the unknown to the must-see.

 **Twins Territory**

It was the mid-1950s, and people in the Twins Cities were looking to bring a professional team to the state of Minnesota. Should the team be in St. Paul or should it be in Minneapolis? That was the common question, and there were two common answers. Boosters from St. Paul wanted the prospective team in their town; boosters in Minneapolis wanted a future team on their side of the river.

After feuding over the issue, the two sides went their separate ways. St. Paul built Midway Stadium, which would become home to the St. Paul Saints. Meanwhile, Minneapolis boosters built a ballpark in Bloomington, Minnesota. Their ballpark was named Metropolitan Stadium, and it became home to the Minneapolis Millers.

Neither ballpark guaranteed anything for either city, but the conversation began to heat up. It was 1956 when the Millers moved into Met Stadium, and while the news wouldn't come until some four years later, it did finally come. The state of Minnesota would get a professional baseball team. The Washington Senators would become the Minnesota Twins and make their home at The Met, and in Minneapolis' territory.

Following the ever-so-popular "Get to Know 'Em" ad campaign that debuted during the 2001 season, the team's new motto that debuted prior to the 2005 season sure had a lot to live up to. The new slogan was simple: "This is Twins Territory." Fans heard it on the radio, they saw the catchy commercials on television and everywhere else they looked—in the team yearbook, on banners, and seemingly anywhere else the Twins plastered their message.

## 3 Million Fans

After the Twins surged in the final months of the 1987 season to make the playoffs, they surprised the league by knocking off the Detroit Tigers in the ALCS to reach the World Series for only the second time in team history. They then proceeded to beat the St. Louis Cardinals for their first championship.

Those facts are commonly known.

What often goes under the radar is that during the next season in 1988, the Twins actually won more regular season games, posting a record of 91–71 in the American League West. But the Oakland Athletics did better, and the Twins failed the make the playoffs. The Twins did win in something, though; they had more fans push through the gates than any other team in baseball.

That season, the Twins became the first team in American League history to surpass the 3 million mark in single-season attendance. That plateau has become more common in recent years, and the Twins only passed it again during their inaugural season at Target Field during the 2010 season.

The center of Twins Territory was the Metrodome at the time, but this new message was key on setting the record straight. Twins Territory wasn't just under that Teflon roof, it wasn't just in Minneapolis, and it wasn't just in the Twin Cities. For that matter, Twins Territory wasn't just in the state of Minnesota.

When Calvin Griffith moved the team from Washington to Minnesota in the fall of 1960, his biggest goal was to unite the cities of Minneapolis and St. Paul. With the team set to play its games in Bloomington, Minnesota, on Minneapolis' side of the river, they had effectively won the territorial battle that had occurred in previous years. But this new baseball team wasn't the lone product of one major city; it was the team for Minneapolis, St. Paul, and, for that matter, a team for the entire Upper Midwest.

"You must latch onto our boys like milfoil on a boat prop," called out the voice in one of the many early Twins Territory commercials. "For this is your state. This is your team. And this is Twins Territory."

Latch on is what fans did from day one when the Twins took the field for the first time on April 21, 1961, at Metropolitan Stadium.

The Twins quickly became successful, making it to the World Series as soon as 1965, and they quickly became the beloved team for the area people who had no other team around to call their own.

Today, Twins Territory spreads much farther than the Twin Cities, and much farther that the state's border. You can catch the team on the radio in Bismarck, North Dakota; Pierre, South Dakota; Sioux City, Iowa; New Richmond, Wisconsin; and on dozens of other affiliate stations all across the states of North Dakota, South Dakota, Iowa, and Wisconsin.

What started as a battle between two cities has since become a friendship. And what started as a team for the state of Minnesota has since become a team with a strong fan connection across several states in the Upper Midwest. The center of Twins Territory today may be Target Field, but the Minnesota Twins and their followers branch out much farther.

Twins Territory has no boundaries.

Wherever you may be, if the Twins are your team, then *you're* in Twins Territory.

 **Live the Fantasy**

From a young age, we dream big. We dream of putting on the uniform and taking the field that the superstars we grew up watching or heard about once did. Eventually, reality sets in, we look ahead to other things, and over time we settle for a simple trip to the ballpark as spectators. We officially put away and give up that once awe-inspiring, far-fetched fantasy.

"I always dreamed about the 3–2 pitch with two outs and the bases loaded," Twins reliever Pat Neshek once said when looking back on his childhood. "I always thought I was the hitter who would hit the home run. I think that was the scenario I played out hundreds of times against the garage wall. I would pitch the ball so it would have extra carry and then fly into the street simulating a home run."

For Neshek, that common childhood dream became a reality, but for many the dream eventually fades as we realize our life has a different direction planned, one that doesn't include hitting game-winning home runs or making catches like Kirby once did in the World Series.

While the dream might fade as we get older and move on to other things, the fantasy never does. It can't. That fantasy of making a marvelous catch or running down the chalk baseline always remains, regardless of age and regardless of reality. No matter where we may be, it's never too late to daydream about that childhood vision, and it's never too late to wonder what it might have been like had things fallen into place many years ago.

And, for a week at least, it's never too late to live that dream, to turn it into reality.

"It's neat," former Twins pitcher Juan Berenguer told the *Cape Coral Daily Breeze* from Fort Myers, Florida, in 2009. "You see a couple guys here who are 65 years old. They may run slow, but they have it in their heart, they have a dream to play professional baseball, and that's what it's all about at the fantasy camp."

Yes, fantasy camp, where you can take the field, put on the uniform, and live a dream that for so long felt like just that. For a week in the winter, you can head to Fort Myers, Florida, to the Twins' spring home. There, you'll live the life of a major league player—hitting, fielding, and possibly even pitching. And who knows, maybe you'll pull a muscle or feel some soreness, allowing you to fully revert back to your childhood days at the ballfield.

From legends like Bert Blyleven, Harmon Killebrew, and Tony Oliva, to guys like Gene Larkin, Tim Laudner, and Ron Coomer, the camp is filled with many Twins greats, and normally around 100 aspiring participants ranging from players still younger than

Jamie Moyer, to guys (and sometimes ladies) who could potentially be their grandpa (or grandma).

That's the beauty of it. There is nothing quite like living your longtime fantasy, and there is nothing quite like camp. When else can you step to the batter's box against Blyleven and maybe even make yourself look foolish chasing a curveball? When else would you ever have the opportunity to step onto the same field as Killebrew and Oliva, two of the greatest hitters in team history? But that's why they call it fantasy camp. These moments are things many can only call a childhood fantasy, but ones that you can turn into the truest reality for seven days.

"Playing brings back memories of my dad and my own kids. When I was real young, the first thing I wanted to be was a cowboy. Then I wanted to be a baseball player. Then reality set in and I went on to other things," camp participant Scott Willis told ESPN.com's Jim Caple in 2008. "Now I'm sort of reverting to childhood again."

We may have moved on to other things in life and created new dreams and aspirations since those days of pretending to be a major league ballplayer in the front yard, but no matter how old, it's never too late to revert back to those moments, for just a few days, and live the dream.

# Visit Cretin-Derham Hall

There are hundreds just like it all across the country, and it doesn't quite compare to a major league ballpark. But the field that sits beyond Cretin-Derham Hall High School in St. Paul, Minnesota, isn't just your typical high school ballpark. Sure it has a mound, bases, and all of the other essential components of a baseball field just like the others, but the names on the scoreboard in right field make it a bit different, they tell the story of how special and different this field is from the others in the state.

It was 1974, and stepping into the batter's box at this ballpark as a senior was Paul Molitor. He excelled in many sports, but the following year he headed to the University of Minnesota, where he played baseball until the Milwaukee Brewers drafted him in 1977. In 21 seasons at the major league level, including three with the Twins, Molitor hit .306, collected 3,319 hits, and launched 234 home runs on his way to baseball's Hall of Fame.

He was legendary alumnus No. 1.

About 17 years removed from Molitor stepping into the box there, catcher Joe Mauer was behind home plate on the same field. Like Molitor, he was exceptional in multiple sports, but that summer after his senior year, he was selected with the first overall pick in the 2001 draft by the hometown Minnesota Twins. During that senior season, Mauer hit .605, and during his high school career he struck out just once. Today, he has won three batting titles and has established himself as one of the best catchers and hitters in the game of baseball.

He is legendary alumnus No. 2.

"It's amazing all the people who went here," Mauer said of his alma mater after the Twins selected him in 2001. At the time he was

### Cretin-Derham Hall's Other Notable Alumni

John Albers (Former CEO, Dr. Pepper)
Kate Millet (Author)
Chris Coleman (Mayor, St. Paul, Minnesota)
Matt Birk (NFL Center)
Steve Walsh (Former NFL Quarterback)
Chris Weinke (2000 Heisman Trophy Winner)
Tim Tschida (MLB Umpire)
Mark Wegner (MLB Umpire)
Ryan McDonagh (12th Pick, 2007 NHL Draft)
Seantrel Henderson (2009 *USA Today* Offensive Football Player of the Year)

referring to Molitor and other alumni such as NFL center Matt Birk, among many others. Today, as the scoreboard in right field indicates with the inclusion of his name, he is included in that outstanding group.

As you head to the field, you'll see a barbershop kitty-corner from where the action takes place. The shop is named Schmidty's Sports Barbers, and throughout the year, about once per month according to some stories, Mauer makes a return to this legendary part of town where he once spent much of his time hitting the ball around the field.

Many across the Midwest can pinpoint the names of Molitor and Mauer when the words Cretin-Derham Hall are muttered, but the uniqueness goes even further. The neighborhood that both players are from, Highland Park, is the hometown of not just those players, but also Jack Morris, the man who won Game 7 of the 1991 World Series. And Hall of Famer Dave Winfield was born less than a mile away.

As you pull up to the diamond at Cretin-Derham Hall in St. Paul, you won't see anything spectacular. There is no fancy seating or spectacularly designed field. It's your typical old-school high school ballpark with a scoreboard in right field and a hill in left, and the players who take the field are amateur athletes who dream of being the next big alumnus. There are two players in particular who once graced this field, though, and they're two of the greatest names to put on a Twins uniform.

# 97 Wally the Beer Man

He has never stepped up to the plate or even ran out from the dugout, but in Minnesota his name is legendary and his voice lets fans know when it's time to play baseball. Away from the ballpark his name is Wally McNeil, but when he enters the gates for each home game, he instead becomes Wally the Beer Man to the hundreds of fans whom he reaches each game, and the thousands of others whom he has served over the course of several decades.

"Cold beer here!" shouts Wally from the aisle.

With just those three words, in his deep and memorable voice, fans turn. As they turn, they see a man now in his mid-seventies who has become an iconic beer vendor not just in the state of Minnesota, but all across the country. The guy has his own bobblehead, he has appeared in commercials, and in 1987 *Sports Illustrated* ran a story exclusively on him. He is, if you will, the embodiment of beer vendors.

To the general eye, selling beer at a baseball game is just another typical part-time job. In reality, it isn't quite that simple. It's baseball, a sport, and there are fans, so the word *beer* alone does much of the work. But it's the special beer vendors at ballparks across the country, the ones who go above and beyond and are recognized by their signature call or style, who connect best with the fans and become easily identified. Wally is one of those vendors.

Wally first became a vendor in 1970. That year he began selling beer at the Minneapolis Auditorium, where he worked wrestling and boxing matches. In 1982 the Twins moved to the Metrodome, and Wally joined them for his first season as a vendor at games. He was 48 years old at the time, but as the Twins left the Dome some 28 seasons later, he was still there and ready to move to the team's new home at Target Field.

"It's the best part-time job a guy could have," Wally once said.

He calls it a part-time job, but Wally's presence goes well beyond his role at the ball diamond. He works games for the Vikings, Timberwolves, and Wild, among other teams. Today he is nearing three decades with the Twins, and overall he has been a vendor for 40 years. But even with those other events, baseball is what Wally does best.

"You've got six, seven, 10 games in a row, and you're there each night with a lot of the same people," Wally said. "They don't forget you."

How could anybody forget him? When you hear the call for ice-cold beer and see fans getting a baseball card of a beer vendor, you know the guy is special. Wally the Beer Man will long be remembered after he calls it quits, but he says he'll be making his way around the ballpark for as long as he possibly can.

"If you're not having fun with what you do, you shouldn't be doing it," Wally once said when talking about his job as a beer vendor. "I'm in good health, and I'll probably be doing this as long as the Lord lets me."

And fans will continue to turn when they hear that signature voice.

# 98 Venturing Online

It has become a new world in a sense, a new place to communicate and a new place to make friends. The Internet is a part of life that continues to evolve every day, and for many, it's a place where the Minnesota Twins are always alive. Whether there is a game taking place or not, and whether it's the heart of baseball season in mid-summer or during the doldrums of winter, baseball is always being talked about—and sometimes argued.

To some it sounds weird, but most of the people online readers "know" or discuss their favorite team with in reality have no idea who the person on the other end really is. There may be the name or nickname that accompanies each comment, but overall the identity and story behind each virtual being is rarely ever known.

Regardless, some of the liveliest discussions and some people's best friends are now in a virtual world.

In 2002 blogging was just beginning to take off, and Twins fan John Bonnes decided to jump on board. It wasn't supposed to be anything major, "an experiment" is what he called it, but what followed was the first serious baseball blog focused on the team in Minnesota, and a new way for fans to communicate and sometimes vent.

"It was an experiment, nothing more," Bonnes recalled of his plan to start a blog. "I wanted to see what I could write about every day, and after a couple of weeks, it was obvious that the answer was baseball. So I renamed the site TwinsGeek.com, and went from there."

What happened from there was a revolution in the way fans could consume Twins baseball. With both the Internet and the arrival of blogs, the Twins were always active, and fans no longer needed to wait until the papers hit the streets to get the latest information. Every injury, every roster move, and for that matter every happening with the team could be found within minutes, and there was now a new way for fans to connect across the country and across the world to share their passion for the team.

"The online experience just gives fans another way to connect over something they care about. When TwinsGeek really broke through to a larger audience, that was the biggest feedback I received—something like, 'Thank God I found you. Now I know someone else who cares about this stuff as much as I do,'" said Bonnes. "I've met dozens of friends through my blog, and it's a heck of a lot more fun to follow my team than it used to be because of it."

Through the online world, you can always be in touch with the team you love, and venture in a new direction. Whether it be statistical analysis, feature stories, or just general discussion, the online world contains a variety for every type of fan. It's a new way to enjoy the game, and all fans should take part.

"The Twin Cities has the most vibrant baseball community in the country—and that's not hometown boosterism. That's largely due to the work of people like Aaron Gleeman, Anne Ursu [Batgirl], and Seth Stohs, who started conversations on the Web that people wanted to join and emulate," said Howard Sinker, online sports coordinator for the *Star Tribune*. "The *Star Tribune* was pretty early to the party, first with John Bonnes blogging at TwinsGeek and then with three separate baseball blogs. It's not only that there are more baseball blogs here than in other parts of the country—an anecdotal rather than an analytical conclusion, by the way—but many of them are very, very good."

And if you jump on board, you're sure to find something you enjoy.

# Good-bye, Metrodome

From Opening Day on April 6, 2009, against the Seattle Mariners, the same team that helped open the first regular season at the Metrodome 28 years earlier, fans knew. Heck, everybody knew. On October 4, 2009, the Minnesota Twins would play their final regular season game under the roof that had created so many memories in its nearly three decades as the team's home.

But everybody who had banked on attending that landmark game aimed for the wrong date. Sure it was *supposed* to be the end. And sure, the greatest players *were* coming back to celebrate the memories. But the crowd of 51,155 on that Sunday afternoon never did see the final regular season game under that Teflon roof.

After the Twins beat the Kansas City Royals 13–4, the ceremony to say farewell to the Metrodome ensued. But the Twins were tied atop the American League Central, and there would be one more regular season game two days later.

Nevertheless, the show went on.

**All-Metrodome Team**
Manager: Tom Kelly
Starting pitchers: Bert Blyleven, Brad Radke, Johan Santana, Frank Viola
Relievers: Rick Aguilera, Joe Nathan
Catcher: Joe Mauer
First base: Kent Hrbek, Justin Morneau
Second base: Chuck Knoblauch
Shortstop: Greg Gagne
Third base: Gary Gaetti
Outfielders: Tom Brunansky, Dan Gladden, Torii Hunter, Kirby Puckett
Designated hitter: Paul Molitor

Everybody showed up. There were recent players such as Denny Hocking, Jacque Jones, and Corey Koskie to help celebrate the division titles in 2002, 2003, 2004, and 2006. There were players on hand such as Kevin Tapani, Jack Morris, and Tim Laudner to help celebrate the team's championships in 1987 and 1991.

The All-Metrodome team was honored one by one. Players such as Brad Radke, Greg Gagne, Dan Gladden, Paul Molitor, and Bert Blyleven showed up. Even Johan Santana sent his praise for the fans through a video message from New York.

Nearly everybody had returned to the Metrodome to help share the memories, to help relive the greatest moments in Minnesota Twins history. But there was one player missing. Not just any player, but as the great Bob Casey had once called him, "The greatest Minnesota Twin ever." On that day, there was no Kirby Puckett.

Instead, in the outfield with the other greats, was his jersey. As videos showed No. 34 making some of the most memorable plays in baseball history, tears fell from players and fans alike. His son would take down the final number remaining on the countdown to outdoor baseball.

The farewell tour had started six months previously almost to the date. At the time it seemed so far off, and it never seemed like fans could possibly miss the place that was best suited for football. But in that moment, with all the players and memories, it began to sink in that this was finally it. The place filled with the greatest joy in team history was closing its doors to baseball.

Giving the farewell speech that day was Kent Hrbek, the hometown kid who won two titles with the Twins while spending every one of his 13 seasons at the Metrodome.

"I wrote this speech thinking this was going to be it; it's not 'it,'" Hrbek told the crowd. "You guys went and screwed up my whole speech. We've got to come back here on Tuesday and drink some more beer."

And they did.

There would be one more regular season game at the Metrodome. But on that day the Twins said good-bye to the memories that the Dome had created: the moments that brought cheers, the plays that brought smiles, and even the times that brought many tears.

As the ceremony concluded, a video played of team greats Harmon Killebrew, Rod Carew, and Tony Oliva raising the flags at the newly built Target Field on the other side of Minneapolis. The Twins had spent 28 seasons under the Teflon roof creating enough memories to last a lifetime, but this day was the beginning of the end for baseball in the Metrodome; the Twins were getting ready for a trip across town.

# 100 Hello, Target Field!

For years it was a frustrating battle with seemingly no end it sight. Eventually, after years of making the playoffs and advancement in talks, legislation was passed and construction on a new ballpark began. Still years off, however, outdoor baseball seemed nothing more than a dream. On April 12, 2010, something happened, though; baseball under the sky in downtown Minneapolis changed from a dream to a reality.

On that sunny spring day, fans filled the plaza hours before first pitch. This was actually the third game for the Minnesota Twins at Target Field; they had played two exhibition games prior to the season. Fans had arrived early for Opening Day in years past at the Metrodome, but this was different. It was the beginning of something new for the Twins, and this time it was for real.

Before the gates even opened, an uncharacteristic three hours before the first pitch, fans lined up around the ballpark. Inside, ready to open their respective gates were team greats Harmon Killebrew, Tony Oliva, Kent Hrbek, and Rod Carew, along with Kirby Puckett's son. As the clock struck noon, the players opened the gates and greeted fans, along with a new era of Minnesota Twins baseball.

"To see our fans in their ballpark sharing their team, and seeing downtown Minneapolis as the epicenter of Twins Territory was very rewarding," said team president Dave St. Peter of that moment. "Knowing the franchise was secure over the long-term after some years of uncertainty, it doesn't get much better than that."

As fans piled into the ballpark, they were handed Homer Hankies, and before the game, 11 pennants were raised above left field by past players such as Jim Kaat, Frank Viola, Shannon Stewart, and Brad Radke to commemorate each of the team's championship seasons both in the division and in the league. These acts helped carry the team's great moments of the past into the future.

If sitting under the blue sky with the sun shining down during batting practice wasn't enough to make fans realize this moment was indeed happening, the pregame ceremony certainly did it. As

*Construction workers who helped erect Target Field present the flag during the National Anthem on Opening Day, April 12, 2010, the first regular season game in the Twins' new ballpark.* Photo courtesy Alex Halsted

players from both teams lined the base paths and as the National Anthem played with construction workers holding a flag spanning the entire outfield, F-16 planes zoomed across the stadium up above. It was time to play meaningful baseball outdoors for the first time in nearly three decades.

The day went according to plan for the Twins. The hometown kid, Joe Mauer, collected three hits, the Twins scored first and never looked back, Jason Kubel hit the first meaningful home run at the ballpark, and fans had something to cheer about as the game ended. Holding a 5–2 lead over the Boston Red Sox, the final inning was something like a playoff atmosphere. The excitement showed as a sellout crowd rose to its feet while the team capped off its first

## Tour Target Field

As you approach Target Field in downtown Minneapolis, there are plenty of things to see around the new home of the Minnesota Twins. You can see the murals, the statues, and the banners. Inside, the experience continues with historic touches around the restaurants and things such as retired numbers on the administrative building and pennants hanging above the Home Run Porch in left field. But there is only one way to go beyond the surface, to see everything Target Field really offers, and for all Twins fans, it's a must.

Take a tour.

For about an hour, you'll walk around a silent, empty ballpark and see things you never would have seen had you not taken the time for a tour.

Along the way you'll learn about the history of the team and the construction of Target Field. You'll see the clubs that are filled with pictures, history, and countless memories, including the Champions Club that holds both World Series trophies. From the closest spot to home plate in the dugout to one of the farthest spots up above on the Roof Deck, you'll also get views that otherwise are hardly possible to capture.

It's only 60 minutes of one day, but for those moments, you'll feel like you're part of the team, and you'll see the best aspects that the newest home of your favorite team has to offer.

victory at Target Field. It was just one game, but to Minnesotans and fans across the Midwest, the day meant much more. Watching baseball in its desired state, with grass and nature in full effect, was finally back. And after loving the Metrodome only conditionally for years, the new ballpark was something fans could truly love and express without fear of being scoffed at.

"The return of outdoor baseball has been met with incredible enthusiasm," said St. Peter. "People take tremendous pride not just in the team, but [in] the ballpark. We have a ballpark that fans can be proud of and call their own."

The day and year marked the opening of a new ballpark for the Twins, but its meaning went much deeper. After beginning the previous decade with the threat of the elimination of Twins baseball through contraction or relocation, Target Field effectively secured baseball in downtown Minneapolis for many years to come and kicked off an era that will carry on well past that first game and long after the first year.

# Acknowledgments

As I entered high school at Newman Catholic in Mason City, Iowa, I had no idea what I wanted to be or where I wanted to go with my life. Like so many other kids, I grew up dreaming of being the star and hitting the game-winning home run in the World Series on a 3–2 count with two outs in the bottom half of the ninth inning. Eventually you realize that dream might be a little far-fetched, and there comes a time when you must begin searching.

I was just a high school freshman in 2006, but if there was one thing I did know, it was that I was obsessed with sports and the Minnesota Twins in particular. That year, right with the team's incredible second-half comeback, I began blogging. This continued for several years, and while I made no money, I was beginning to do what I now love, and opportunities opened that I could have never imagined.

There are moments in life that you never forget, whether it is time spent with family and friends or some other special moment. In my life, in addition to the great moments spent at the ballpark with my family and many of life's other events, I remember where I was when I first saw my name in a publication. There are actually two key occurrences, with the first coming in the summer of 2008. I had checked the mailbox day after day until I finally received it— a large manila envelope addressed to me. I'll never forget the feeling when I opened that *GameDay Magazine*, and at the age of 16, saw my byline published for the first time. Another moment I won't soon forget came the next spring while attending Opening Day at the Metrodome. My dad stepped to the program booth and purchased a copy of *Twins Magazine*. As I flipped through, there was my name, published in the Official Publication of the Minnesota Twins, the team I had grown up admiring.

These details are important because it begins a long list of people I must thank for the great opportunities I've been blessed with at my age, and for where I find myself today as the author of *100 Things Twins Fans Should Know & Do Before They Die*. I must start by thanking the two people responsible for opening the first door and in part, making this opportunity to write a book possible. John Bonnes and Molly Gallatin, if it weren't for you two, I wouldn't be writing this. The two of you helped me realize my calling; you helped start this path.

On multiple occasions while talking with my high school guidance counselor, Mr. Mark Neibauer, he jokingly told me to remember to mention him when I won a Pulitzer Prize. I haven't quite reached that, but he sure got me thinking about things like this. I must thank my three high school English teachers, Mrs. Patty Ohl, Mrs. Becky Rother, and Mrs. Debbie Potthoff. In so many different instances, these instructors provided advice and compliments that helped me believe something of this magnitude was possible.

After being published for the first time, I began to imagine what it would be like to one day write a book. I could have never anticipated it happening at this point in my life, nor did I know how stressful and thought-provoking it could be. Nevertheless, this project has been an amazing experience, and I must thank Tom Bast and Adam Motin of Triumph Books and Jennifer Barrell of Prologue Publishing Services. I'll forever be thankful that Tom asked me to write this book, Adam provided great advice and spent an immense amount of time to turn this book into what you see, and Jennifer did great work editing the manuscript.

There are so many other people who helped make this book what it is. Thank you to the people who have helped put me in touch with players and other personnel, including Lynette Gittins, Mike Herman, Bryan Donaldson, and Patrick Donnelly. Thank you to so many players, team personnel, and others who provided both information and quotes, including Ron Shapiro, Dave St. Peter, Patrick Klinger, Craig David, Rob Antony, Howard Sinker, Roy Smalley, Seth Stohs, Joe Christensen, Kirk Hardcastle, Kevin Dutcher, and finally Clyde Doepner, a man who has so much great Twins knowledge and took an immense amount of time to accommodate my needs.

I must begin to end this long list by thanking the rest of the faculty at Newman Catholic as well as my many classmates and friends. There were a lot of memories shared, and your support is to be commended. Thank you to Thomas Peterson; we spent hours upon hours talking about the Twins at work, and it never seemed to get old. Also thank you to Dylan Montz, my college roommate, and friends Tyler Glover, Shawn Bowie, Lilly Petersen, and Kirsten Leeper. Beginning college while doing a project of this size isn't easy, but this book was certainly made easier than it could have been because of these friends.

Last but certainly not least, my family.

To my grandparents and extended family, who have always shown great support. And thank you to my parents, Lori and Tony, and my sisters, Katelyn and Paige. You all made me who I am today, and you never were annoyed by my constant sports talk (well, maybe just a *little*).

I was only months old when Kirby Puckett put the team on his back and helped the Minnesota Twins win their second championship, but he once said something that has always stuck, "You can be what you want to be. If you believe in yourself and you work hard, anything, and I'm telling you anything, is possible."

Now more than ever, I've begun to find out how right Mr. Puckett was.

# Sources

A number of books, media guides, magazines, newspaper archives, and online resources helped with the completion of this project. While many of the quotes found in this book were gathered first-hand, there were so many other outlets that helped provide an additional perspective or information on a player, game, or key event, and in some cases they provided quotes that helped put the finishing touches on a section.

Baseball-Reference.com is an invaluable resource for any baseball fan or writer, as is RetroSheet.org for any fan looking to get every last detail from any game in Minnesota Twins history. These two sites were crucial in looking at particular games with play-by-play breakdowns and in providing stats and interesting facts on individual players.

There were many other resources that helped shape this journey, and they include:

## Books

Aschburner, Steve. *The Good, the Bad, and the Ugly: Minnesota Twins.* Chicago: Triumph Books, 2008.

Berkow, Ira. *Carew.* New York: Simon and Schuster, 1979.

Brackin, Dennis, and Patrick Reusse. *Minnesota Twins: The Complete Illustrated History.* Minneapolis: MVP Books, 2010.

Grow, Doug. *We're Gonna Win, Twins!* Minneapolis: University of Minnesota Press, 2010.

*Minnesota Twins Media Guide* (2010)

*Minnesota Twins Yearbook* (2006, 2010)

Rippel, Joel. *Minnesota Sports Almanac.* St. Paul: Minnesota Historical Society Press, 2006.

Smith, Curt. *Voices of Summer.* New York: Carroll & Graf Publishers, 2005.

Wright, Dave. *162–0: The Greatest Wins!* Chicago: Triumph Books, 2010.

## Magazines
*Baseball Digest* (George Vass)

*Sports Illustrated* (Ben Reiter, Steve Rushin, Ted Williams, John Underwood)

*Twins Magazine* (John Nemo)

## Newspapers
*Cape Coral Daily Breeze* (Dave Devereux)

*Minneapolis Star Tribune* (Jim Souhan, Joe Christensen, Tom Briere, Patrick Reusse, La Velle E. Neal III, Mike Kaszuba, Mark Brunswick, Paul Levy, Judd Zulgad, Tim Harlow, Aimee Blanchette, Howard Sinker, Norman Draper, Kurt Chandler, Mark Vancil, Bill Ward)

*New York Times* (Claire Smith)

*St. Paul Pioneer Press* (Bob Sansevere)

## Websites
Baseball-Reference.com

Baseball-Almanac.com

Bobble Heads (Bobble-Heads.com)

Cool of the Evening (Jim Thielman)

ESPN.com (Rick Weinberg, Tim Kurkjian, Jim Caple)

MLB.com (Kelly Thesier, John Gilbert, Mark Sheldon, Alden Gonzalez)

Minnesota Monthly (John Rosengren)

Minnesota Public Radio (William Wilcoxen)

Minnesota State University Reporter (Doug Monson)

NBC.com (Bert Blyleven)